Lesbian Death

Desire and Danger
between Feminist and Queer

MAIREAD SULLIVAN

UNIVERSITY OF MINNESOTA PRESS

MINNEAPOLIS • LONDON

A different version of chapter 2 was previously published as "A Crisis Emerges: Lesbian Health between Breast Cancer and HIV/AIDS," *Journal of Lesbian Studies* 22, no. 2 (2018): 220–34; Taylor & Francis Ltd., http://www.tandfonline.com. Portions of chapter 3 were previously published in "Kill Daddy: Reproduction, Futurity, and the Survival of the Radical Feminist," in "Survival," special issue, *WSQ* 44, no. 1/2 (Spring/Summer 2016): 268–82; copyright 2016 Mairead Sullivan.

Published by the University of Minnesota Press
111 Third Avenue South, Suite 290
Minneapolis, MN 55401-2520
http://www.upress.umn.edu

ISBN 978-1-5179-1001-3 (hc)
ISBN 978-1-5179-1002-0 (pb)

A Cataloging-in-Publication record for this book is available from the Library of Congress.

Printed on acid-free paper

The University of Minnesota is an equal-opportunity educator and employer.

Contents

Preface

In the winter of 2020, as I was completing the first draft of this manuscript and Covid-19 was barely on our radar, Showtime was in the midst of a queer lesbian revival of sorts. The long-anticipated *L Word: Generation Q* brought the stylized high life of Los Angeles lesbians back to our Sunday nights. When the first *L Word* came out, I was a young queer living through the harsh winters of Boston with my own stereotypes about life in LA. Nearly every Sunday across the show's six-season run, I crammed into a friend's living room or sidled up to a packed bar to watch, and also to lament, what felt like the impending end of queer politics and the mainstreaming of gay and lesbian life. So, it seems apt that I would be completing this book—now a middle-aged queer living in LA—with just enough time to mention *The L Word*'s newest iteration. Even more striking for this project, however, is the new queer drama that immediately followed *Generation Q*'s Sunday night slot: *Work in Progress*.

Work in Progress offers a stark contrast to the glamour and drama of queer life in Los Angeles's eastside neighborhoods, *Generation Q*'s new locale.[1] The show's main character, Abby, is a middle-aged, self-described fat, butch, queer dyke living with obsessive-compulsive disorder and a plethora of depressive and anxious symptoms. In the first episode, Abby gives herself six months to overcome her sense of despair before ending it all. She counts out 180 almonds, lays them out on her counter, and begins her commitment to her own suicide. In a short time, however, Abby's life takes an upturn when she begins dating twenty-two-year-old trans man Chris. After mistaking Chris for a cute baby dyke, Abby quickly falls into the new rhythms of queer and trans identities that Chris and his friends represent.

In episode 2, Abby ventures out with Chris to a queer sex club, referred to in the episode notes as a "queer wonderland" (Mason 2019). The club pulses with electronic music and queers of all manner of gender presentation and sexual interest fill the space. The sides of the dance floor are lined with art for sale, booths with homemade leather and kink goods, and a rotating showcase of queer performance art. Abby knows she has been to the venue before but cannot quite place it. When she orders her next drink, she asks the bartender about the bar's history. It has been many things, they report, including, perhaps, once a lesbian bar. Abby immediately flashes back to a previous iteration of the space, simply called "The Lesbian Bar." In the Lesbian Bar, the lights are turned up and friends gather in small masses. The space is bland, and the night's entertainment is two white, feminine women with guitars playing slow, weepy music. One singer's tank top is clearly emblazoned with a Dyke March logo. The music fades into the background of the scene but one line from the music clearly rings out: "I'm begging you to be so careful with me." Around the room, couples slowly sway, some gently making out. The juxtaposition of the queer sex club, pulsing with public sex, leather, and bondage, with the Lesbian Bar situates the show's premise within a number of lesbian logics that I take up in this book: the lesbian is gone, subsumed by queer's expansions; that *lesbian* is dowdy, unstylish, unsexy. I was shocked, then, when a subtitle marked the year of the Lesbian Bar as 2007. I am far closer in age to Abby than Chris, but I have never marked myself on *that* side of the lesbian–queer divide.

I have never perfected the elevator pitch for this book. For strangers and outsiders to queer politics and queer studies, when I report that I am writing a book about the panic that no one wants to identify as lesbian, they quickly report that they know many lesbians! For myself, when I share with other queers and academics that I am writing a book about the lesbian question, I rush to assure that I am taking to task a virulent strain of anti-trans rhetoric that has taken up the lesbian as in need of protection from "trans." I am quick, too, to promise I am not trying to save the lesbian or recuperate *lesbian* in any way. But I am also struck by how much I and many others find deep pleasure in naming the lesbian as part of our culture—indeed, our politics—even if we do not claim *lesbian* as an identity. That I find it so anxiety-producing to create a project on the lesbian is precisely why I have written this book. I have written this book because I am not a lesbian. I have written this book because associating my work with *lesbian* makes me endlessly nervous. I have written this book because I find so much richness in lesbian histories and lesbian culture. I have written this book because I have spent endless hours in archives of lesbian activists, and I have loved every minute. I have written this book because lesbians have saved me, gave me a home, gave me language, showed me a future. I have also written this book because *lesbian* has been weaponized, used to instigate, justify, and perpetuate anti-trans violence and vitriol. I have written this book because I want the generations that worry that *lesbian* has been or is being forgotten to know that we remember. I have written this book because I feel myself holding on to the political and identarian commitments that served me but no longer serve my students. I have written this book because I feel scared to be branded as a lesbian scholar (rather than a scholar of the lesbian). I have written this book because I cannot let *lesbian* go. Mostly, I have written this book because I really do love lesbians.

Introduction

Lesbian Disruption

> What is a lesbian? A lesbian is the rage of all women condensed to
> the point of explosion.
>
> —Radicalesbians, "The Woman-Identified Woman"

The lesbian is dead. Or so the story goes. If she is not dead, then she is
dying, a victim of new constellations of gender and sexuality. Or, perhaps,
she is a victim of her own making. If it is not that no one wants to be a
lesbian anymore, then it is that the generation for whom "lesbian" was a
salient political claim has so well succeeded in their goals of lesbian mainstreaming that *lesbian* no longer carries political weight. Conversely, the
story is that *lesbian* is too readily aligned with gender essentialism and anachronistic rejections of avant-garde cultures; *lesbian* has been superseded by
queer, now *trans*, left to the trash bin of yesterday's mistake.

This book starts from the current anxiety that lesbian identity has reached
extinction. I am particularly struck by the claim that "no one wants to be a
lesbian" against increasing visibility and representation of people who call
themselves lesbians in social, political, and popular culture (Cauterucci
2016). The recent loss of lesbian space, specifically bars, bookstores, and
music festivals, has led to an increasing anxiety that the lesbian is reach-
ing extinction, especially as she is figured as the anachronistic holdover of
feminist commitments to "woman identification" in distinction to the anti-
essentialist impulses of queer and trans politics. Curiously, this anxiety
emerges against the backdrop of both an increased visibility of LGBT communities and a rising interest in 1970s feminism, often aestheticized in relation to the lesbian. The death of the lesbian is one of many stories that
continues to animate much critical work in feminist and queer studies.[1]

I

Lesbian Death reads how the lesbian is conceptualized in relation to death from the 1970s onward in order to argue that *lesbian,* as a border claim between *feminist* and *queer,* offers disruptive potential while also pointing to certain failures of lesbian projects. I frame the lesbian in relation to death—from the literal death imagined in the lesbian breast cancer epidemic to the murderousness invoked in the specter of lesbian separatism to the framing of so-called lesbian bed death as the logical outcome of the feminist sex wars—in order to, simultaneously, dislodge the lesbian from the demand that she be either feminist or queer as well as to hail the possibilities of the lesbian's extinction. By engaging these histories of lesbian death, I locate the current anxiety around the death of the lesbian as something more than the simple loss of an object—that is, the loss of an identity—but also as hailing the loss of a promised political project. To this end, across the project I track how these mourned lesbian projects are often coded as white. I take up these current anxieties in order to demonstrate that such fears are actually about the loss of the lesbian's political claim, especially in cases where whiteness is a central point of lesbian political legibility. In this way, I reposition the anxiety around the death of the lesbian as an anxiety around the loss of whiteness in defining lesbian legibility rather than an effect of queer's antifoundationalist commitments. By so doing, I argue away from the use of the lesbian as an object of inquiry and argue instead for the analytic potentials of *lesbian* as disruption.

This project began over ten years ago in the kitchen of the house where I lived with other transmasculine queers and gender deviants. On any given night, there were between five and ten residents and only two bathrooms. The five of us who paid rent were all heavily involved in queer politics around housing, labor, public health, and queer youth social services. One night, as we prepared for another thematic potluck and game night, my roommate declared, "I think we need to reclaim *lesbian.*" I was appalled. We were queer. "Lesbian," I protested, was never a label that I would want to claim. It is too centered in "woman," I complained. "Exactly," they replied. We need to reclaim *lesbian* to reclaim feminism. I have thought back on this conversation many times over the past ten years. The conversation took place mere feet away from a mantle where we proudly displayed speculum trophies; these were awarded, if I remember correctly, at the annual fundraiser for Massachusetts's crowdsourced abortion fund. We were laying out dishes labeled with dietary restrictions: vegan stews, gluten-free pasta salads, hummus and chips pillaged from the dumpster of a suburban

Trader Joe's. While our living arrangement was not a co-op in the formal sense, we did share resources—including a well-stocked root cellar full of vegetables earned from our time-shares at a local farm and a veritable bike shop in the basement—and split household costs based on income and room size. Only rarely was there a cis man in the house, and if there was, they were so swishy and queer and punk it was hard to mark them through a hetero masculinity. The house had been in our local queer community for about a year when I moved in, and there was frequent roommate turnover during the two years that I lived there. I moved in when my ex-girlfriend's new partner was moving out of town with her, taking the new partner's former room. Others came and went often also in pattern with the beginning or ending of new romantic relationships.

When my roommate proposed we reclaim *lesbian,* I refused with a staunch righteousness. *Lesbian* was too mired in woman-identification, hardly the language my roommates and I used. *Lesbian,* in my mind, was out of date and out of style. *Lesbian* was an embarrassing failure of coalition politics, an exclusionary project of middle-class white women, and, more contemporaneously, *lesbian* named the violent exclusion our trans women friends faced at avowed lesbian spaces like the Michigan Womyn's Music Festival and elsewhere. *Lesbian,* I argued, could not capture my or our social and political commitments. But, as I tour that time in my memory, I cannot help but identify *lesbian* in that space. Even if we were not, and are not, lesbians, we were certainly inheritors of political and social movements that called themselves "lesbian." We took such pleasures in the ways we engaged those inheritances, in our potlucks and our Ani DiFranco sing-alongs. But it was also reflected in our politics, how we split the rent based on income, in our monthly house meetings that foregrounded feelings and process, and in our commitment to think this space as a political space.

This project approaches the lesbian with ambivalence—that is, with both love and hate. Such ambivalence is my own and, as I will argue, is central to the ongoing debates around lesbian death and survival. Recognizing these ambivalent relations to *lesbian,* my argument is simple: the lesbian disrupts. Over and over again, especially in the last fifty years, the concern and conundrum around lesbian identity and lesbian politics is marked by a state of disruption. That disruption can come in the form of bars closing, the ends of musical festivals, the disavowals of an identity across generational lines. The disruptions are also marked through specific events and protestations: the disruption imagined by the presence of trans women in lesbian space, especially as such disruption is juxtaposed against the very real and violent disruption of trans-exclusionary protestors and gatekeepers; the imagined disruption of lesbians of color and class-conscious lesbians derailing the claims of women's liberation, especially as such disruption is juxtaposed against the very real disruptions of white women's racism, demanded tokenism, and rejection of the legitimate dissent of lesbians of color. When one starts with the lesbian as disruption, one unseats "lesbian" as an identarian claim that is far too policed and far too contested. This is not to say that such identity does not remain available, indeed viable. It does, of course. But rather, to engage disruption is to confront the messiness, the impossibility of that identification as well as the violence of the policing around who has a legitimate claim to the project. What is more, to think the lesbian as disruption opens *lesbian*, in all its messiness, to critical work around the aforementioned disruptions. In other words, anxieties about the lesbian's salience are part of this disruptive machinery. Rather than fight against it, I aim here to think with this disruption.

By aligning the lesbian with disruption, I do not mean to imply an everlasting use value for the disruption or for lesbian identity. Sometimes the lesbian disrupts in ways that are productive, perhaps even progressive. Other times, the lesbian disrupts in ways that are violent, that exert harms. Many times, the lesbian disrupts in ways that are banal and boring, sexy and sensational, divisive and demanding. Put more clearly, I am not arguing that we need the lesbian to do disruptive work or that we must reclaim *lesbian* for that disruption. Rather, I argue that the lesbian's disruptive potentials are central to many of the attachments that inform the current anxiety about the lesbian's death. Indeed, by naming lesbian disruption I aim to take seriously two sides of the same narrative: why lesbian is falling out of favor and why some are clinging so hard to this term. Herein, I join a conversation that Jennifer C. Nash (2019, 13) calls "the introspective turn" in which women's studies has begun to engage its "critical attachments, political desires, and prevailing narratives . . . that resurrect terms like 'lesbian,' 'woman,' and 'second wave feminism.'" Building on these works, I aim to connect an anxiety in the study of lesbians with an anxiety that is ripe in the wider cultural milieu of the lesbian. In order to do this, I trace the lesbian to sites of feminist and queer contestation.

In my attention to the lesbian as disruption, I am guided by Sara Ahmed's figure of the feminist killjoy. The killjoy, as Ahmed (2010) argues, is the figuration of a feminist as herself the problem, the violence, that her politics names. Ahmed reads the killjoy through the political and social imperative of happiness. When the feminist names evidence of sexism and racism, for example, she becomes an accuser. In this way, the killjoy disrupts the comfortable stasis—that is, the happiness—of things as they are. Her refusal to ignore systems of violence is itself read as a violence because she refuses to be happy in current conditions. Following a history of lesbian feminist activism, the lesbian is often figured as an emblematic feminist killjoy. And, yet, in aligning the lesbian with disruption, I stop short of marking the lesbian as always a killjoy. I resist claiming the lesbian as an emblematic killjoy figure—even as I argue that the attachments that inform the current anxieties about lesbian death are attachments to the promises of killjoy politics—because doing so risks reifying the lesbian as a valorous feminist figure beyond critique. Indeed, what most concerns me in the anxiety of lesbian death is the read that younger generations who refuse lesbian identity are killing the lesbian's political promise. In this read, those who refuse lesbian identity themselves become the problem, the killjoys, rather than the conduits to more capacious projects.

Framing my inquiry here in terms of lesbian extinction, as some call the end of lesbian identity, might make for a softer metaphor than lesbian death (Morris 2016). And yet, death, more so than extinction, calls forth many of the other analytics that I attach to the lesbian, including loss, aggression, murderousness, and bed death. What is more, many of the ideological battles of academic and political feminism are narrated as wars: think, for example, of the sex wars, the theory wars, the butch–FTM border wars, the intersectionality wars, or, more recently, the TERF (Trans-Exclusionary Radical Feminist) wars (Duggan 1998; Halberstam 1998; Nash 2019; Pearce, Erikainen, and Vincent 2020).[2] With the exception, perhaps, of the intersectionality wars, the lesbian has played a central role in these battles, and these conflicts are often traced as fomenting moments in the end of lesbian identity. So-called casualties of war, a flippant term, are not victims of extinction but victims of mediated death. And, while the current climate crisis might offer a different take on the root causes of extinction, we often imagine extinction as a slow and toxic process. By contrast, the stories of lesbian death are rife with claims of willful antagonisms and attacks.

Contra the anxieties that the lesbian has reached her end, I want to explore ongoing attachments to and ongoing disavowals of the lesbian precisely because the lesbian is a "bad object." I take my use of the term *bad object* from Jennifer C. Nash and Samantha Pinto (2020, xi), who name "bad objects" as those sites of "feminist thought that have atrophied in an accumulation of negative affect, particularly around their identification with whiteness." In so doing, I engage what Elizabeth Freeman (2010, 62) diagnoses as "temporal drag"—that is, "the gravitational pull that 'lesbian,' and even more so 'lesbian feminist,' sometimes seems to exert on 'queer.'" Because of the lesbian's presumed attachment to the "bad" aspects of feminist pasts, to invoke her today is to risk being accused of "bad" politics. What is more, many, most especially antitrans activists, have weaponized *lesbian*. When weaponized, *lesbian* loses its allure as a feminist promise and, instead, becomes what we must disavow in order to also disavow the violence that is enacted in the name of the lesbian. Across the book, I attempt to hold these competing commitments in tension. I want to take seriously both that following the lesbian can lead us to some failures of the feminist past but also that many lesbian feminist projects continue to inform world-building and world-changing projects today. Simultaneously, however, I take seriously that *lesbian* today names real violence, especially against trans women, that we cannot ignore. My aim here is not to lessen anxiety about lesbian loss. Indeed, this project may incite new or revive old anxieties about the lesbian's place in emerging constellations of genders and sexualities. Rather, my hope is that this book disrupts some of the anxieties and attachments that the lesbian provokes today. At its root, this project is about playing with the fun that can be had with the lesbian while also engaging the critical limits of the capital L Lesbian.

Across the project, I use *lesbian* variously as a noun, as in "I am a lesbian," and as an adjective, as in "lesbian breast cancer." This bifurcation of *lesbian* as object or descriptor is central to the anxieties that I trace here. In other words, I am deliberate in my choice to separate lesbian as a kind of person from *lesbian* as a political or social signifier. Because I am interested in *lesbian*'s mobility, I often use *lesbian* as a kind of floating signifier and, in so doing, also sidestep the imperative to make *lesbian* legible as either noun or adjective. My refusal to specify *lesbian* also mimics the unspecificity I find in the anxiety over the lesbian's demise. For example, in Bonnie J. Morris's *The Disappearing L,* she proclaims: "*Dyke* identity, that specific nomenclature of the fierce woman-identified woman, has been replaced by the more inclusive *queer,* as a new era of thoughtful GBT activists proclaim their disidentification with the categories 'woman' and 'lesbian'" (2016, 2). And yet, in the very next paragraph, Morris argues that "we are witnessing the almost flippant dismissal of recent, late-twentieth century lesbian culture" (2). Here, lesbian identity and lesbian space become one and the same. In this project, I reject this slippage. Rather, I allow *lesbian* to float, often untethered to either persons or places. By disentangling *lesbian* from these slippages, I hope to offer both new ways to claim *lesbian* and an inroad to claiming a lesbian-informed politics without the label "lesbian." Because I am interested in the attachments that inform the anxieties that attend to lesbian death, I am leaving to the side many important questions about what constitutes lesbian identity or lesbian space or the term *lesbian*. I follow *lesbian* without regard as to whether there is continuity across these lesbian sites or with attention to what holds these uses of *lesbian* together. Rather, I am interested in the disjunctures that occur when I follow *lesbian* both through the framework of death and across some of the primary sites where *lesbian* disrupts both *feminist* and *queer*.

WHAT IS A LESBIAN?

"A lesbian is the rage of all women condensed to the point of explosion"— so begins the manifesto "The Woman-Identified Woman" (Radicalesbians 2018, 221). On May 1, 1970, in response to the continued sidelining of lesbian concerns in the mainstream women's liberation movement, a group calling themselves the Radicalesbians staged a protest at the Second Congress to Unite Women (Jay 2000). As the meeting was called to open, the Radicalesbians cut the lights and the sound. When the lights returned, women across the theater had removed their jackets and shirts to reveal t-shirts in various shades of purple screen printed with the words "lavender menace." As the protestors made their presence—and their lesbian status—known, they also distributed a ten-paragraph manifesto: "The Woman-Identified Woman." The manifesto was a rebuttal to Betty Friedan's quip, reported by Susan Brownmiller in the *New York Times Magazine* six weeks earlier, that lesbians in the women's liberation movement were a "lavender menace." Friedan, famously the author of *The Feminine Mystique*, was also a founding member of the National Organization for Women (NOW). Founded in 1966, NOW was established with the explicit goal of expanding civil rights protections to women, most notably in the realm of employment discrimination, and on legal access to abortion. By 1970, NOW had become one of the most recognized and mainstream feminist organizations in the United States.

In memories of these early days of women's liberation, the lavender menace action stands out as an inaugurating moment of lesbian feminism. "The Woman-Identified Woman" is a political manifesto and is one of a number of events and actions across the 1970s that mark the emergence of the feminist-as-lesbian, to use Victoria Hesford's (2013) term. The Radicalesbians and the many aligned groups that followed understood "lesbian" not only as a sexual identity but also as a political commitment and response to the structuring of "woman" in a misogynistic and heterosexist society. The commitment to lesbianism as a political framework is one defining feature of 1970s radical feminism, a feature best captured in the phrase often attributed to Ti-Grace Atkinson: feminism is the theory, lesbianism is the practice (Koedt 1973). Despite the fact that many early radical feminist groups, including the Redstockings, were, like NOW, accused of similar antilesbian sentiment, historical memory often aligns the strategies of radical feminism with lesbian feminism, specifically lesbian separatism.

Separatist politics, especially the myriad brief attempts at separatist communities such as the Furies, often fell apart over issues of both class and race.[3] Separatist living communities, however, were not the only form of separatist politics. Indeed, many of the most potent manifestos of the 1970s stake themselves in lesbian or separatist politics. Or, as in the case of the Combahee River Collective's "Black Feminist Statement," others stake themselves in response to the limits of separatism. By 1977, when Combahee distributed their statement, so-called radical (and predominantly white) feminism was waning. Under this shift, separatism persisted as a form of cultural feminism focused on women's inherent femininity (Echols 1989). The Combahee River Collective built on the revolutionary movements that drew from feminist, Black power, and socialist movements of the previous decades. In the institutionalized story of feminism, the years after Combahee mark the emergence of the Kitchen Table Press and the publication of a number of foundational works of Black and women of color feminism, including *This Bridge Called My Back, But Some of Us Are Brave,* and *Home Girls* (Hemmings 2011; Aanerud 2002). Rarely do any of these three texts, however, find themselves mourned in anxieties about the end of lesbian feminism. In this way, then, feminist historiography tends to align lesbian feminism of this era with the failures of feminist separatism.

Though "lesbian" has never been a stable category, by the early 1980s the buildup and fallout of the pornography debates continued to unsettle the lesbian's already challenged singularity. In the late 1970s, pornography became a central concern to some feminist activists, beginning on the West Coast but quickly migrating east (Bronstein 2011). One notable event of early 1980s feminism was the Scholar and Feminist Conference (also known as the Barnard Conference on Sexuality) from which the so-called sex wars emerged (Vance 1984). Most famously, the battle over pornography, and concomitantly other forms of obscenity and issues of censorship, reached an apex at the Scholar and Feminist Conference's 1982 gathering. Organizers convened the 1982 gathering under the rubric of sexuality; it cleared a battleground for the growing debate between groups like Women Against Pornography and the growing lesbian sadomasochism (S/M) and propornography movement. The Barnard conference was a flashpoint that represents the critical split that defined feminist politics across the 1980s.

The lesbian straddles both sides of the sex wars. Whereas, as Carole S. Vance (1984) notes, feminism's earlier sex panic—the panic that launched the lavender menace—regarded the threat of the lesbian as a masculine, and thus sexualizing, impostor in the women's movement, the Barnard conference inaugurated a new sex panic over questions of pornography and lesbian S/M practices. If 1982 was the pinnacle of the sex wars, I argue that this era also marks the end of the lesbian's assumed association with feminism. The Barnard conference and its attendant fallout split gender from sexuality. That is, gender, read as "woman," became the proper object of the antipornography feminism, whereas sexuality, understood as practices within social, became the object of sex-positive feminists.[4] Importantly, the sex wars hit their zenith against the backdrop of the early days of the U.S. AIDS crisis. The pro-sex feminists, whose sexual politics largely coalesced around lesbian S/M, found they had more in common with gay men under the conditions of the AIDS crisis than they did with cultural feminists. To be sure, gays and lesbians had been in community, political and otherwise, since the revolutionary movements of the 1960s. As the memory of this time goes, however, lesbians—namely, pro-sex lesbians—redirected their political efforts to caring for and fighting with gay men in the crisis years of the HIV pandemic (Stoller 1997). A feminist emphasis on antipornography specifically and sexual violence writ large defines 1980s feminist movements, at least in the wave metaphor of feminist progress. While the lesbian certainly trails some aspects of this split, a point I take on in chapter 4, lesbians, as a political class, found more ground in the AIDS crisis than they did in the mainstream feminist movements across this decade. This is not to say that there were not lesbians, indeed many lesbians, involved in the feminist movements of the 1980s. Rather, "lesbian" as a political claim was more visible in the work of pro-sex movements and specifically in the joint activism in response to AIDS. In this way, the 1980s are a kind of dead zone for an imagined solidified lesbian politics.

By the end of the 1980s, lesbians who were earlier involved in the pro-sex side of the sex wars were heavily involved in the radical groups that had developed in response to the AIDS crisis, including Queer Nation and ACT UP. In cities across the United States, lesbians were forming their own chapters and subgroups in groups like ACT UP.[5] By contrast, across the 1980s, mainstream feminism focused largely on issues of domestic violence, rape, and abortion access. In 1991, public accusations of sexual harassment against now Supreme Court Justice Clarence Thomas during his nomination proceeding catalyzed younger women to get involved with feminism.[6] At the turn of the decade, these young women, both queer and straight, were coming of age—and political consciousness—in the shadow of the AIDS crisis and its concomitant sex panic. This historical moment brought with it not only the gains of the sexual liberation movements but also a deeper understanding of both the promises and limitations of feminism as an organizing principle.

Whereas gender and sexual politics in the early 1990s were reinvigorated in relationship to both feminist and queer movements, a normativizing, or mainstreaming, gay and lesbian movement also took hold. Across the 1990s, white, class-ascendant, gender-normative lesbians became aligned with a kind of stylish chic.[7] *Rolling Stone* magazine even named "lesbian" the "hot subculture" of the year (Swisher 1993). Curiously, the story of lesbian style at this time is one of leaving behind the antistyle of lesbian feminism and embracing a new cosmopolitanism. Activist and political reads of early 1990s lesbian chic mark the arrival of the lesbian as style as the end of the lesbian's political claim. By contrast, in narratives of third wave feminist engagements, *dyke* emerges as the political moniker for lesbian commitments, whereas *lesbian* tracks more closely with the mainstream gay and lesbian movement.[8] By the end of the 1990s, the hallmarks of 1970s feminism that were, perhaps, most associated with radical and lesbian feminism had reached a more feminist-oriented mainstream. Lilith Fair, for example, a touring music festival with a lineup of all women performers, was the top-grossing traveling tour in its initial year. Across the 1990s, lesbian as a lifestyle is cleaved from feminism as politics but, concomitantly, feminism, particularly in its form as commodity, evacuates the lesbian.

Perhaps no moment better narrates the lesbian's crossover from feminist bad girl to mainstream commodity, and with it her emergence into twenty-first-century consumer culture, than the high-production cable TV series *The L Word*. Set in Los Angeles's trendy West Hollywood, *The L Word*'s cast was primarily white and comfortably gendered feminine. Modeled after the wildly popular pseudofeminist *Sex and the City* franchise of the late 1990s, *The L Word* offered lesbian identity as simply another drama point in city life for twenty- and thirty-something working women. The show attempted to address contemporary political issues, including censorship of sexually explicit art, addiction, gender transition, and, of course, gay marriage. Even so, the show did not portray lesbianism as the unifying framework for any specific political commitment. While *The L Word* received numerous critiques for its failures of lesbian representation, it also enjoyed a wide and sustaining audience, ultimately producing six seasons. *The L Word*'s popularity demonstrated the appeal of lesbian representation that went beyond feminist archetypes and offered lesbianism as just another facet of urban life. Indeed, *The L Word* set the groundwork for more casual representation of lesbians as everyday people in the years since.

If, as I argue, the lesbian who is dying is a lesbian claimed in citation to the 1970s feminist movements, then the sex wars of the early 1980s are the first marker of her death. The sex wars also return us to a time when academic feminism and activist feminism were more clearly in bed with each other, so to speak (Corbman 2015). By this I mean that it is almost impossible to separate the concerns of feminist scholars and feminist activists in these conversations. Indeed, on both sides, whether marked through Carole S. Vance's *Pleasure and Danger* collection or the strategic partnership of Catharine MacKinnon and Andrea Dworkin, activists and academics were working together. Though I reject the forever debates of theory and praxis, the sex wars are a notable time when the schism was felt cleanly across both activist and academic commitments. The historiography of queer theory also marks this time—that is, the schism of the feminist sex wars—as one of queer theory's inaugurating moments. Those of us raised on a certain strand of academic queer theory are familiar with Gayle S. Rubin's "Thinking Sex" as one among many origin stories. This queer historiography credits "Thinking Sex" with separating the analytics of sex

from the analytics of gender (Rubin 2011). In this move, sex—and with it
sexuality—becomes the purview of the queer whereas gender—and with
it the violence of gender in a system of heterosexuality—becomes the purview of feminism. The early 1990s alongside the rise of queer politics in
relationship to the AIDS crisis marked a renewed anxiety in relation to the
loss of the lesbian.[9] Or, rather, this time marked a shift from the demarcating of who is not a lesbian and the policing of the border of lesbian identity to the perception that lesbian identity and thus lesbian life were being
subsumed by a sex-positive, masculinist queer polemic. By the turn of the
twenty-first century, worries about the lesbian's persistence were many.

NARRATING THE LESBIAN'S DEMISE

For over twenty years, any critical engagement with the lesbian must make
mention of her demise. For example, in her introduction to *Lesbian Rule*,
Amy Villarejo (2003, 7) states: "If the term *lesbian* is in its final hours, slowly
to be taken over by the term *queer*, let this book then stand as an elegy to
it." In 2007, the *Journal of Lesbian Studies* produced a special volume of two
double issues: "Twenty-First Century Lesbian Studies." The editors invited
submissions with a number of provocations, including: "Does 'lesbian' have
continued relevance as an identity descriptor or political position?"; "Are
we now 'post-lesbian'?"; and "Does lesbian studies have a future?" (Giffney
and O'Donnell 2007, 8–9). In her afterword to *The Lesbian Premodern*, Robyn
Wiegman calls the lesbian's erasure a "field forming complaint" (Wiegman
2011, 208). Bonnie Morris's *The Disappearing L* has positioned the lesbian
as "a dinosaur facing extinction in this new queer jungle" (2016, 1). More
recently, the *Journal of Lesbian Studies* called for papers under the rubric
"Is Lesbian Identity Obsolete?" Many proclamations of lesbian's demise
are stated without evidence. In this way, stories of lesbian death take on
the quality of what Clare Hemmings (2011, 19) calls "technologies of the
presumed." The proclamation that the lesbian is under attack or in her
twilight, then, becomes both a commonsense narrative and the grounds
on which most critical engagements with the lesbian must be staked.[10]
Each proclamation of the lesbian's demise, those listed above and myriad
others, carries with it two assumptions. The first assumption is that there
is an empirical decline in lesbian identity and the lesbian's political purchase. Put more simply, either no one wants to be a lesbian or *lesbian* just
does not mean what it used to. The second assumption is that the arrival

and presumed rise of queer theory and queer politics has both subsumed and actively erased lesbians and lesbian politics.

I begin this book by outright rejecting its premise of lesbian death. The lesbian lives. If this book starts from the provocation that the lesbian is dead, it also starts from the promise that the lesbian who lives is multiple. Quite simply, "lesbian" persists both as an identity category and as an adjective to describe everything from bars to bookstores to commercial cruises. The lesbian that is dead, or the lesbian that some imagine is dead, I argue, is a singular lesbian. This dead lesbian arrives not as fact but as the persistent object of an anxiety that lesbian identity is waning. Because it is the anxiety, rather than the lesbian, that is both persistent and consistent, the presumed dead lesbian herself is hard to pin down. For this reason, it is hard to point to what, outside of the nebulous markers "queer" or "trans," is trying to kill the lesbian or how we might mark her death. There are the obvious signs: the closing of bars and bookstores, the end of music festivals, the proliferation of new labels and identities. But these ends are also always beginnings. Even more so, that these ends generate such anxiety helpfully points us to the question of lesbian persistence. By this I mean that for every marker of lesbian death there is a return force that proclaims the lesbian's persistence. Bar closings provide the best example. When a lesbian bar closes, as in the case of the Lexington Club in San Francisco, there is an outpouring of support and demand for the need for lesbian space. Thus, often the responses to the closing of lesbian spaces are forceful proclamations that lesbians exist and that they need their own spaces. Within this logic, it is hard to argue that the closing of lesbian space is the end of the lesbian as either a kind of individual or collective.

Rather than prove the lesbian's ongoing existence, I explore the singular lesbian that is both disavowed and anxiously guarded—and I argue that they are the same—that haunts the lesbian through a contemporary association with 1970s feminism. I am not alone in naming lesbian figurations today as haunted by the 1970s.[11] Rather than disavow or interrogate this connection, I want to take seriously the attachments and the disavowals that inform that haunting today. Thus, this book takes as axiomatic that the lesbian who is mourned and the lesbian who is disavowed have specific—that is, both explicit and implicit—connections to the memories and attachments to a now past lesbian political project with roots in 1970s lesbian feminism. The ways that lesbian demise is staked in relation to the queer's rise most clearly mark the temporality of the lesbian as in the past. The queer, in this story, either subsumes the lesbian to its project or offers progress by virtue of its annihilation of the lesbian. The lesbian, in this story, is often invoked as from another time. Taking this "pull of the past" further, I argue that the lesbian's "temporal drag," to use Elizabeth Freeman's (2010) term, is actually a doubling. That is, the lesbian, in this story, is often invoked *as* evoking another time. More specifically, the time that the lesbian evokes is the 1970s. The dying lesbian cannot escape the 1970s, which is another way to say the lesbian, as Freeman and others argue, cannot escape this strand of feminism.

Understanding lesbian disavowal—that is, the real refusal of some younger queers to claim lesbian identity—as a grappling with the legacy of 1970s feminism opens new avenues of inquiry outside of the simple idea that lesbian identity is suddenly out of fashion or has been killed by queer identity. Lesbian disavowal takes on two primary forms, both of which disavow the lesbian's connections to the perceived failures and violence of "second wave feminism" (L. Wilson 2018). The first, and I would argue primary, disavowal is disidentification with the lesbian because the lesbian is understood to be a marker of trans exclusion. This form of lesbian disavowal is very clear-cut in that queers who have come of age in the twenty-first century have witnessed the mobilization of the lesbian, specifically lesbian spaces, as the battleground for women identification that is avowedly, often violently, exclusionary of trans women and, especially, trans lesbians. Trans-exclusionary movements often group themselves under the rubric of "radical feminism" and, in this way, imply associations between radical and lesbian feminism of the 1970s and trans-exclusionary feminisms today. Thus, when young queers report that they do not find home in lesbian identity, when they refuse to identify as lesbians, they are often rejecting the trans-exclusionary practices that are so often proclaimed as "lesbian" proper.

The second form of disavowal is a general dismissal of the lesbian's association with anachronizing and essentializing tenets of lesbian feminism, specifically as lesbian feminism is understood to be a whitewashed failure of separatist feminism with roots in the 1970s. In this form of disavowal, accusations of anachronism and essentialism stand in for critiques of whiteness (Hemmings 2011; Musser 2015; Mitchell 2019). Lesbian disavowals on the basis of essentialism or anachronism mirror what Clare Hemmings (2011) calls the "political grammar" of feminist theory. Specifically, disavowals of the lesbian because of her close association with second wave essentialism route lesbian identity into logics of loss whereby we must necessarily lose the lesbian in order to leave behind the failures of 1970s mainstream feminism. These failures that we must leave behind are both gender essentializing and white. Dismissals on the basis of the latter, I argue, have the strange, and perhaps unintended, effect of reifying the lesbian—and, specifically, lesbian feminist politics—as a project of white feminism. Here I join Finn Enke (2018, 10), who notes that: *"1970s feminists* is often used as short hand genealogy of today's racist and trans-exclusionary feminist (TERFs)."* As Enke demonstrates, this easy association between "racist and trans-exclusionary" feminism today and the shorthand "1970s feminists" risks eliding the many and multiple contributions of queers and lesbians of color and trans women activists of this time.

Disavowals of lesbian identity, disavowals whose specter stokes the most anxiety of the lesbian's death, can point us to important questions about the lesbian's ongoing political and theoretical purchase. Those who worry that the lesbian is coming to an end narrate their experience of lesbian disavowal quite differently but through the same stories. In Morris's *The Disappearing L,* for example, she laments the loss of "women-only" spaces as the canary in the coal mine, so to speak, of the end of lesbian identity. At the launch of Georgetown University's LGBT center, Morris observes that in a series of photos overlaid with the statement "I AM . . ." not a single subject included the declarative "I AM a lesbian" (Morris 2016, 13). Morris takes this absence of lesbian identities as evidence that younger people have repudiated lesbian history. In the pages that follow, Morris outlines over thirty years of her own involvement in lesbian, or women only, cultural spaces. What Morris and others miss is that it is this very rigid definition of *lesbian,* one that is tied to a rigid definition of *woman,* that younger generations reject. Moreover, Morris's extensive, and indeed exciting, experiences in lesbian feminism are not the only story or only sites of lesbian feminist culture or lesbian feminist histories.

Anxieties about lesbian loss are often drawn across generational lines.[12] Older generations often lament that younger people do not know their history or, even more damning, that younger people do not care to know their history (Munt 2007). By contrast, younger generations often engage in political and social formations that either outwardly reject their fore-bearers or that imply a kind of ahistorical newness. It is easy for the younger generation to dismiss the worries of the elder generation as mere nostalgia. Conversely, it is easy for the elder generation to dismiss the concerns of the younger as a forgetting or rejecting. The lesbian's generational anxieties mirror and attach to dominant frameworks of feminist theoretical and political progress narratives. Like the apocalyptic modus operandi of women's studies, as Robyn Wiegman (2000) names it, wherein the expansion of gender and sexuality projects spells the end of feminism, the lesbian generational anxiety names a past success that has been lost or even killed. The lamenters often attribute younger generations' disavowal of lesbian identity to a historical ignorance. In so doing, the lamenters suggest that if young queers today knew the pleasures and promises of the past, they would be more likely to take up the banner of "lesbian." Quite to the contrary, however, the generational divides that such proclamations respond to are specifically invested in disavowing a very well-known history. In *Object Lessons,* Wiegman (2012) notes that critiques of "woman" as an essential category fail to be read as an invitation to expand its foundational claims but, rather, are always read as an annihilative strategy. The same can be said of the lesbian. This is especially true at the moments in which the lesbian is asked to release some attachments.

Whether as lost in the past or too clearly subsumed in a normative present, the lesbian gets caught in the border wars between the feminist and the queer (Stein 2010; Garber 2001). Most often, the lesbian arrives as the figure who highlights the need for queers to take feminism seriously.[13] Despite the persistence of claims that queers—and their academic counterparts, queer theorists—dismiss the lesbian as anachronistic, I have found few instances of this outright dismissal. Rather, the lesbian has been taken to task or not engaged with at all. But even this claim is not entirely born out. The out-of-time-ness that queer theory purportedly accuses the lesbian of is typically marked through her association with a militant, killjoy feminism often gathered under the rubric of radical feminism and, again, with hauntings of 1970s feminism. Calling the lesbian anachronistic is another way of saying "dowdy"; that is, out of style, out of date. This antistyle association of the lesbian and feminism is so engrained in the story of lesbian demise that it has become both a joke and a presumption. As Hemmings (2011) notes, accusations of the lesbian's anachronism stand in for dismissals of 1970s feminisms and accusations of bad essentialisms. The lesbian's dowdiness takes on many different forms. Freeman (2010, 61) calls this figure the "archetypical humorless lesbian feminist." Wiegman (2012,

102) argues that "'the lesbian' . . . has been reduced, unsexed, domesticated, uglied, and abjected by forces too numerous to list, including those of feminist and queer theory." The lesbian's reduction and domestication is echoed in Karen Tongson's (2011, 58) naming of 1970s feminism, and by association its lesbian avatar, as "emotional earnestness" and Scott Herring's read of lesbian separatism as "anti-fashion" (Herring 2010, 80). Elsewhere, Heather Love (2011, 180) aligns the lesbian identity she will not relinquish with "the wide stance, the longing, the social work, the sluttish classicism, the frumpiness, the bad relationships." Jaime Harker (2018, 14) argues, "Queer genealogical narratives tend to scapegoat lesbian feminism, seeing it as inferior discourse that gave way to the more sophisticated, transgressive, and transformative potential of queer theory." Linda Garber (2001, 1, 17) opens *Identity Poetics* claiming that "queer theory labels lesbian feminist essentialist (an academic code word for unsophisticated if not stupid)" and later states that queer theory "tends to characterize 1970s lesbian feminism as unreflexively essentialist." All of these formations of the lesbian reflect a commonsense understanding of the lesbian as from the past and, thus, not in the present.

Nearly all proclamations of the lesbian's death mark this death in relation to the queer. Indeed, the increasing institutionalization of queer studies has led to increasing claims of lesbian erasure (Morris 2016). Most claims that the queer has an antagonizing relationship to the lesbian trace this split to a genealogy of queer inaugurated in the late 1980s and early 1990s with the concomitant rise of groups like ACT UP and Queer Nation and the publication of Judith Butler's *Gender Trouble* and Eve Kosofsky Sedgwick's *Epistemology of the Closet*. These works stake themselves in response to some limits of feminism. In this framework, the queer takes on both the work of gender subversion and the work of sexuality as an expansive and theoretically rich site of inquiry over and against feminism's perceived insistence on the violences of both gender and sexuality. This insistence of the queer's separation from feminism—perhaps, even, the queer's antagonism to feminism—continues to generate anxieties about the lesbian's proper home. I must also note, however, that the queer against which the lesbian is measured tracks most closely with what we might call white queer studies or white queer politics (Halberstam 2005; Muñoz 2006). That is, the queer theory and, even, queer politics that many name as antagonistic to both feminism—notably, feminism as a specific project of liberalism—and the lesbian are queer theory projects that fail to think racialization and racial formation as central to and produced by heteronormative functions of colonialism and imperialism.

In this project, I reject the defensive stance that the lesbian so often needs to take on in relation to the queer. Whereas white queer theory, at least when understood as the killer of the lesbian, forces the lesbian to choose between style and anachronism, queer of color critique grounds itself in women of color, and specifically Black, lesbian feminism that is rooted in the revolutionary and liberatory movements of the mid- and late twentieth century (Tompkins 2015).[14] This stark contrast shows that the lesbian who many imagine is irrelevant to queer theory is coded as white and is overly marked by her inability to engage questions of race and class. Put more directly, if the queer killed the lesbian but queer of color critique is lesbian, then the queer that kills the lesbian is a queer that is mired in an inability to think beyond whiteness or to think critically about whiteness. Furthermore, if queer of color critique grounds itself in the social, political, and theoretical work of Black and women of color lesbian feminists, then this queer can hardly be said to be killing the lesbian. Ergo, the queer that generates such anxieties of lesbian erasure generates those anxieties in relation to whiteness, and thus the lesbian that fears erasure is herself marked by whiteness.

One cannot write about this anxiety about the death of the lesbian without also writing about what have been branded trans-exclusionary radical feminists, or TERFs. Activists have mobilized the moniker "TERF" to name anyone who uses the label of "radical feminism" to make pointed and vitriolic demands for the exclusion of trans people, specifically trans women, from feminist and lesbian spaces and politics.[15] Those who espouse trans exclusion often call their stance "gender critical." Trans exclusion in gender-critical frameworks is predicated on a curious paradox. On the one hand, trans exclusion accuses trans people, especially trans women, of buying into an essentialized gender category that gender-critical feminists reject. On the other hand, gender-critical politics are built on claims to unitary experiences based on essentialized experiences of sex distinction—in other words, gender—to dictate their own borders. This group is a small but vocal minority. Nevertheless, the reach of trans-exclusionary rhetoric is so wide that anyone who calls themself a lesbian—or, in my case, studies the lesbian question—must simultaneously disavow TERFdom. In the vast space between those who, instead, disavow the lesbian for its association with trans exclusion and those who identify as lesbian are many who would say they are not trans-exclusionary but who, nevertheless, reproduce many of the central tenets of trans-exclusionary rhetoric. Namely, these narratives reproduce the doubling down on the presumed monolithic experience of girlhood as the central framework for woman identification or, alternatively, the worrying over the preservation of "women-only" spaces. Adjacent to, if not always produced by, trans-exclusionary rhetoric, the panic over the relationship between trans identities and lesbian identities arrives in two modes: the panic that "good lesbians" are leaving the club for the safety or salacity of gender expansion or the vitriolic policing of lesbian space over and against trans women's claims on women identification. Both panics are expressed in the guise of protection and consolidation of lesbian identity, which has become nearly synonymous with lesbian space.

Lesbian identity, and its association with lesbian space, is no longer the grounds for a unified lesbian politics. Relatedly, lesbian politics, at least in its association with certain strands of 1970s radical feminism, no longer clearly equates to lesbian identity. In other words, many, perhaps even most, people who identify as lesbians today do not do so out of a commitment to an avowed feminist politic. What is more, many people who share political and social commitments with some of the radical tenets of 1970s feminism do not identify as lesbians. This, it seems to me, is the crux of the problem. Lesbian politics may no longer register under the title "lesbian." For example, every fall, over fifteen thousand lesbians gather in Palm Springs, California, for the annual Dinah Shore Weekend (the Dinah). For five days, lesbians of all ages, races, and genders from all around the world gather for all-night clubbing, raucous pool parties, and an ever-expanding lineup of big-name musicians and headliner celebrities. Rarely, if ever, does the Dinah attract a kind of worried outrage that lesbian identity is going extinct. Concomitantly, the Dinah never announces the persistence of lesbian identity. Though, if one needs evidence that lesbian identity persists, indeed thrives, I suggest a trip to Palm Springs next fall.

The challenge that the Dinah presents to the anxiety over the lesbian's demise, however, is that the Dinah is most definitely not a political space. That Dinah Shore Weekend, and other gathering spaces like it, does not reassure the worried parties about the lesbian's persistence helpfully points us to the root of that worry. Quite simply, the fear that lesbian identity is no longer viable is a fear that lesbian identity is no longer a political claim.

By "political claim," I mean that lesbian identity, according to this worry, no longer registers a politic commitment in which lesbianism is the ground for imagining and building different worlds. In the lament that young queer people should not abandon lesbian identity, I hear the demand: if you are queer and feminist, you must claim "lesbian." Here the lesbian mirrors the queer in the attachment that Kadji Amin (2019, 277) diagnoses in queer studies as "affectively haunted by the historical and political moment of the U.S. 1990s in which it emerged." Similarly, the affective attachment that guides worry over the lesbian's demise is haunted by the historical and political moment of the 1970s in which this figure emerged. In order to explore these attachments, I engage a methodology that Kaitlin Noss (2013), following Elizabeth Freeman (2010), names as "Deep Lez." Deep Lez is a framework that engages the pleasures of fomenting moments of lesbian feminism while also sustaining an accountability of the forms of racism and transphobia that plagued many of the most guarded lesbian feminist projects.

In what follows, I trace this haunting of the lesbian as the lesbian is figured through her emergence in the 1970s. In this way, I follow a method Amin calls "attachment genealogy." Like Amin (2019, 278), I am interested in "exposing, fragmenting, and reworking [the lesbian's] historical inheritances to enable [the lesbian] to do different work in new contexts." I focus specifically on the tension that the lesbian highlights between feminist and queer political and intellectual commitments. I am, admittedly, narrow in my focus. I join, however, a number of recent engagements with the lesbian's political and intellectual claims that productively engage this tension. Like Lynne Huffer (2013), whose queer feminist ethics of sex reads queer theory's commitment to antifoundationalism through lesbian figurations via Luce Irigaray, I am also interested in the pressure the lesbian can assert on queer theory's antisocial thesis. Similarly, I follow scholars like Angela Willey (2016), who offers *dyke* as an ethical and relational signifier that is explicitly political in ways that *lesbian* fails to be, and Kevin Henderson (2017), who reads foundational lesbian theorists, in this case Monique Wittig, as offering inroads to more expansive lesbian queer projects today. In taking seriously lesbian meaning today, *Lesbian Death* joins more recent returns to the politics and praxis of 1970s lesbian feminism while simultaneously following this figuration of the lesbian, via radical feminism, to lesbian nostalgia and lesbian anxiety in their contemporary forms.[16]

SCOPE OF THE BOOK

In the chapters that follow, I present case studies that group *lesbian*, the adjective, with different conceptions of death. In chapters 1 and 2, I tackle questions of both lesbian loss and lesbian progress. In chapters 3, 4, and 5, I offer case studies that read the lesbian with death in the defining feminist or lesbian political modes of the 1970s, 1980s, and 1990s. Of course, marking the feminist past as divided by these decades is reductive at best and counter to feminist revolutionary work at worst. Nevertheless, these decades provide a loose but necessary boundary to the stories I am telling. As Victoria Hesford (2013) demonstrates, 1970 is the year that announced the women's liberation movement with its attendant figure of the feminist-as-lesbian. 1981 saw the first report of the AIDS crisis, and 1982 is the most recognizable marker of the sex wars. The rise of lesbian-specific activist groups grown out of ACT UP and Queer Nation and the inauguration of the so-called third wave of feminism marks the early 1990s. So, these boundaries are not about siloing modes of thought and activism but about concrete events that anchor the story of the lesbian that I tell herein.

In her book *Why Stories Matter: The Political Grammar of Feminist Theory*, Clare Hemmings (2011) argues that in its engagements with its recent pasts, mostly the 1970s, 1980s, and 1990s, feminist theory relies on three narrative strategies: namely, stories of progress, loss, and return. Stories of progress narrate feminism as ever evolving, thanks in large part to the activism of and better incorporation of mainstream feminism's others—namely, women of color. In distinction, stories of loss lament the depoliticization of feminism and the refusal of new generations to take up the feminist banner. Finally, stories of return promise that we can mine our feminist pasts for their use today even while holding us accountable to the failures and short-sightedness of our past. Hemmings warns that these narrative conventions contribute to a demand that the feminist political project be unifying and that, if only we find the right formula, we can assure feminism as a utopian project that can capture all. The political grammar that Hemmings names is also the political grammar of lesbian death. Indeed, as Hemmings tracks these genres, "lesbian" emerges as a central and contested category that figures prominently in each of these modes. Thus, I structure my exploration of lesbian death through these narrative categories. Of course, in this I also risk promising a utopian or unifying vision. My only hope is that in so doing, we can move beyond these narrative structures and embrace "lesbian" as a capacious and mobile category.

Many who fear that the lesbian has reached her end worry that lesbian loss is the unfortunate by-product of lesbian progress (Morris 2016). Following this worry, I offer a reading of both lesbian loss and lesbian progress that puts pressure on these prevailing narratives. In chapter 1, I trace three of the most prominent narratives of lesbian loss today: the closing of lesbian bars, the end of the Michigan Womyn's Music Festival, and the continued rise of queer theory as the vanguard approach to gender and sexuality studies. These are not the only signs of the lesbian's demise. Nevertheless, the first two have received widespread media attention. A central animating concern of this chapter, indeed of the whole book, is why queer theory's and queer politics' perceived erasure of the lesbian continues to generate such anxiety. Foreshadowing the following chapters, I argue that the nostalgia for a lesbian culture that many worry is lost is marked by whiteness as well as the promises of early lesbian feminist projects. Pivoting from this claim, I ask what lives on in the aftermath of lesbian loss.

In chapter 2, I ask how AIDS changed the lesbian in order to position her in the current regime of LGBT civil rights projects. This chapter tells the story of the emergence of "lesbian" as a biopolitical category—that is, a category marked for the promotion of life—specifically as such a category is measured through the investments of the U.S. government in the late 1990s. Tracing the rise of lesbian breast cancer activism in concert with the HIV/AIDS crisis, I demonstrate that "lesbian" becomes consolidated as a biopolitical category through multiple and, at times, contradictory articulations of the overlap between feminist and queer health concerns. I make this argument through an analysis of three archives: the work of San Francisco AIDS czar and lesbian health activist Jackie Winnow, the work of Bay Area Breast Cancer Action in concert with ACT UP Golden Gate, and the media maelstrom that followed the National Institutes of Health's declaration of a lesbian breast cancer epidemic in 1993. The consolidation of "lesbian" as a biopolitical category has the effect, I argue, not only of normalizing but also of devenomizing the political category of "lesbian."

In chapters 3 and 4, I trace the lesbian's political history in relationship to the queer with specific attention to a strand of queer theory that is most often accused of refusing the lesbian, the so-called antisocial thesis (Halberstam 2008). In these narratives, I use the lesbian to explore the limits of queer theory's antisocial thesis, especially as Lee Edelman and Leo Bersani articulate it. Simultaneously, however, I ask after the limits of a lesbian politics that cannot expand beyond a single-identity framework. In chapter 3, I shift to understand the lesbian's association with death as a murderous feminist impetus toward annihilation. Chapter 3 explores the histories of lesbian separatism as a defining political commitment of 1970s U.S. radical feminism. In this chapter, I read radical feminist separatist texts *SCUM Manifesto,* the C.L.I.T. papers, and "Lesbians in Revolt" alongside queer theorist Lee Edelman's rejection of reproductive futurism. Redeploying one of Edelman's key terms, I argue that the radical feminist persists as a sinthomosexual figure. Lesbian separatism is the hinge of this persistence, which I mark through a cultural understanding of political lesbianism as a direct threat to reproductive futurity. I argue that separatist feminism's threat to futurity figures more violently than Edelman's sinthomosexual by connecting the rhetoric of lesbian separatism to a murderous impulse and nihilistic negativity.

Connecting feminism's murderous impulses to a more individualized effect of killjoy feminism, in chapter 4 I shift to explore how a sexological panic around "lesbian bed death" is symptomatic of a wider fear that feminism's logical end is the death of sex. This chapter traces the rise of the phrase *lesbian bed death* with Leo Bersani's "Is the Rectum a Grave?" and Andrea Dworkin's *Intercourse.* Usually misattributed to Philip Blumstein and Pepper Schwartz's 1983 *American Couples, lesbian bed death* names the presumed waning of sex and desire in long-term lesbian couples. Rejecting this narrative, I offer an alternative genealogy connecting the phrase to Jade McGleughlin's speech at the Sex and Politics Forum during the 1987 March on Washington for Lesbian and Gay Rights. Countering the sexological narrative that feminism's attention to the power imbalances of sex has a disruptive effect on lesbian libido, I argue that, in fact, normalizing gay politics has a disruptive effect on lesbian publics. Coupling this narrative with the fallout of the feminist sex wars and the overarching concern with sexual violence, I argue that the specter of lesbian bed death reflects an anxiety that the feminist demand to address the reality, and ordinariness, of sexual violence will have a killjoy effect on sexuality. Rather, I position lesbian bed death against a backdrop of queer and feminist resistances to the normalizing politics of both mainstream gay and lesbian movements and the legislative initiatives of antipornography feminism. Chapter 5 takes up the question of lesbian aggression. In this chapter, I read the ways in which aggression attaches to the lesbian through three events: the political work of the Lesbian Avengers, the criminalization and incarceration of a group of Black lesbians known as the New Jersey 4, and more recent claims on lesbian victimization as made by antitrans activists under the banner of radical feminism. Across this chapter, I read the ways that aggression becomes legible in connection with the lesbian in order to argue that aggression works differently in different contexts and when attached to different bodies.

In the Conclusion, I offer two different modes for looking back at lesbian politics today. First, I read current social and political movements for their citations of past lesbian projects and politics. Second, I invoke nostalgia as a frozen and melancholic attachment to the past. I reject this mode of engaging in the lesbian's past lives. Reading back through the text, I argue that nostalgia clings too hard to that which must be let go in order to see the lesbian's persistence today. The lesbian that is mourned in current anxieties about lesbian death must release some of the project's critical attachments in order to assure the capaciousness that the lesbian has always promised. This is not to say that these anxieties are without merit or, even, necessity.

The reader will note that my case studies give primary attention to sites, figures, and movements that are largely associated with white feminism and white lesbian feminism even more specifically. This move is deliberate. I do not aim here to hold these case studies as emblematic of lesbian politics or as definitive of a universalizing lesbian claim. Rather, I trace these cases as sites of attachment in the ongoing anxieties over the death of the lesbian. Because this tracing has led me, primarily, to cases that are marked by whiteness, my cases studies here are also overwhelmingly white. This is not to say that lesbians of color have not been involved in and even central to the case studies I present here. Moreover, this is not to imply that lesbians of color do not worry over the end of lesbian politics or repeat many of the same fears in relation to queer and trans politics that I explore herein. To the contrary, lesbian culture and lesbian politics have always been important sites for cross-racial identification, coalition, and solidarity (Strongman 2018). In highlighting these cases, I am not implying or creating a kind of dividing line between white lesbians and lesbians of color. What I am doing, however, is tracing the attachments that are most cited in the fears over the lesbian's pending extinction. In examining these sites of attachment, I highlight where the promises of coalition and the potential of the lesbian as a unifying, though never universal, framework fails. I will return to this question in the Conclusion to think about how we might mobilize lesbian social and political histories for the social and political needs of today.

1 Lesbians Killed the Lesbian Bar

Lamentations of Loss

> Laments about the loss of lesbian community spoke to the loss of a center, of a sense of certainty and unity. For a brief period in the early 1970s, there was a burst of extraordinary solidarity, a feeling that lesbians shared a common oppression and a collective sense of identity.
>
> —ARLENE STEIN, *Sex and Sensibility*

On July 1, 2015, an essay in the *Huffington Post* proclaimed the death of the lesbian (Anderson 2015). In the opening comments, author Aimee Anderson recalls a lecture given by Jack Halberstam ten years prior. In the lecture, Halberstam, according to Anderson's memory, noted that a culture so informed by male sexual desire will forever disavow female masculinity. Echoing the butch–FTM border wars that were central to Halberstam's (1998) earlier work in *Female Masculinity*, Anderson repeats the tired trope that the rise in public acceptance of trans identities is, in effect, killing the lesbian. She marks the evidence of this lesbian loss in three places: the closing of numerous lesbian bars and bookstores, most notably San Francisco's Lexington Club; the widespread boycotts and subsequent end of the Michigan Womyn's Music Festival; and a queer investment in gender proliferation and the rejection of binary gender logics. The year 2015 was a turning point for anxieties around lesbian loss. On April 30, the Lexington Club, long lauded as San Francisco's last lesbian bar, closed its doors. Just weeks prior, Lisa Vogel, founding director of the Michigan Womyn's Music Festival, a holdout "separatist" space with roots in 1970s feminism's music and back-to-the-land cultures, announced that 2015 would be the festival's last year. Just one year prior, Laverne Cox, a Black trans woman actress and activist, was featured on the cover of *Time* magazine under the proclamation "The Transgender Tipping Point" (Steinmetz 2014). The *Huffington Post* essay proclaiming the death of the lesbian was one among many to take up the question of lesbian death in this time frame.[1]

While anxiety about lesbian identity and lesbian anachronicity is hardly new, the shifting terrains of lesbian and queer life across the past decade have amplified these anxieties. This more vocal anxiety, I argue, cannot be disentangled from the rise in attention, both politically and culturally, to trans identities and experiences. And yet, these claims of lesbian death are not solely in response to wider cultural conversations about gender. In this chapter, I move to explore the attachments that are central to recent lamentations of lesbian loss. Specifically, I argue that fears around the loss of lesbian space and lesbian identity reflect both tacit and often explicit transphobia, as well as the inability of white, middle-class lesbian leadership to address issues of classism and racism with their conception of lesbian spaces, lesbian politics, and lesbian studies. Each closure of a lesbian bar or ending of a dedicated community space brings to the fore the same anxieties: namely, that no one wants to be a lesbian anymore, that there are no more lesbians, or that those who still identify as lesbian are being run out of the very spaces they created. To be clear, numerous lesbian bars, an incredible amount really, have closed in the past two decades (Mattson 2019). Moreover, the closure of the Michigan Womyn's Music Festival—which was among the last holdouts against corporate, or profit-based, music festivals with explicit roots in the radical feminist movements of the 1970s—marks a shift in the terrain of "women's music" culture. Additionally, as I outlined in the Introduction, the context for and meaning of lesbian identity, both for those who claim it and in the wider feminist and queer political and social milieus, is different today that it was for generations prior. All of these are true. What interests me, however, is how each of these truths is assumed to point to the end of "lesbian" as a meaningful identity or organizing rubric rather than to open the lesbian to more capacious projects.

Anxieties around lesbian extinction center a sense of loss. I approach this anxiety around lesbian loss with both skepticism and seriousness. I approach this anxiety with skepticism because I find much of it to be an affective rejoinder without evidence. Or, more astutely, the anxiety is often short-sighted, which tells us something about the desire for capital *L Lesbian*.

Quite simply, what many imagine is lost in these ends of lesbian space is a specific form of radical political movement-making that germinated in the mid- to late twentieth century out of the need for lesbian-centric spaces. What makes this argument simple is that it is easily addressed or dismissed by stating that the old-timers have not caught up with the times; the radical political movement-making persists—it just looks different. Such a response is true, to a certain extent. Yet, the argument also requires more complexity. As I outlined in the Introduction, lesbian politics, and subsequently lesbian space, have always been contested. Much of this contestation is rooted in both transphobia and white centricity. The contemporary panic around lesbian erasure imagines an orchestrated effort to disenfranchise and subsequently drive out a "lesbian" specificity rather than a movement to drive out anachronistic essentialist and transphobic spaces and practices, spaces often defined through the centrality of whiteness and the failures of coalition.

In this chapter, I take up three themes of lesbian loss. These themes are the claim that the closing of lesbian bars is evidence of lesbian mainstreaming and thus lesbian obsolescence; the fear of the loss of "women-only space," especially as such spaces have been contested sites of trans inclusion; and the proclamation that queer theory has rendered both lesbians and lesbian studies passé. I explore these themes by paying attention to three specific case studies that emerged at roughly the same time, around 2015. My cases studies are the closing of San Francisco's last lesbian bar, the Lexington Club (the Lex); the closing of the Michigan Womyn's Music Festival (or Michfest, as it was known to serial attendees); and Valerie Traub's *Thinking Sex with the Early Moderns*, specifically her chapter "The Sign of the Lesbian" and the two seminars she convened, with Sue Lanser, that she references in this chapter. I have chosen these case studies in part because at least two—the closing of San Francisco's long-standing lesbian bar and the end of the Michigan Womyn's Music Festival—fueled national conversations on the inevitable death of lesbian identity.[2] Both the closing of the Lex and the end of the Michigan Womyn's Music Festival received widespread coverage in gay and lesbian and mainstream media. I have chosen to focus on Traub's *Thinking Sex with the Early Moderns* because she nicely outlines the sense that feminist and queer studies have forgone lesbian analytics. These cases are useful not only because they are likely to be familiar to many but also because they line up with the final legalization of gay marriage in the United States. In June 2015, two months after the closing of the Lex and two months before the final Michfest, the U.S. Supreme Court legalized same-sex marriage. It is no coincidence, I argue, that in a cultural moment that many argued would be the end of gay politics, fears of lesbian obsolescence reached a new fervor (Sycamore 2013). In the cases below, I explore both what is left behind and what attachments endure for a lesbian project that many imagine to be lost.

THE END OF THE LESBIAN BAR:
WHEN THE LEXINGTON CLOSED

When San Francisco closed its last lesbian bar, the loss reverberated around the city. The year was 1991 and Amelia's, the last standout of San Francisco lesbian bars, closed and reopened as the Elbo Room, ostensibly because of waning patronage from local lesbians (Stein 1997, 184–85).[3] Once heralded as the epicenter of gay life in the United States, the changing demographics of the city coupled with the growing normalization of gay and lesbian life, as the locals reported, converged to erase San Francisco's last lesbian-only space. The irony of a gay city without a lesbian bar was not lost on the *San Francisco Examiner* journalist who noted, "More lesbians than ever live in San Francisco, but the last lesbian bar is set to close" (quoted in Stein 1997, 184). It would be six more years before San Francisco got another lesbian bar. The Lexington Club, San Francisco's next great lesbian bar, opened in 1997 in the heart of the Mission District and quickly took up the moniker of San Francisco's sole lesbian bar.

In 2005, my friends and I set off on a one-week road trip from Boston to San Francisco. Our destination was the Lexington Club. Social media, as we know it now, was in its infancy. We knew that the Lex was the revered lesbian bar of San Francisco, but all we could picture was what we had read about in guidebooks or heard about from others' visits to the lesbian holy grail. At a bookstore in Denver, I found one such guidebook and wrote down the address of the famed club. To this day, I swear that book promised floors of DJs, mirrored walls, and a proverbial bacchanal of lesbians of all varieties. Imagine our surprise to arrive in San Francisco and head to the corner of Nineteenth and Lexington, where the Lex's neon sign hung above the door, to find a one-thousand-square-foot dive bar whose bathroom door barely closed.

The Lex was a cramped, dark space, squarely between the Mission and Valencia corridors. The door to the bar was positioned exactly at the corner. The service bar ran parallel to the wall at the left side. The bathrooms were at the end of the bar. A juke box and a DJ booth were along the wall to the right of the door. This area would often be used as a stage for poetry readings and other performances. There was a pool table in the middle of the room. Most nights, small tables lined the walls and people were packed in like sardines. The bar had classic dive bar hallmarks: it was cash only; the lone bathroom was covered in graffiti; the decorations, which rotated by season and theme night, were likely purchased from a local dollar store or Party City. The staff were well-known locals, often the most lusted-after queers, and themselves a kind of queer family structure. While the Lex was dubbed a lesbian bar, it drew patrons from across the queer spectrum. The bar's commitment was as a queer gathering space that would be accessible to all. Indeed, their famed tagline was "Never a cover."

In 2015, the closing of the Lexington was emblematic of two national trends. First, San Francisco had become the epicenter of a shifting economy, driven largely by big tech and Silicon Valley start-ups.[4] Second, the closing of the Lex provided further confirmation of a nearly decades-long decline in dedicated lesbian spaces in major urban areas (Mattson 2019). Lesbian bars, along with women's bookstores and lesbian-run coffeehouses, were closing at breakneck speed.[5] These two cultural shifts—for which the Lex is but a symptom—cannot be disentangled. The rise of techno giants, like Amazon, has, at least in perception, sped the decline of women's bookstores, and shifting urban demographics have driven underearning queers from the urban centers they once inhabited. This trend, of course, is not specific to lesbian bars. Lesbian bars, like other small businesses, suffer from rising rents on the properties they inhabit, as well as the exile of the communities they serve under the same financial duress (Podmore 2006).

Most people assume that lesbian bars close for one of two reasons: lesbians' thin wallets or the lack of a sexually driven party culture for queer women. Both claims imagine that there are lesbians who, under the right circumstances, would continue to patronize lesbian-specific spaces. This framework imagines lesbians as a group distinct from the younger queer folks who keep lesbian nights and lesbian politics alive. Lesbian bars and lesbian spaces have always been much more than a cruising scene.[6] And yet, lesbian bars and lesbian places have also always been a space of desire and sex (a point to which I will return in chapter 4). The closing of the Lex had less to do with the spending power of its patrons, or lack thereof. Rather, according to owner Lila Thirkield, the rising rents on both commercial and residential properties in the area forced the bar's clientele farther and farther away from the Mission neighborhood (Placzek 2015). For the Lex and other lesbian bars across the country, it is often a potent mix of declining consumer power, rising commercial rents, and economic policy that disadvantages small business owners that drives lesbian bars out of business. Such realities are not specific to lesbian bars. In many ways, the closing of lesbian bars and spaces simply mirrors wider industry trends.[7]

Many of the exposés lamenting the death of the lesbian have appeared in mainstream crossover publications like the *Huffington Post, Slate,* and the *Daily Dot.* Lesbian-centric outlets have carried their share of lamentation, but the de rigueur proclamations of death that followed the end of the Lex may better point to the saturation that queer spaces are experiencing. That these elegies are published in mainstream press points to how lesbian life and lesbian cultures have been, at least to a certain extent, incorporated into the wider cultural milieu. An often-told rejoinder in the death of lesbian bars is that the mainstreaming of gay and lesbian life has meant that previously inhospitable spaces—namely, straight bars—have now become more accepting to gay and lesbian clientele. By this logic, acceptance in straight bars renders the need for lesbian bars obsolete. But, as Jen Jack Gieseking (2020) argues, such logics tend to obscure the various ways that lesbians and queer folks make community within and beyond established norms of space and place.

The closing of lesbian bars across the country, indeed across the world, prompts the question of what constitutes a lesbian bar. In the case of the Lex, the bar had always been home to a gender-diverse crowd of young queers and punks. The Lex is not an old school lesbian bar with roots in the midcentury; it opened in the Mission neighborhood of San Francisco concomitantly with the shifting demographics of that neighborhood in the late twentieth century. Indeed, the opening of the Lex itself signaled a wave of gentrification in the then dominantly Latino Mission District led by queers and artists, many of whom were white. Just south of the Lex, the Bernal Heights bar Wild Side West has been lesbian owned since its beginnings in 1962. In the aftermath of the closing of the Lex, Wild Side West has stepped in to claim the moniker of San Francisco's longest-running lesbian bar. While the bar's website makes this proclamation, Wild Side West does not claim to be an exclusively lesbian-serving establishment. Perhaps this is because the bar is located in the rather sleepy neighborhood of Bernal Heights. Anecdotally, Wild Side West has long been understood as the stomping ground of older lesbians.[8] Wild Side

West claims to attract locals of all kinds, again making it not so much a party destination as a local watering hole. The nostalgia for the bygone era of lesbian bars has the short history of a single generation. Indeed, the way in which the Lex maintains the tagline of "San Francisco's only lesbian bar" implies that it is and was the only lesbian bar to ever exist in the city. Even to declare the Lex the last standing lesbian bar negates the myriad of spaces that cater to San Francisco's gender and sexual minorities who may, by declaration or not, fall under the rubric of "lesbian."

In the wake of the end of lesbian bars, many lesbian and queer communities in major cities in the United States rely on specific nights that rotate their location. When the Lex closed, the bar's owner shifted their focus to a second Mission bar under their ownership, Virgil's Sea Room. Virgil's Sea Room was a short distance away from the Lex, still in the Mission, and next to the long-running Latinx gay bar El Rio. El Rio once described itself as "A neighborhood Bar, Community Space, Garden and the kind of spot you bring your Mama too [sic]" (El Rio, n.d.). In other words, El Rio is so much more than a bar. El Rio also hosts a number of rotating parties that specifically and explicitly center queer of color communities. Many of the anxieties about the loss of lesbian bars claim that without this space, lesbian culture is disappearing too. These claims imagine that young lesbian, queer, and trans people do not have a culture. And yet, as El Rio and myriad other queer establishments, promoters, and partygoers make clear, a radical, political, community-oriented gay culture persists, with or without the lesbian bar.

With each closing of a lesbian bar, we shorten the history of how we track lesbian space. When Amelia's closed in 1991, communities mourned the loss of a dedicated lesbian bar. Regardless, lesbians continued to congregate, making space and making politics (a point that I pick up in the next chapter when I turn to San Francisco as the site of lesbian breast cancer activism).[9] By the early 1990s, however, the commitments of earlier lesbian feminism's anticapitalism were waning. As Katie Hogan (2016) documents, during this same time women booksellers began to abandon their collectivist strategies in order to keep up with the growing corporatization of the bookselling industry. Bookstores and bars differed because bookstores were about selling a product that was not available elsewhere. Bars, however, were about tapping into a consumer market. The lament of the loss of the lesbian bar helps highlight the centrality of the gay market to the establishment of many of these spaces. The mourning of the closing of lesbian bars imagines that what is lost is an ethos of 1970s separatism when, in fact, what is lost has roots in the rise of gay consumerism in the 1990s. In this way, the entanglement of lesbian space with capitalism and the shifting market economies post-Reagan can be displaced through claims of violence and exclusion.[10]

Arguments about women's, and lesbians', lack of capital betray the lack of anticapitalist frameworks in response to such closures. In other words, this argument imagines that if only lesbians could make more money and better participate in the market economy, they would be better consumers and their cultural establishments would thrive. Elsewhere the argument goes that lesbians have become too mainstreamed. These two arguments are somewhat in contradiction to each other. On the one hand, the implication is that lesbians have not been afforded the pleasures and leisures of mainstreaming and, thus, cannot be good consumers. On the other, it is that lesbians have been afforded the economic benefits of mainstreaming and now consume elsewhere. What is missing here is the middle ground of anticapitalism. As Gieseking argues, even in the absence of dedicated spaces such as bars, a "dyke politics" of anticapitalist commitments, with roots in the political inheritances of lesbian feminism, persists. Gieseking (2020, 26) notes, "These politics take the form of do-it-yourself events, sliding scale fees or free spaces, nonprofit jobs, a focus on community building and activism . . . as well as informal economies." Of course, we should be wholly concerned with the ongoing erasure of queer and lesbian spaces. And yet, when these lamentations focus on individual market actors and pin the survival of lesbian spaces on whether or not lesbians are spending their dollars in or out of the community, we end up with a failure to conjure the real histories of anticapitalist political frameworks of which lesbians were a part. When the loss of lesbian bars is imagined as the loss of the cultural markers of 1970s feminism, a focus on the patrons, rather than the social and economic context, betrays the forgotten commitments of the supposedly lost political project.

MICHIGAN WOMYN'S MUSIC FESTIVAL

In 2015, after forty years "on the land," the Michigan Womyn's Music Festival held its final August gathering.[11] The Michigan Womyn's Music Festival began in 1976 as a yearly gathering of women (mostly lesbians) on rural land near Hart, Michigan, for a week of music and community. Michfest was one of hundreds of women's music festivals that grew out of and developed in tandem with the feminist separatist and back-to-the-land movements of the 1970s.[12] In its final years, many of the most famous supporters and performers at Michfest formally withdrew their support and participation as part of a larger backlash against the festival's trans-exclusionary policies. Michfest was a lightning rod for accusations of lesbian anachronicity and transphobia.[13]

For forty years, Michfest was an annual pilgrimage for thousands of women and lesbians from around the globe. The week was anchored in music with performances by women-only bands, largely lesbian folk and soul groups, in the afternoons and evenings. Festivalgoers—or "festies," as they were known—would camp out on the over six hundred acres of land. Attendees shared communal meals and communal showers. Many found new lovers and rekindled old flames. In addition to music, Michfest also featured a number of workshops ranging from S/M basics to antiracist trainings, as well as an ever-growing crafts market. The vibe was basically Woodstock meets a women's studies conference. While music was the raison d'être of the festival, the primary attraction was the matriarchal society that the group erected in the confines of "the land." From its inception, Michfest was a separatist space. The ethos of the gathering was a world built *for* women *by* women. In her extensive ethnography of the culture of women's music festivals, Bonnie J. Morris (1999, 60) describes Michfest as "an entire city run by and for lesbian feminists. Utopia revealed." For weeks before the start of the festival, workers on the "long crew" meticulously built stages, eating areas, and outdoor showers. In less than a month, a small society was erected with its own rules, habits, and traditions. Like a city, the land was marked by its neighborhoods. Attendees could choose to reside in areas designated as sober or for late-night partiers. There was an area for S/M practitioners and an area with quiet hours. There was dedicated space for musical artists and long-haul festival workers. While attendees paid hefty sums for festival entrance, the festival also required that attendees volunteer for work shifts. Every attendee contributed to the inner workings of the small society, from serving food in the communal kitchen to directing traffic at the front gates. The only task not done by attendees, and the only time men were allowed on the land—they were often greeted with a rolling chant, "man on the land," to announce their presence—was the daily cleaning of the so-dubbed porta-janes.

Many women describe Michfest as home. Home, for attendees, was marked by the one week every year where they could live free from the confines and the violence of patriarchal society. This utopia promised a safe space for all lesbians and women. Such promises, however, can rarely ever match the ideal. The question of difference and the difficult conversations regarding who the space served were central to the festival, as well as separatist space writ large, from its inception.[14] Across the festival's forty years, activism and mobilization by groups of women—most notably women of color, disabled women, and S/M practitioners—led to meaningful change in both the everyday operations of the festival and the experiences of festivalgoers. Early activism on the part of Black and women of color attendees led to dedicated space for women of color, ongoing workshops on the persistence of racism in lesbian communities, and designated sacred drum circles for women of color only (Morris 1999). Activism by disabled women led to changes in the built environment, sign language interpreters on the paid staff, and, again, meaningful moments for social and political education on ableism. In the early 1990s, S/M practitioners dropped flyers from crop planes to protest the policing of their spaces at Michfest (Morris 1999, 165). The result was a designated space, the Twilight Zone, for S/M play parties and sanctioned S/M workshops, so long as they did not include live demonstrations.[15]

In 1991, Nancy Burkholder arrived on the land for her second Michfest.[16] She had attended the year prior and made the return trip with her friend Laura, driving through the night from their home in Western Massachusetts. Nancy had come out as a lesbian five years prior to her first trip to Michfest. Like all festival attendees, Nancy had found home in lesbian community and was eager for her week in this sacred lesbian space. When Nancy and Laura arrived at the festival, they quickly volunteered for their work shifts and offered Laura's car to help deliver attendees and their belongings to their campsites. After setting up their own tents, Nancy and Laura returned to the front gates to await the arrival of a friend on a nighttime shuttle. At the front gates, Nancy and Laura joined other women around a welcome site campfire. While they were waiting, two festival organizers approached Nancy and demanded to know if she was a man. Nancy immediately produced her driver's license—sex designation F—and, despite the indignity, even volunteered for a genital screening. Neither her legal nor genital status as a woman were convincing to the organizers, who insisted that only "womyn-born womyn" were allowed at the festival. Nancy was not even allowed to return to her campsite to collect her belongings. She waited alone by the front gates while Laura retrieved her tent and other items. Producers permanently barred Nancy from the festival—though she would return in protest—all because she was a trans woman (Burkholder 1993).

The year that Nancy was kicked out of the festival, most attendees were unaware of what had transpired. But by the next year, hundreds of women had heard about what happened to Nancy and were outraged. Many women returned to the festival and vowed to protest the "womyn-born womyn" policy. Attendees, often wearing pins asking "Where's Nancy?," set up educational booths and distributed flier debunking "gender myths." The year 1992 was also the first year that Michfest organizers included the language of "womyn-born womyn" in the official program for the event (Fredrickson 1993b). While Burkholder did not attend the 1992 festival, her friends circulated a survey to collect festivalgoers' thoughts and opinions on the inclusion of trans women in the space. Overwhelmingly, respondents reported that they felt trans women belonged at Michfest (Fredrickson 1993a). Based on this information, Burkholder returned in 1993 with fellow activists prepared to lead teach-ins and workshops on trans experiences and trans inclusion at Michfest. Again, organizers ejected Burkholder and her friends from the grounds, but they hosted their workshops at a campsite outside the front gates (Fredrickson 1993a). Organizers dubbed this space "Camp Trans."[17]

Between the summer of 1993 and the summer of 1994, activists across the country held educational programs and fundraisers in support of Camp Trans. Camp Trans returned in 1994, this time with a permit to camp across from the front gates, a formal program of events and workshops, and the backing of many prominent lesbian and trans activists, including Riki Wilchins, Jamison Green, Leslie Feinberg, and Minnie Bruce Pratt. The week of actions culminated in a group of organizers, both trans and cis, entering the festival, guarded and escorted by the activist group the Lesbian Avengers ("Camp Trans Welcomes You" 1995). While Camp Trans, as a formal gathering outside the gates, fizzled across the late 1990s, the "womyn-born womyn" policy, which most festival attendees rejected, was an ongoing point of contention both inside and outside of the festival. In the early 2000s, activists reestablished Camp Trans and the battle over Michfest's admittance policy remained a central point of contention at the festival. In a press release in 2006, Vogel held fast to the womyn-born womyn policy while also refusing to outright state that trans women were not allowed. This fine line between outright refusal to welcome trans women and a refusal to explicitly state their exclusion became a focal point of festival politics in its last decade. The responses to Michfest's transphobic policies bled into local scenes where those who opposed the Michfest admission policy chastised and boycotted performers and community organizers who did not speak out against Michfest (Trigilio 2016). In 2013, activist Red Durkin created a Change.org petition asking performers to boycott Michfest until Vogel and organizers reversed the womyn-born womyn policy. In response to Durkin's petition, many attendees refused to travel to Michfest. Even more damningly, a number of regional and national LGBT organizations joined the boycott, including Equality Michigan, the Human Rights Campaign, the National Center for Lesbian Rights, and the National LGBTQ Task Force (Holden 2015).

At the close of the 2014 festival, Vogel and organizers released a response to the summer's protests and boycotts. In a letter titled "We Have a Few Demands of Our Own," Vogel set out four demands of critics of the festival's policies. The demands included admonishments to detractors to stop accusing the festival of transphobia, to acknowledge the necessity of female-defined space, to recognize the unique experience of the space, and to turn their energies back toward patriarchal systems. They also invited their critics to dialogue. In the letter's opening paragraph, Vogel (2014) states: "We reiterate that Michfest recognizes trans women as women. . . . We do not fear their presence among us." The problem, as Vogel frames it, is not the presence of trans women—as well as, presumably, their friends and lovers—but rather the purported erasure of lesbian specificity, a specificity that, in her telling, is tied to an imagined shared experience of girlhood socialization. This doubling down on a monolithic girlhood, or experience of being socialized female, is central to the boundary lines Vogel and a minority of lesbian community gatekeepers draw to mark trans women as exterior.[18] While Vogel acknowledges that trans women and trans men have been a part of the festival across its forty-year history, it is the ethos of the space that she argues is threatened if the participant policies expand beyond the marker of womyn-born womyn. In the statement, Vogel offloads the meaning of *lesbian* and of female identity from individuals and bodies and locates *lesbian*'s specificity within the space of the festival. Vogel states, "It is not the inclusion of trans women at the festival that we resist; it is the erasure of the specificity of female experience in the discussion of the space itself that stifles progress in this conversation." The space, Vogel reiterates, is a lesbian space, defined by lesbian culture. This curious slippage has a number of implications. First, lesbian culture is certainly not monolithic. However, the lesbian culture that Vogel is referring to can be understood as reflective of the wider history of lesbian space as defined through 1970s feminist movements, specifically around music festivals and bookstores (Enke 2007; Hogan 2016). In this story, such a culture is defined by both its failures at combating racism and its violent exclusion of trans women (Enke 2018; Heaney 2016). The commonsense story of lesbian culture to which Vogel refers, then, is the very environment she and organizers are being accused of fostering. Second, Vogel is volleying the accusations back to the detractors by implying that the problem is not the exclusion of trans women, an exclusion that she refuses to make explicit, but rather trans women's demand to be recognized as within the defining frameworks of lesbian space.

Michfest was not alone in perpetuating debates about trans women's access to and inclusion within avowed lesbian or women's spaces. Across the first decade of the twenty-first century, numerous organizations, including rape crisis centers and women's health centers, were mired in their own contentious conversations about the inclusion of trans women as both service seekers and service providers. Michfest, however, uniquely leveraged lesbian specificity as the justification for the exclusion for trans women. One tactic that Michfest organizers and defenders used was to compare lesbian separatist spaces to women of color spaces, especially the necessity of the women of color tent at Michfest. Indeed, analogies to the experiences of women of color animate many of the arguments against the explicit inclusion of trans women in lesbian space. In this strategy, the women of color tent becomes justification for the necessity of "womyn-born womyn"–defined space. The women of color tent came to be in response to the experiences of persistent racism in the early days of the festival. As Laurie J. Kendall (2013, 69) reports, in the early 1980s festival organizers responded to the demands of women of color—who instituted the women of color tent—by inviting more performers of color, upping BIPOC representation to a dismal 15 percent. Such numbers, which organizers reported as a major achievement, demonstrate the relative dearth of women of color in these separatist spaces. This is not to say that women of color do not exist in, benefit from, and desire these spaces.[19] Rather, this narrative tool highlights how white women continue to imagine lesbian identity as a shared and unifying claim that is analogous to racialized identities but not co-constitutive. In so doing, the framers of this narrative recast whiteness as central to the space while allowing the supposed special interests of racially marginalized groups protection within.

When trans women's exclusion is analogized to space for women of color only, as Keridwen N. Luis (2018, 211) notes, such rhetoric "likens trans women to white women attempting to 'crash' women of color space, attributing social power to them (trans women) not congruent with reality." The analogy also fails to acknowledge the myriad, often a representational majority, women who were regular festival attendees who advocated and actively fought for trans women's inclusion. For trans women and their friends and lovers, including trans women in lesbian separatist space was not antithetical to the separatists' ethos but, indeed, in line with it. Trans women and their friends and lovers were not arguing that trans women be included as an outsider group allowed on the inside. To the contrary, women supporting inclusion argued that trans women's experiences and existence were central to their experience of lesbian identity and sisterhood. Or, as protestors inside the festival put it, "Trans women belong here."

LESBIAN STUDIES IN QUEER TIMES

In January 2014, and again in April 2016, Valerie Traub and Sue Lanser convened two seminars, first at Harvard and then at the University of Michigan, with the goal of reinvigorating lesbian scholarship. Both seminars brought together a number of established scholars whose work crossed between the lesbian and the queer.[20] The brief description of the first seminar, began with the following claim: "The last two decades have seen a dramatic increase in the exploration of 'lesbian' history and representation, yet this scholarship continues to be sidelined not only in disciplines such as history and literature but in women's studies and queer studies as well." The seminar, thus, begins from a paradox: there has been an increase in scholarship on "lesbian" history, but this scholarship is being devalued.[21] The use of quotes around *lesbian* invites the question of the meaning of this term. Unlike the debates around bar culture and music festivals, the academic debates as to the place of the lesbian are more fraught with inspecificity. The seminar Traub and Lanser convened at Radcliffe dodges specificity through the various uses of *lesbianism* and *"lesbian"* history. Moreover, the goals of the seminar seem to be at odds with the proposition offered in its title. To write lesbianism into history and representation would be to recover a lost or, perhaps, never seen history. Whereas, the organizers assert, there already is not only a "lesbian" history but also a cadre of scholars who have done the work to name and study this history. The problem, then, is not so much the lack of history as the lack of interest in such history. The anxiety about lesbian studies and a perceived waning of interest in such a field is expanded in Valerie Traub's *Thinking Sex with the Early Moderns*. "Lesbianism," Traub (2016, 268) proclaims in the text, "has all but disappeared in the stories that queer theory tells about itself." The statement has no citations, though it speaks with the certainty of fact and with a commonsense knowledge that it assumes the reader shares. It is not clear, however, exactly what story queer theory tells about itself. Queer theory is neither a coalesced discipline nor even a solitary conversation. One might assume that Traub means a specific lineage of queer theory that stretches from Butler and Sedgwick with strong roots in psychoanalytic thinking and Foucauldian critique.[22] But even this lineage cannot reasonably be argued to have dispensed with the lesbian altogether.[23]

I turn here to Traub because her chapter "The Sign of the Lesbian" nicely captures the ongoing anxiety that lesbian studies scholars articulate in relationship to the queer.[24] Even more so, Traub's insistence that the lesbian's analytic purchase has hit its swan song overlooks the ways that the lesbian survives, and even thrives, beyond a framework of "female same-sex desire." Across the text, Traub attends to the epistemological slipperiness of sex—sex as practices, as a series of acts, as libidinous desire—that cannot be neatly categorized through contemporary frameworks of identity. In the whole of the project, but especially in the chapter "The Sign of the Lesbian," Traub rejects an approach to history that searches for lesbians in the past as defined by what *lesbian* means in the contemporary. In response to this challenge of history, Traub (2016, 267) offers the "sign of the lesbian," following Robyn Wiegman, in order to "explore how same-sex desire and practice most explicitly marked by gender might yield theoretical resources for queerly rethinking the history of sex."[25] In this argument, Traub's chapter enacts two important gestures. First, Traub repeats the straw argument that the lesbian, whether as identity or as an interest for contemporary scholarship, has fallen out of fashion as a result of the queer's promised plenitude. Second, Traub's reliance on "same-sex desire and practice" evacuates any politics from the lesbian. The latter is especially crucial because the former relies on a sense of the lesbian as apolitical, or even worse myopically feminist, in relationship to the queer (Martin 1994). These two gestures converge to produce Traub's elision, if not outright dismissal, of engagements with contemporary forms of queer theory and lesbian

studies that root themselves in women of color and Third World feminisms, most specifically those works and conversations that fall under the
banner of queer of color critique.

In short, Traub's project in *Thinking Sex with the Early Moderns* is to
reject methods and orientations of both queer studies writ large and queer
history specifically that rely on contemporary frameworks of identity to
understand the social relations that mediated sexual practices in the past.
Rather, Traub insists on the opacity of sex to any totalizing field of knowledge. The text's central argument is the culmination of a protracted debate
among queer scholars who work in literary formations prior to the nineteenth and twentieth centuries. Within these debates, Traub herself was
accused of historical teleology, wherein the events of the past become the
necessary precursors for present. Traub's text, then, despite its title, begins
not with the early moderns but with a series of diagnoses, and concomitant disagreements, that she has for contemporary queer studies. Admittedly, these diagnoses are beyond the scope of this project. What I am
most interested in, and what offers the most resonance for this project, is
Traub's (2016, 18) secondary argument—namely, her assertion that "the
gendered specificity of female embodiment offers an especially valuable
resource for thinking sex." Traub twins history and lesbianism together as
the forgotten others of queer theory's presentism and masculinist impulses.
The key here, for my argument at least, is Traub's ready association of
lesbianism with the feminine in this configuration and, more specifically,
with a form of relation that she calls "female-female." Ironically, Traub
presents a singular "queer" in her allegations of the lesbian's evacuation
from the queer project.

Claims of the lesbian's erasure from the queer tend to rely on a singular definition of both *queer* and *lesbian*. This singularity is especially true in
Traub's telling. The queer that Traub and others accuse of forgetting the
lesbian stands in for a lineage of queer theory that tends to ground itself
in the experiences of gay white men. Traub anchors queer theory in two
texts: *The Routledge Queer Studies Reader* and *Sex, or The Unbearable.* The
reader, published in 2013, presents a broad series of essays that provide a
kind of state of the field. While it is true that *lesbian* does not appear in the
title of any of the essays, a deeper scratch reveals lesbian figures, lesbian
concerns, and lesbian histories abundantly peppered throughout. It is hard
to say, thus, that this field of queer theory has dispensed with the lesbian.
Sex, or The Unbearable, a short, experimental piece of writing published in

2013 by Lauren Berlant and Lee Edelman, does not mention the word *lesbian*. To be clear, Traub presents these two texts, as well as essays that inform Berlant and Edelman's project, in order to demonstrate queer studies' apathetic, if not antagonistic, relationship to history—which Traub aligns with the material—in favor of theory. Traub aligns the lesbian with this historical-material. Thus, according to Traub, it is the lineages of queer studies that she alleges reject history that are to be understood as the same lineages that reject the lesbian. This framing has the curious effect of affirming queer studies as only and always theory and as only and always disavowing the lesbian. I want to make clear here that my concern is not with Traub's overarching argument, per se. Rather, I am concerned with both these moves outlined above, a move that itself erases deep strands of queer studies that root themselves in feminist and critical race concerns, as well as the singularity of Traub's definition of *lesbian*.

The sign of the lesbian, as Traub offers it, is mired in a commitment to a singular kind of supposedly female embodiment as the ground for its signification. In other words, Traub's lesbianism relies on an idea of "female same-sex desire"—she slips between defining *lesbianism* as "female same-sex desire," "female same-sex relations," and "female homoeroticism"—that conjures or implies an embodied sameness. Put more bluntly, despite Traub's insistence that *lesbian*, as a word, has a fluid and changing history, her anxiety over *lesbian*'s loss points to a commitment to a lesbian framework that mirrors Michfest's womyn-born womyn policy. This is especially true if we consider that Traub's insistence in the project is on the epistemological promises and challenges of sex as an event or an action. Whereas Traub resists "lesbian" as identity, this resistance has the effect of rendering the sign of the lesbian as a practice between two "same" bodies. In this way, Traub marks the border of the lesbian thus: she is both what is left out of queer studies and she is the same-sex practices that are not called on for critical work today.

When Traub and others define *lesbian* as the entity that the queer erased, both *lesbian* and *queer* remain remarkably ill-defined. To be sure, Traub's project in *Thinking Sex with the Early Moderns* argues for an expansion of queer studies away from the postmodern frames of literary studies to take seriously both history and historiography. Nevertheless, within this argument, if not central to it, Traub offers a succinct narrative of lesbian anxieties between the feminist and the queer. At the end of the chapter, Traub slips from "lesbian studies" to "lesbian history," a move that makes her whole project make a different kind of sense. To argue for the value of the lesbian as a historical analytic, which I take to be Traub's project, is quite different from demanding that more value be given to lesbian studies in current times.[26] Whereas women's studies aligns itself with a progress narrative of better incorporating race and sexuality, lesbian studies, as Traub describes it, defines itself through an exclusion narrative. By this I mean that lesbian studies, in Traub's telling, is an elusive endeavor, one marked largely by the negligence of the fields of queer studies and women's and gender studies. The doubling down on the exclusion narrative of lesbian studies, against the backdrop of the explosion of intersectionality as women's studies' central project, furthers the separation of "lesbian" from other political categories, most specifically that of race. Traub's concern with the lesbian's historiography serves as a crucial point here. Of course, the concern with historiography highlights the challenge of how to account for experiences and practices that we might group under "lesbian" but that predate the formation of the lesbian as she is understood in a feminist and queer framework. And yet, in order to make this argument, Traub makes broad claims about the evacuation of the lesbian today that she herself is guilty of perpetuating.

If the lesbian that Traub fears is lost is defined by her exclusion from queer theory, then she is also white. As I noted in the Introduction, it is a very narrow segment of queer theory that can be reasonably argued to ignore lesbian politics or lesbian subjectivities. Indeed, queer of color critique is grounded in Black and Third World lesbian activism and writing. Traub, however, references works of lesbians of color and the work of queer of color critique only in a brief footnote. In a chapter subsection titled "The Embarrassment of Lesbian Studies," Traub (2016, 281), without evidence, laments, "Many women of color, youth, and genderqueers view lesbianism as a white, middle-class identification, and have no interest in being 'hailed' by it, whatever their sexual inclinations." This statement aligns "women of color, youth, and genderqueers" with the project of the queer, as Traub defines it, in their refusal of "the sign of the lesbian." Even if we are to take as true that "women of color, youth, and genderqueers" refuse to claim *lesbian*—and, to be clear, I do not take this as fact—I am left to wonder what about "the sign of the lesbian" fails to serve the social or political needs of women of color, youth, and genderqueers. By aligning lesbianism with a materiality, specifically a materiality that the queer refuses, Traub suggests that female same-sex desire is rendered banal. In so doing, especially as juxtaposed to the claim that "women of color, youth, and genderqueers" refuse *lesbian,* Traub aligns the lesbian with white women's sexuality. It is, in this context, a white woman's problem to understand sex, even lesbian sex, as too vanilla to be politically useful. By this I mean: white women's lesbian sex does little to disrupt cultural narratives of deviance that attach to other bodies in the service of systems of domination. But without a wider political claim, white women's privatized lesbian sex does not offer much cultural or theoretical purchase.

As I outlined in the Introduction, it is not clear to me that the lesbian has been cast out from queer theory. Which is not to say that there are not strands of queer theory that fail to attend to lesbian possibilities (a point I address more in chapters 3 and 4). Traub's claims, and those of others that echo them, have the double effect of rendering both the lesbian and queer theory as a singular logic. In other words, they imply that both "queer theory" and "lesbian" are well-defined and discrete categories. The idea that queer theory has a rigid boundary is expressed most forcefully in the claim that the lesbian has been excluded from this boundary. To be sure, other responses to early work that falls under the rubric of queer theory have been clear about the exclusions of that work.[27] To name such exclusions, however, does not necessitate diagnosing queer theory as rigidly guarded from the infiltration of certain subjects. Indeed, critiques of the race and class exclusions of early queer theory focus on how such exclusions are developed from the place of narrow-minded, single-axis politics rather than from a deliberate casting out of nonwhite subjects. Although Traub cites Roderick Ferguson as one example of scholarship that theorizes Black lesbian sexuality, she overlooks decades of queer theorizing—often cited under the rubric of queer of color critique—that is avowedly interested in the lesbian, specifically as the lesbian is figured by women of color feminism. The same strands of queer theorizing that have elided the lesbian—in Traub's telling, Edelman, etc.—have been called to task for their failure to address the racialized political economy of queer theorizing. An attention to queer of color critique might suggest, contra Traub et al., that the lesbian is, indeed, central to the queer studies.[28] This lesbian, however, is not the Eurocentric lesbian of early modernity.

The lesbian who is mourned, who is called back or lost, in each of the above examples—I would argue, including Traub's—is a lesbian figured through 1970s feminist projects. That is to say, there is one specific lesbian who is lamented in this anxiety. This lesbian is white, she is culturally salient, and she is a single-axis lesbian. Such construction of the lesbian has the effect of freezing her in a specific time. In this way she is neither ahistorical nor transhistorical but singular. Bonnie J. Morris and the defenders of Michfest policies imagine that the lesbian exists only in history, that she is the "disappearing L." Traub, however, imagines that the lesbian is erased from history. Both want this past lesbian to be useful today. The only thing that grounds this lesbian figuration, however, is the use of the word *lesbian*. But, even more so, the sense of loss enacts this lesbian figuration—a loss that is occasioned by exclusion.

THE AFTERLIVES OF LESBIAN LOSS

What are the afterlives of these proclaimed losses? When the Lexington Club closed its doors in 2015, the PlumpJack Group bought the space. This restaurant group was founded in the mid-1990s by Gavin Newsom. Newsom's group has replaced the Lex with a cocktail bar named Wildhawk, a reference to nineteenth-century San Francisco local Lola Montez, "a European transplant hell-raiser with a firecracker persona" (Wildhawk, n.d.). As a diversity point, it touts that its head bartender is a woman. The replacement of the Lex with a trendy cocktail bar whose selling point is female empowerment aptly highlights how such social issues cannot be addressed through single-axis nodes of difference and certainly not without an examination of political economy. Gavin Newsom is well known for his activist stance in favor of gay marriage. In 2004, in the wake of a national doubling down against gay marriage, Newsom, then mayor of San Francisco, defied both state and federal statutes and began issuing same-sex marriage licenses at city hall. The run of his resistance lasted four weeks. This move is often heralded as his most important political decision. While Newsom himself is heterosexual, and has been embroiled in a notable sex scandal, he has won cult status among mainstream LGBT communities. Likewise, Wildhawk using their woman head bartender as a selling point makes women-centered space a commercial draw.

The Michigan Womyn's Music Festival grew out of the feminist music movements of the 1970s. Outside of Michfest, Olivia Records was one of the most noted and lauded institutions of women's music. Founded in 1973, Olivia Records was an all-female recording company often credited with some of the most foundational women's folk music. Today, many remember Olivia Records for the very public battle among the collective over the place of trans women in lesbian separatist space. In the late 1970s, there was a small but vocal outrage at recording engineer and trans woman Sandy Stone's inclusion in the separatist collective. Contra the Michigan Womyn's Music Festival, the Olivia Records collective was steadfastly in support of Stone and her position in the collective. In the historiography of trans women's exclusion from lesbian space, Olivia Records' defense of Stone stands at the root. In the early 1990s, as the folk traditions of the 1970s gave way to the punk-influenced riot grrrl movements and the rise of hip-hop cultures, Olivia Records' work was waning and the collective was slowly disbanding. Though they were still making records and producing concerts, individual finances were tight and many of the original members left to pursue other projects. Reportedly on the suggestion of a concert-goer, Judy Dlugacz, one of the few remaining members of the collective, moved the music of Olivia Records from the stage to the seas. In 1989, Dlugacz announced what would be the first Olivia Cruise, setting sail from Miami in February 1990. By 1993, more than six thousand women had sailed with Olivia Cruises, and with the release of their final album the company shifted focus to the cruise industry full time (Post 1990). Today, Olivia Cruises produces nearly twenty trips per year, ranging from tropical cruises to African safaris to high-end trips like "Wonders of Japan Luxury" (Olivia, n.d.). In 2017, Olivia Cruises was listed as the third largest LGBT-owned company in the Bay Area, with annual revenue of $23 million (Cooper 2018). In other words, what was once the most lauded example of lesbian separatist potential is now one of the highest-grossing corporations catering to a neoliberal lesbian consumer. While the commitment to providing lesbians and their friends with women's music and dedicated lesbian space remains, it is nearly impossible to trace any of the original political commitment that drove lesbian separatism as a project of radical feminism.

The lesbian losses that some attribute to queer's rise are less clear. As I have demonstrated, there is an ongoing, even axiomatic, anxiety about queer's disavowal of the lesbian. Aside from lesbian bars and separatist spaces, there is not a single or well-recognized moment to mark this loss. And yet, as I have shown, the anxiety about the space for lesbian contra queer is ubiquitous. There has not, despite the story this anxiety tells, been a precipitous drop in lesbian studies, especially in a framework of studies about lesbians. To the contrary, as I explore in the next chapter, there continues to be an ever-expanding arena, not to mention financing, for lesbian studies, both empirical and beyond. Put quite simply, there are still lesbian nights and bar cultures informed by dyke sensibilities. Across 2018, there were at least three new feminist bookstore openings. There are still lesbian music spaces, the corporate success of Olivia being just one example. There are endless lesbian studies, but many are interested in the lesbian as empirical fact. Over the four years of the Trump presidency, there has been a return to the aesthetics and rhetorics of 1970s lesbian feminism, a point I take up more in this book's Conclusion. But these, too, have become commodified. Without a focus on political economy, the lesbian becomes another cog in this neoliberal framework.

LESBIAN LOSS AND THE DESIRE FOR SAMENESS

While some things have changed, much has stayed the same in the stories of lesbian loss from the early 1990s to today. Take for example Arlene Stein's (1997) ethnography of lesbian generational divides. Her early chapters—interviews with women who came of queer age in the 1970s amid the Gay Liberation Front, the women's liberation movements, and the rise of Black power–influenced critical race politics—highlight again and again the painful inability of lesbians to identify a single coherent identity or political claim. Indeed, what marks this time most forcefully is the turmoil and interpersonal disputes. Stein follows many narratives that brush aside concerns of class or race as growing pains of a movement trying to find its footing. And yet, in the concluding chapter on 1990s women, Stein echoes the sentiment that there is a coherent past from which new lesbians are attempting to distance themselves.

The contemporary stories that animate anxieties of lesbian loss, similarly, are about needing sameness—specifically, a same history, a same politics, and, especially, a same identity. Clare Hemmings (2011) notes that feminism, in the stories it tells, is caught up with an idea about difference. By contrast, the pursuit of sameness informs the meaning of *lesbian* as it is marked through ideas of women and women's space, specifically as informed by a certain strand of 1970s feminism. The feminism of the 1970s also saw the creation and expansion of women's spaces such as health clinics, community spaces, and social service organizations (Batza 2018). Many of these organizations set the groundwork for the queer community's response to HIV. Yet rarely are anxieties around lesbian death mapped onto these locations. Shifts in lesbian space map quite neatly to shifting economic programs, specifically the rise of neoliberalism.[29] And yet, much of the most vocal hand-wringing about the fate of the lesbian and lesbian space does not engage with questions of neoliberalism or the shifting economic land-scapes. Indeed, the most oft-reported refrain is that the dwindling of avowed lesbian space is part of a generational shift informed by the rise of queer theory and trans identities, as well as the shifting terrain of dating in the age of social media and a mass-mobilized internet culture. What is disappearing, then, is not only lesbian space but a sustained critique of and engagement with the histories of anticapitalism and antipatriarchy that informed earlier political movements under the moniker of *lesbian* (Hennessy 2018).

The attachment to a singular vision of lesbian identity and politics, one squarely rooted in a supposedly lost lesbian past, undergirds the centrality of whiteness to these anxieties. Here, I am not necessarily connecting whiteness to an empirical fact but rather to an ideology of privilege that refuses coalitional work and maintains a focus on sameness. Much of the lamentation of lesbian loss is rooted in attachments to projects that refuse to imagine an expansive definition of lesbian culture or lesbian politics. In Nan Alamilla Boyd's history of gay San Francisco, she identifies two modes of political engagement for gay constituents. The first mode was made through involvement with homophile organizations, such as the Daugh-ters of Bilitis, and centered the fight for individual rights. The second mode was enacted through bar culture and fought for the right to public assem-bly. The first, Boyd (2013) argues, was a politics of sameness and one that was more readily associated with the identity claim of "lesbian." The sec-ond was a politics of difference, one that predates current queer modes of engagement. This distinction, I argue, is the crux. Individual lesbians are here to stay. Many individual lesbians, though certainly not all, are happy to be a part of the mainstreaming of gay and lesbian life. But it is the insis-tence on a capital *L* Lesbian that makes it seem like certain spaces are dis-appearing. But maybe, the lesbian is something else besides the Lesbian.

Across these frameworks of lesbian loss, those who fret about the les-bian's demise cling to the enactments of an earlier lesbian politics. As I have outlined, lesbian spaces (such as bars), separatist ethos (like the found-ing imperative of Michfest), and even the political and theoretical poten-tial of the lesbian as analytic were the enactments of an avowed, if often vexed, feminist politics. What is left in these attachments, however, is only the enactments. Those who mourn or lament the lesbian's demise long for the heady potential of lesbian politics. The hand-wringing and defensive-ness that attach to these lost spaces, places, and analytics today, however, arrive without a politics. Quite simply, the attachments to these prior modes of lesbian politics come at the expense of engaging new modes of political engagement that follow the political potential that the lesbian once promised, even if they eschew earlier practices.

The lamentations of lesbian loss that I have outlined here arrived at the time of the legalization of gay marriage in the United States. A number of years ago, I heard a longtime gay activist remark that gay marriage, somewhat convolutedly, was made possible by the horrors of the AIDS crisis. In this statement, of course, he echoed years of theorizing under the rubric of homonormativity. That is, the idea that normative sexual practices rooted in the frameworks of heterosexuality, when made available to gay and lesbian subjects, would allow them access to market promises of neoliberal subjectivity. In this story, the lesbian is appended to the gay as a kind of barnacle along for the ride to state-based, or market-based, recognitions. Following this story, I move in the next chapter to chart the path of lesbian mainstreaming as distinct from, though related to, the process of gay men's mainstreaming through an attention to lesbian biopolitics.

2 Marked for Life

Breast Cancer and Lesbian Biopolitics

> A biopolitical paradigm . . . takes two different areas of concern—
> the meaning of biological difference and the status of socially
> subordinated groups—and weaves them together by articulating a
> distinctive way of asking and answering questions about the
> demarcating of subpopulations of patients and citizens.
>
> —STEVEN EPSTEIN, *Inclusion:*
> *The Politics of Difference in Medical Research*

In 1999, the Office of Research on Women's Health at the National Institutes of Health (NIH) published a 250-page report titled *Lesbian Health: Current Assessment and Directions for the Future* (Solarz 1999). The Institute of Medicine Committee on Lesbian Health Research Priorities commissioned the report as part of a number of initiatives to expand research on women's health in marginalized communities. In addition to developing better standards of care for lesbians, as well as identifying lesbian-specific health risks, the report sought to confirm or deny a number of misconceptions regarding lesbian health. While lesbian health had long been a concern of feminist and LGBT health activists, this publication marked the first time that lesbian health needs were articulated within the purview of state-based health organizations.[1] The publication of this document marks, as Steven Epstein (2003) notes, the solidification of "lesbian" as an identifiable and measurable category—most notably, as a category that came to be a concern of the state. Put differently, this publication marks a significant attempt to consolidate "lesbian" as a biopolitical category.

49

I turn in this chapter to one underexplored narrative of the lesbian's rise to mainstream recognition. As I demonstrated in the previous chapter, many attribute lesbian loss to mainstream acceptance of lesbian life and lifestyles. Oftentimes this shift in mainstream acceptance is understood in relation to a benevolent, heteronormative public's increased tolerance of homosexuality. In this narrative, gay marriage becomes the signifier of mainstream acceptance. As others (Duggan 2004) demonstrate, marriage as a political goal based on acceptance and equality masks the manner in which marriage serves the economic and social benefits of an already privileged class, even if such subjects are minoritized through sexuality. Others attribute the shifting acceptance of the lesbian across the 1990s to increased media representation, specifically the advent of "lesbian chic" (Mckenna 2002; Walters 2003; Rand 2013). Both gay marriage and the rise of lesbian chic are part of a wider trend toward assimilation through what Sara Warner (2013) calls "homoliberalism." *Homoliberalism* names a gay and lesbian political agenda driven by "individual economic interests, a privatized sexual politics, and a constricted notion of national-public life" (2). While engagements with the histories and dangers of homoliberalism are many, there has been little attention to how shifting public health models influenced how the lesbian comes to count, so to speak, in wider projects of social inclusion and rights-based political movements.

The fight for recognition in order to access the benefits and privileges of citizenship defines many rights-based projects for social inclusion. Across the twentieth and into the twenty-first centuries, claims for citizenship rights through liberalism have been made in relation to claims on the body. For this reason, exploring how the lesbian comes to be associated with claims on the body, as in "lesbian breast cancer," is central to understanding how lesbian identity becomes aligned with a project of normativity. The ways that certain communities make claims for citizenry rights in relation to the body, per the work of sociologist Nikolas Rose (2006), is called biocitizenship. *Biocitizenship* names, simultaneously, the ways that new categories of citizenry come to count and the modes of political action available to make claims for recognition.[2] In order to access biocitizenship, a community must first claim recognition through biopolitical categorization. The meeting of HIV / AIDS activism and breast cancer activism in the 1990s provided the conditions for these claims for lesbian communities.

My use of the term *biopolitical category* is drawn from philosopher Michel Foucault's (1978, 140) articulation of *biopower* as "an explosion of numerous and diverse techniques for achieving the subjugation of bodies and control of populations."[3] *Biopolitical category*, then, names one mechanism through which a certain population, in this case lesbians, comes to be counted under the purview of the state and as part of a system of biopower. I am interested here in the conditions that made possible the consolidation of "lesbian" as a category of citizen—that is, a category of people that the state has a special interest in demarcating—as well as how the "lesbian" category emerges in relation to the body. That is to say, I am interested, first, in why it became necessary to count lesbians, so to speak, within the framework of public health. Second, I am interested in what events preceded the consolidation of "lesbian" as a measurable category in our current biopolitical regime. This demarcation of "lesbian" as a biopolitical category—a categorical claim that can then be used for rights-based claims—has the effect, I argue, of shifting the political purchase of the lesbian from a radical project of antinormativity to a liberal project of inclusion. In other words, through this demand for biopolitical recognition, *lesbian* no longer names an antinormative rejection of the mechanisms of heteropatriarchy when it becomes a demographic category that the state recognizes as a kind of person.[4]

The growing conversation around an epidemic of breast cancer that seemed to be afflicting lesbians in the early 1990s was a central factor in the publication of the NIH report on lesbian health. The emergence of the so-called lesbian breast cancer epidemic, as it was staked in relation to the narratives of the AIDS crisis, I argue, was a major factor in the consolidation of "lesbian" as a biopolitical category. Specifically, I argue that the category emerged at this moment from the multiple, and at times contradictory, rhetorics of vulnerability that bridged activist and academic work on the two diseases. In this chapter, I examine the political relationship between breast cancer and HIV/AIDS, particularly during the early 1990s. I have identified this period as a time when the relationship between these two diseases was mobilized in a variety of ways that emphasized the particular vulnerabilities faced by specific communities based on both gender and sexual orientation. In reading three different activist and political narratives that paired breast cancer with HIV/AIDS, albeit in different ways, I demonstrate how the pairing of these two diseases worked to articulate the specificities of lesbian health. In other words, I argue that these multiple ways of bringing together women's health concerns, as articulated through breast cancer research and activism, and gay health concerns, in the context of the AIDS crisis, created the conditions of possibility for the lesbian to be counted as a biopolitical subject.

My argument picks up from Steven Epstein's work in *Inclusion: The Politics of Difference in Medical Research*. Epstein (2009) demonstrates how social differences are measured on the body within the frameworks of public health and how this measurement affects the allocation of resources for health research and pharmaceutical development. Within this narrative, Epstein documents the many ways that scholars and activists articulated, and demanded, recognition of lesbians as a subset of women in need of special attention. He notes, "Crucially, proponents of lesbian health research were able to benefit from positioning themselves as a specific subgroup of women to which the new [Department of Health and Human Services] infrastructure devoted to women's health ought reasonably to attend—that is, women's health provided a strategic wedge for lesbian health advocates" (264–65). In other words, as the bioregime of late twentieth-century public health began to respond to feminist demands for more attention to women's health, lesbians were able to articulate their place within the needs of women's health but with an added attention to the specific needs of sexual minorities. Following Epstein, I turn here to demonstrate that "lesbian," as a biopolitical category, emerged as part of a political model of visibility and inclusion (Rand 2013). For lesbians, this emergence not only shifts political claims but also interestingly mobilizes both feminist and queer projects. That is, the biopolitical category of "lesbian" relied on both the gender-based health disparities articulated in the claims for women's health and the sexuality-based health disparities noted in the claims for gay men's health. Most notably, however, activists and researchers were able to articulate the relationship between these diseases in different ways. While, as I discuss below, there is much to be wary of in the consolidation of a biopolitical category, there is also much to be drawn from the ways in which *lesbian* continues to exceed the referent of either *woman* or *gay*.

Across this book, I explore how the lesbian tracks between feminist and queer projects. Specifically, I track the lesbian as disruption. My attention to disruption in this chapter is somewhat counterintuitive. If AIDS politics were the breeding ground for an articulated queer politics, lesbian breast cancer politics, by contrast, has been, I argue, central to the mainstreaming of gay and lesbian life. The AIDS crisis in the United States was a central catalyst for later gay and lesbian civil rights projects, from the repeal of sodomy laws to the federal recognition of same-sex marriage.

The cleaving of the queer from the gay and the lesbian as a political mode, however, enacts a rejection of the various forms of normative subjectification that have informed and influenced this trajectory. While, as I argue below, lesbian breast cancer activism sutures political claims made through both the AIDS crisis and earlier feminist health movements, this suturing disrupts only in so much as it takes the venom out of the lesbian as a political claim in its own right. Put most simply, the consolidation of "lesbian" as a biopolitical category marks the lesbian for the promotion of life. This promotion of life has implications for both how the lesbian can be mobilized politically but also for who counts under the category of "lesbian."

I focus in this chapter on two related events. First, I track the work of Jackie Winnow and the San Francisco–based Breast Cancer Action. Across literature on the histories of breast cancer in the United States, there are frequent references to the work of San Francisco breast cancer activists working in tandem with HIV / AIDS activists. Winnow, as I outline below, was a seasoned lesbian activist working in HIV / AIDS activism when she was diagnosed with breast cancer. Second, I focus on the oft-cited National Lesbian Health Care Survey (Bradford and Ryan 2006) that produced early narratives of lesbians' greater risk of breast cancer. My focus here is on narratives of lesbian progress that render "lesbian" a monolithic entity. While it is not possible to make a one-for-one line between the consolidation of "lesbian" as a biopolitical category and the current perceptions of lesbian erasure, I do mean to suggest that stories of lesbian progress can have unintended consequences. Even more so, in this chapter, I highlight the ways that the lesbian's incorporation into recognizable life renders impotent lesbian political projects that root themselves in nostalgia for feminist radicalism.

BUILDING A CANCER MOVEMENT

San Francisco was a particular hotbed for political and social activism around HIV / AIDS and breast cancer in the early 1990s, making it an exemplary site of inquiry. I focus here on three distinct but converging narratives of the relation between breast cancer and HIV / AIDS.[5] First, I explore how San Francisco AIDS-professional-turned-lesbian-health-activist Jackie Winnow mobilized disparities between HIV / AIDS funding and breast cancer funding to articulate the need for a specifically lesbian health movement, one which, I argue, grew out of a tension between women's health movements and gay health movements. I then turn to the development of San Francisco–based Breast Cancer Action and its connection to ACT UP/ Golden Gate. These two organizations paired breast cancer and HIV/ AIDS in order to fight against an established medical system, specifically for access to experimental drugs and for the inclusion of patient voices in the Food and Drug Administration. Finally, I examine the media maelstrom that surrounded a 1993 press release claiming that lesbians were at a much higher risk for breast cancer than their heterosexual women peers. The press release drew explicit connections between the epidemic status of HIV/AIDS and that of breast cancer for lesbians. Additionally, it affected a shift in understanding lesbianism as a subset of women's health to a risky health behavior in its own right. The emergence of "lesbian" as a biopolitical category, I argue, relied on the overlapping crisis narratives attached to both breast cancer and HIV/AIDS through political concerns with both women's health and gay health.

Jackie Winnow was diagnosed with breast cancer in 1985. Following a long history in gay and lesbian activism, Winnow was working as the les-bian/gay community liaison to the San Francisco Human Rights Commis-sion at the time of her diagnosis. Years later, Winnow (1992) recalled the invisibility she felt as a person with breast cancer in the gay and lesbian community, which was so heavily focused on AIDS at the time. Winnow recognized that the gay and lesbian community had done an exemplary job of creating the kinds of informal social service networks that allowed people with AIDS to continue to live with dignity and independence even as their health deteriorated. She demonstrated that these same kinds of networks had not been developed for women coping with cancer, and particularly not for the women who were often left out of more main-stream health care: lesbians, women of color, and poor and working-class women. Recognizing this lack of services and building upon the model put forth by AIDS activists in San Francisco (often referred to as the "San Fran-cisco model"), in 1986, Winnow, along with Carla Dalton, founded the Women's Cancer Resource Center (WCRC) in Berkeley, California. The WCRC followed the model developed by the nascent AIDS movement in order to create a resource for women with cancer outside of the formal networks of institutionalized health care. The main focus of the WCRC was patient education and empowerment, as well as facilitating connec-tions to resources and alternative therapies.

In 1989, Winnow gave the keynote address—"Lesbians Evolving Health Care"—at the Lesbian Caregivers and the AIDS Epidemic Conference in San Francisco. Her speech served as a kind of call to arms for a specifically lesbian-focused health movement, one that could bridge lesbian women's experiences in earlier feminist health movements of the 1970s with the kind of feminine labor of care they were taking on within the AIDS crisis. The speech, given at a number of subsequent conferences regarding lesbian health, opened with a comparison of the morbidity and mortality rates of breast cancer and AIDS. Citing a recent *San Francisco Chronicle* article on the growth of community resources for the nearly one hundred women with AIDS living in San Francisco, Winnow (1992, 68) noted the lack of such resources for the "approximately 40,000 women . . . living with cancer in the San Francisco/Oakland area." Drawing on an interpretation of Alfred Kinsey's studies of sexual orientation that estimated that 10 percent of the population was predominantly homosexual (Kinsey, Pomeroy, and Martin 1948), Winnow (1992, 68) extrapolated that 4,000 of the 40,000 women were lesbians and "about 4,000 women [were] dying." Though Winnow was quick to assure her audiences that she was not suggesting less resources for HIV/AIDS, her argument, nonetheless, relied on the rhetorical power of pointing to the disparities in both funding streams and rates of diagnosis and death in San Francisco between women with AIDS and women, specifically lesbians, with breast cancer.

If AIDS initiated a specifically gay men's (and mostly white) health movement, with the notable institutionalization of gay health clinics in major cities, Winnow was among the primary voices advocating for an attention to the specificity of lesbian health concerns.[6] For Winnow and the WCRC, the needs of lesbians were more structural and social than connected to any epidemiological factors associated with lesbian identity. While Winnow was concerned with the rise of cancer rates and the lack of research progress, she was not interested in claiming that lesbians were at particular risk for cancer compared with, for example, middle-class heterosexual women. Rather, according to Winnow, lesbians, as well as other marginalized women, were invisible within established medical models of care and therefore had a particular need for community and social support, a need that she stressed was not addressed within either the mainstream efforts at supporting women with cancer or the gay and lesbian efforts at supporting people, mostly men, with HIV.

While Winnow and the WCRC were primarily interested in providing direct support and health services for women with cancer, activists like Elenore Pred were outraged at the slow pace of research on breast cancer prevention and the stagnated "slash, poison, and burn" approach to treatment.[7] In 1990, Pred and others came together to form Breast Cancer Action (BCA), a Bay Area activist group dedicated to direct action protests to effect change in funding streams for breast cancer research. Also inspired by the AIDS movement, BCA sought out strategic partnerships with AIDS political organizations, most notably ACT UP. ACT UP (AIDS Coalition to Unleash Power) was a direct action organization dedicated to oppositional politics in the fight against AIDS.[8] It began in New York City in the spring of 1987, with regional chapters and affiliated offshoots soon developing in nearly every major metropolis in the United States and around the globe. By 1990, ACT UP had gained national recognition for its very dramatic zaps, or protests, in response to restrictions on research funding and drug approvals at the federal Food and Drug Administration.[9]

In June 1990, the Sixth International AIDS Conference held its annual meeting in San Francisco. The agenda for the conference included physicians and other health professionals reporting their findings from recent laboratory and clinical studies. ACT UP planned a number of nonviolent demonstrations protesting the continued slow pace of AIDS treatment research and calling out the United States' ban on international travel by persons with HIV. Activists demanded the passage of the Americans with Disabilities Act as a pressing matter for people living with HIV/AIDS. The conference was a major turning point for AIDS activism and AIDS research. The protests gained national attention, prompting the conference organizers to commit to only hosting the conference in countries that allowed HIV-positive travelers, as well as a greater commitment to the inclusion of consumers in the decision-making bodies effecting major research. Internal strife, however, caused the Bay Area chapter of ACT UP to splinter following the conference. From then on, the newly organized ACT UP/ Golden Gate dedicated most of its effort to issues of treatment and research for HIV, while ACT UP/San Francisco, a smaller group, focused more on questioning scientific claims about the causes and relations of the HIV virus to AIDS.

Following their new formation, and just a few months after the founding of BCA, Pred met with ACT UP/Golden Gate leaders. From these meetings, Pred and other members of BCA received training on everything from how to use computers for research (in the very early days of the internet) to strategies for making highly specialized medical knowledge available to the general patient population (Batt 1994, 320). One of BCA's first moves was to create a newsletter focused on patient empowerment. From its earliest days, the newsletter sought to bring information about medical research to the patient community and to urge patients to see themselves as active agents rather than passive recipients of medical knowledge. This model is similar to *AIDS Treatment News,* a publication that began as a grassroots effort to disseminate information on research, clinical trials, and treatment protocols in the early days of the HIV crisis. Almost immediately, ACT UP and BCA began to collaborate on zaps, with their first major zap taking place on Mother's Day 1991 on the stairs of the state capitol to protest the lack of government funding for breast cancer research (Hull 1991).

The concerns of breast cancer activists found voice in the weekly ACT UP / Golden Gate meetings. Pred became a regular attendee and, after her death in 1991, Gracia Buffleben, a "heterosexual housewife and nurse" who was herself battling metastatic breast cancer, assumed Pred's position in ACT UP / Golden Gate's Treatment Issues Committee. Buffleben and her husband, George, immersed themselves in ACT UP's model. As Robert Bazell (1998, 115) reports, "The conservative-looking, middle-aged couple certainly stood out among the tattoos and body pierced ACT-UP crowd." Buffleben soon became BCA's primary liaison to ACT UP, working with the group to collaborate on zaps and other direct actions and joining ACT UP activists on trips to Washington to meet with officials and researchers at the National Institutes of Health and the National Cancer Institute. Through the work of Pred and Buffleben, breast cancer activists and HIV / AIDS activists committed to working together. In doing so, they made clear that their fight was not about a single disease but the power and authority of medical and governmental institutions.

Both ACT UP and BCA were born in response not only to the state violences that were enacted through restricted funding streams and lack of access to experimental treatment protocols but also to the normalizing politics of more visible, and some might say more palatable, service organizations within the realms of these two diseases. While the tension between the more politically oriented breast cancer organizations and those focused on conventional patient care were not so publicly volatile, the differences between the work of groups like BCA and the more mainstream Komen Foundation highlight similar tensions in the breast cancer world as

well.[10] Put differently, BCA marked itself apart from Komen—a largely apolitical, awareness-driven organization—through its political engagements.
By partnering with ACT UP, BCA and its activists were signaling an alliance with, if not a commitment to, the kind of radical queer politics that
so notably marked the first decade of the AIDS crisis.

Another major catalyst in the consolidation of "lesbian" as a biopolitical
category came with the declaration in the early 1990s that lesbians had a
higher risk of developing breast cancer.[11] In early 1993, a study conducted
by Suzanne Haynes (1992) sparked a controversy when she declared lesbians to have two to three times greater likelihood of developing breast cancer than heterosexual women. Drawing from the National Lesbian Health
Care Survey, Haynes concluded that lesbians tended to have a higher incidence of some breast cancer risk factors—namely, obesity, smoking, higher
alcohol consumption, and nulliparity (no pregnancies)—when compared
with heterosexual women. While the findings of the study drew consider-
able attention to lesbian health issues, specifically breast cancer, the mis-
leading rhetoric of Haynes's claim led to widespread confusion. Her study
implied that there was a causal relation between lesbianism and breast cancer when, in fact, that relation is only correlative and deductive. In other
words, certain health behaviors and outcomes, such as those mentioned
above, are noted to be associated with breast cancer risk but do not, in fact,
cause cancer. Haynes's study noted that these specific health behaviors
were known risks for breast cancer and were also reported by lesbians at
a rate of two to three times higher than their heterosexual counterparts.
Taking this information together, Haynes deduced that lesbians, given their
higher reporting of a number of these risk factors, would thus have higher
rates of breast cancer. Despite the many problems that arise with this kind
of glossing of the difference between causation and correlation, U.S. media
outlets quickly picked up on these findings and made the lesbian breast
cancer epidemic major news.[12]

The Associated Press (1993b) issued a news release on February 5, 1993,
announcing, "Lesbians face one in three risk for breast cancer." The article
went on to cite a statistic that lesbians are "80 percent more likely to
develop breast cancer." The article quoted Susan Hester, director of the
Mary-Helen Mautner Project for Lesbians with Cancer, as stating: "When
you compare these numbers with AIDS, it's amazing. It's more of an epidemic, but the numbers are not recognized yet. It's absolutely a plague."
The comparison of lesbian breast cancer to AIDS as both an "epidemic"

and a "plague" had the effect of defining breast cancer more in line with a kind of infectious agent—specifically, one linked to a risky sexuality—that must be curbed through a personal and communal commitment to eradicating the modes of its spread. Curiously, on the same day of the lesbian breast cancer news item, the Associated Press (1993a) highlighted a report from the National Research Council contending that AIDS would not have the kind of widespread societal effects many imagined. Rather, the article states, AIDS would remain within the socially marginalized clusters in which it was already found and would not likely have any greater effect on the wider society. In many newspapers, the headline "Study: AIDS Won't Shake Society" was run on the same page as the announcement regarding lesbians and breast cancer. The juxtaposition of these two articles presented a paradox wherein the claims for a lesbian breast cancer plague relied on the wider understanding of AIDS as a plague-like contagion while such an assertion was simultaneously being contested. The declaration that AIDS would not become the apocalyptic pandemic many feared was itself quite controversial for its implication that the disease would run its course once it had wiped out those marginal communities it had most affected.

In the wake of Haynes's study, many scholars sought to contest the claims of personal risk by documenting the negative consequences of homophobic health-care providers on gay and lesbian preventive care (Terry 1999). This flip in rhetoric from breast cancer in lesbians as a result of individual behaviors to lesbian health risk being measured in the context of environmental and social factors worked to bridge women's health concerns with LGBT health, contributing to the consolidation of "lesbian" as a biopolitical category.

MAKING CONNECTIONS: BREAST CANCER AND HIV / AIDS

Breast cancer activism has often been deployed at the nexus of gender and sexuality. On the one hand, breast cancer reigns supreme as *the* women's health issue of our age. As Samantha King argues in *Pink Ribbons, Inc.,* the rise of breast cancer as a women's issue represents a backlash against feminist threats to femininity, heteronormativity, and even capitalism. Breasts, King (2008, 113) argues, are "a highly valued part of the human body that [are] both sexually charged . . . and symbolic of a woman's role in reproduc[tion]." In this section, I demonstrate that the suturing of breast cancer and HIV / AIDS activism in the early 1990s resists the neat alignment of the lesbian within either the women's health movement or the gay health movement. Rather, I argue, the emergence of a specifically lesbian health movement, and with it the biopolitical categorization of the lesbian, was catalyzed by associations with the AIDS crisis and HIV activism but also required an articulated difference, or lesbian specificity, that breast cancer provided.

At the time that breast cancer was being declared a lesbian epidemic, the public rhetoric surrounding AIDS was moving away from AIDS as a gay disease and toward a deeper understanding of the ways AIDS affected many marginalized communities. The very public death of eighteen-year-old Ryan White in 1990 forced policy makers and the general public to acknowledge new populations that were affected by the disease and the manner in which social stratification contributed to its spread beyond marginalized communities.[13] This shift in the understanding of HIV / AIDS—the shift from HIV as a viral contagion affecting only those who engage in certain risky behavior to a global public health crisis—opened the possibility for health-based political movements that understood social stratification based on sexual identity as equally important as any sort of biomedical causation, if not more so. That is to say, AIDS had made it possible to suture health (or sickness) to social identity. Breast cancer movements needed, then, to be able to articulate a similarly correlative effect.

Jackie Winnow did not claim, as others did, that breast cancer, or even cancer, was the lesbian health issue. Her assertion that breast cancer was emblematic of wider lesbian health needs relied on a comparison with HIV / AIDS activism and community responses, of which she was one of the primary architects. Part of Winnow's rallying cry in her highly trafficked speech was a critique of how the demands of the AIDS crisis, and specifically lesbians' roles therein, relied on a perpetuation of women's roles as caretakers. Winnow acknowledged that lesbians stepped up in the AIDS crisis because of a shared sense that this was happening "in our community." Not only were lesbians witnessing and responding to the deaths of friends and loved ones, much like their gay brothers, but they were also politically motivated to counter the homophobic social and political responses to the crisis. Winnow's concern, however, was that lesbians had abandoned their earlier work with the women's movement and women's community. She lamented the defunding of women's health organizations, the right-wing attacks on women's bodily autonomy, and the decrease in government spending on issues most important to women in the wake of the AIDS crisis.

Winnow's call to arms for a specifically lesbian health movement relied on the viability of a sexual-identity-based health movement, of the kind most readily apparent in the AIDS crisis, and yet her arguments track much more concretely around issues of gender. A paradox emerges in Winnow's argument: lesbians, she claimed, are outsiders to both the women's movement, on account of their gayness, and to the gay movement, on account of being women, and yet they find themselves torn between the demands of the two. In other words, lesbians need both the women's movement and the gay movement, but they find no proper home in either. Doubly marginalized by both groups, Winnow argued that lesbians needed to resist the insistence that they choose between their vulnerability as gay people or their vulnerability as women, between their sexuality and their gender. What is more, class was also a critical issue for Winnow. In many ways, the successes of both the gay male response to AIDS and the mainstream response to breast cancer were reliant on the financial capital of its players. One of Winnow's main arguments was that lesbians, women of color, and working-class women did not have the financial capital that both mainstream and alternative modes of treatment required. Many of the women Winnow worked with were uninsured, and even if they were insured, insurance often did not cover things like support groups. Winnow's call for a specifically lesbian health movement was a call to both recognize and resist the various ways in which lesbian concerns were left out of both the HIV/AIDS movement and the women's health movement. Breast cancer became the emblematic site of this resistance.

Winnow's call for a lesbian health movement staked "lesbian" as a sexual identity that is the same as that of gay men, but when it came to the "health" aspect of the movement, distinctions needed to be made within this sexual identity along the lines of gender. While Winnow acknowledged the needs of women with AIDS in her speech, her introductory statistics served to reinforce a notion that women, and specifically lesbian women, were dying of cancer at a rate that far outpaced the death rate of women with AIDS. Lesbians, this rhetoric implies, may be affected by AIDS but they will not be infected. The sparse number of women living with AIDS in San Francisco, one hundred by Winnow's (1992) report, were not imagined to overlap with the forty thousand with breast cancer, including these four thousand lesbians.[14] Gender here gets displaced onto the predominant frame of gay sexuality that shades Winnow's tracking of AIDS even as Winnow made the move to amplify the importance of women's experience to any lesbian health movement.

Like Winnow's lesbian health movement, Breast Cancer Action relied on the queer capital of the AIDS movement while it also embodied links to civil rights movements and the feminist health movements. Nearly all the profiles of BCA's founder Elenore Pred note her long history as an activist with strong roots in the civil rights, antiwar, and feminist movements of earlier decades. It was these early activist roots that both inspired Pred and prompted her to make connections with ACT UP (Klawiter 2008, 15). Although many of BCA's leaders were lesbians, BCA was not a named lesbian organization. Rather, BCA's connections to ACT UP were drawn through their shared investment in a kind of queering of health politics that also drew upon feminist claims for the specific needs of women. These two organizations were more centrally focused on disrupting the power hierarchies of medical expertise that surrounded both diseases. While they were certainly advocating on behalf of specific patient populations, their focus was less on distinguishing these populations from each other than on addressing social and systemic issues in patient access to care. In other words, the queer alliance of ACT UP and BCA was forged not in a specific identity politics but in their radical upending of the knowledge hierarchies that dominated the medical landscape.

For Winnow, breast cancer highlighted the paradox of lesbian identity as it was staked in both the AIDS health movement and the women's health movement. For Haynes, however, lesbianism was conceptualized not as an identity but as a kind of practice, and a risk-based practice at that. The results drew a connection to AIDS, then, in that both gay men and lesbians were thought to engage in behaviors related to their sexuality—or, perhaps measurable in relation to their sexuality—that marked them as at risk for certain health outcomes—namely, HIV and breast cancer. Drawing a connection between lesbianism and breast cancer through certain health behaviors—behaviors that were noted to be bad because of their associations with a myriad of diseases and social ills, including but not limited to breast cancer—had the added effect of characterizing lesbianism as a set of social practices, such as drinking or smoking, seemingly circulating around sexuality but not sexual in and of themselves.[15] In other words, lesbianism got coded as a risk behavior not because of specific sexual practices but because of specific social behaviors that were associated (and perhaps dubiously, given the critiques of Haynes's research methodology and her findings) with this group identity.

"LESBIAN" AS A BIOPOLITICAL CATEGORY

The past thirty years have seen a significant shift in the public health framing of the lesbian. The Haynes study marked one of the earliest attempts from a national body (in this case, the National Cancer Institute) to measure health disparities in lesbian communities. While lesbians were often included, either implicitly or explicitly, in both the women's health movements of the 1970s and the HIV/AIDS-fueled movements for gay and lesbian health in the 1980s, the early 1990s marked the first attempts to articulate a specifically lesbian measure of health disparity. Haynes's study drew data from the National Lesbian Health Care Survey (NLHCS), which was collected from 1984 to 1985 (Bradford and Ryan 2006). The survey remained the largest data set on lesbian health and life until the early 2000s when national health surveys started collecting sexual orientation measures (Ryan and Bradford 1999). Researchers began publishing on and using the data from the NLHCS in the late 1980s. Haynes's study, in 1993, however, gained the most attention from the popular press and medical establishment. While the NLHCS was the most comprehensive study of lesbian lives and lifestyle to date, no data was collected on cancer experience or incidence. Rather, highlighting lesbian engagement in social behaviors that were presumed to be risk factors for breast cancer drew the association between lesbians and breast cancer. Nevertheless, the contestable methods gave a starting point—and provided the story necessary to secure the requisite funding streams—for numerous follow-up studies seeking to measure lesbian breast cancer risk, a research area that continues to this day.[16]

Since the 1999 publication of *Lesbian Health: Current Assessment and Directions for the Future,* the field of lesbian health has shifted dramatically. Whereas the first NLHCS was conducted largely at bars and in other lesbian-identified spaces, local and national health surveys now include metrics of sexual orientation, measured through self-reporting of both identity and practice. Along the lines of breast cancer studies, there have been more recent attempts to conduct population-based data collection using statewide cancer registries.[17] The increase in studies involving lesbians has, at times, risked reinforcing cultural stereotypes. For example, there was major media backlash after a study of lesbian obesity articulated high body-mass index in lesbian populations as a result of a proclaimed disregard of feminine aesthetics.[18] Aside from producing new knowledge on lesbian health behaviors and outcomes, the articulated need for lesbian health measurements continues to provide funding streams for LGBT-based research under both federal and private oversight. Perhaps unsurprisingly, much of the research on lesbian health lacks an intersectional perspective that is able to consider the complicated intertwining specificities of race, class, gender, and sexuality. Even in the face of continued concern for LGBT cancer rates, research tends to emphasize screening and survivor outcomes over causal factors such as exposure to environmental carcinogens.

The consolidation of "lesbian" as a biopolitical category has been a great success. The suturing of breast cancer and HIV / AIDS—specifically as articulated by lesbian activists such as Jackie Winnow and breast cancer and HIV activists in ACT UP and BCA—allowed the lesbian community to name and address the specific concerns of lesbian health. While lesbians had long been framed through the language of medicalization, the invert model of sexuality, which locates pathology within the body of the lesbian, has since been displaced. The recognition of lesbians as a population of concern has allowed for resources to be allocated for the study and management of this particular population. Moreover, activists and researchers have been able to address many questions and myths that motivated the 1999 NIH publication in the first place.

Even with the gains that this biopolitical categorization has allowed for, there are myriad reasons to be cautious about this process. The consolidation of "lesbian" as a biopolitical category has unfolded against the backdrop of a late twentieth-century intensification of the naming and management of risk. The shift to the management of risk is reflective of a new model of medicalization where disease can be anticipated, and thus prevented, through the identification and mitigation of measurable and identifiable factors that are thought to contribute to the development of disease.[19] The rise of epidemiologies of risk marks a shift in the modalities of biopower such that subjects are compelled, through the demand to reduce risk, to behave in certain ways. In other words, the language of risk shifts the burden of health maintenance onto the individual. These shifts in the field of lesbian health follow what Foucault (1978, 137) terms "a power that exerts positive influence on life, that endeavors to administer, optimize, and multiply it, subjecting it to precise controls and comprehensive regulations." The increasing measurement of lesbian health and sexuality are mechanisms to promote life, to assure the persistence of a certain population within defined mechanisms of control. In the case of gay and lesbian health, these measurements may be used to curtail certain sexual and social practices.

The lesbian as biopolitical subject has the subsequent effect of making "lesbian" appear as a biological category. That is to say, this moment not only consolidates the lesbian for the promotion of life through state-based surveillance but also consolidates the lesbian as a kind of body. I ended the last chapter by thinking through the endurance of individual lesbians with and against the waning of lesbian collectivities. While the consolidation of a biopolitical category may appear to provide the contours for collective identification, the work of biocitizenship is the work of individualizing such categories. Here, again, I want to mark a shift from lesbian collectives to the endurance of lesbian individuals. Under the biopolitical, as I have noted here, being lesbian becomes a risk to manage. Risk in the biopolitical frame is measured through statistical aggregate—that is, risk is measured at the level of the population—but it is managed at the level of the individual. Thus, while *lesbian* names a population to be measured under biopolitical categorization, such a move negates the need of lesbian collectivities. Put simply, if the state is naming the risk, then it is managed. State recognition gives the promise of state protection. With state protection, in a liberal framework, there is no longer a need for community protection.

By the late 1990s, the fight against cancer had become a national priority. In 1998, the *Annual Report to the Nation on the Status of Cancer* for the first time claimed declining cancer mortality (Jones and Chilton 2002). Against this seeming victory, the report also documented a growing disparity in breast cancer outcomes between white women and Black women. Breast cancer risk continues to be mapped to embodied vulnerability despite recent research into the social and environmental factors that contribute to breast cancer incidences. In breast cancer research especially, the search for the root cause of racial disparities continues to refuse social explanation.[20] For both lesbians and women of color, social factors are the primary contributors to disparities in breast cancer mortality. These social factors often look the same for both groups: lack of trust in health providers and lower socioeconomic status. The root social causes of these disparities, however, are mapped differently through homophobia and racism. In this way, these two groups are often disarticulated from each other. That is to say, lesbians as a population group are rarely studied in the context of systemic racism. Indeed, most studies of lesbian health fail to address racial differences.[21]

I opened this chapter by defining *biopolitical category* in relation to Foucault. Biopower, through which the biopolitical is a necessary mechanism, is central to what Rey Chow (2002) calls "the ascendancy of whiteness." Whiteness, then, is a central feature of the populations marked for life and targeted by biopower for optimization. Under neoliberal economic and social frameworks, increased recognition by the state via the biopolitical is considered a net good. Recent queer of color critique, however, draws attention to the necessary conditions for the biopolitical promotion of life— namely, the allowance of death.[22] As Grace Hong (2015, 31) notes, "The protection of life is predicated on the dispersal of death." When subjects are marked for life, life is meted out along lines of race and class respectability predicated, as Jasbir Puar (2007) demonstrates, on the incorporation of good subjects of difference, a designation to which many gay and lesbian subjectivities align. This is not to say that because the state counts lesbians, disparities grow for women of color. Rather, what I am pointing to here is how the disaggregation of "lesbian" from categories of racialization works in service to a project of normalization defined by whiteness.

While I began by naming the rise of biopolitical category as different from the rise of the gay consumer market, these two moments cannot be thought of as separate. Indeed, the health movements that arise from the U.S. AIDS crisis demonstrate that there is a specifically gay and lesbian health consumer market. In this way, the rise of biopolitical categorization is also a project of capital. The mainstreaming of the lesbian, then, is not only about wider social and cultural acceptance. Even more so, this mainstreaming is informed and enforced through shifting economic landscapes and the rise of the gay consumer. In this way, the mainstream lesbian leaves behind her radical roots.

3 Murderous Lesbian Separatism

Killing Daddy

> For a woman to be a lesbian in a male-supremacist, capitalist, misogynist, racist, homophobic, imperialist culture, such as that of North America, is an act of resistance.
>
> —CHERYL CLARKE, "Lesbianism:
> An Act of Resistance"

In 1973, the Los Angeles–based group Lesbian Activist Women, led by Jeanne Córdova and others, hosted the West Coast Lesbian Conference. The conference, held at the University of California, Los Angeles, drew over 1,500 lesbians from across the United States and internationally. The conference was the first large-scale attempt to define a solidified lesbian identity and lesbian political agenda. Despite its broad appeal, the conference was racked by internal struggles and debates. Most notably, the singer-songwriter Beth Elliott—a trans woman, lesbian feminist, and member of the organizing committee—performed on the first night. Within minutes of her taking the stage, the Berkeley-based lesbian feminist collective the Gutter Dykes rushed the stage demanding Elliott's eviction and distributing flyers proclaiming a "man" was in their midst. Robin Morgan, editor of *Sisterhood Is Powerful* and coiner of the concept of political lesbianism, was one of the event's keynotes and decided to adjust her address to staunchly reject Elliott's lesbian identity (Samek 2016; Enke 2018).

In the weeks and months after the conference, the central divisions of the event were played out in the pages of gay and feminist publications across the country ("A Collective Editorial" 2016). Jeanne Córdova (2011) attributed her own nervous breakdown in the months that followed to the calamity of the debates, as well as the role *Lesbian Tide*, a periodical which Córdova founded, played as the clearinghouse for airing the conversations. What emerged from the debates was not a unified lesbian community or political agenda or even a sense of warring factions within the movement. Rather, the split that emerged was ideological, borne out between the sense of a need for individual lesbian identification against a need for a coalitional politics that addresses the systemic cause of lesbian oppression. The conference proceedings are filled with real fears of physical violence that was being threatened by the Gutter Dykes and their supporters (McLean 1973). Indeed, as Elliott documents, she and others were threatened with real violence, often death threats, for years (Nettick and Elliott 2011).

I open with the West Coast Lesbian Conference because it provides a nice origin story for how 1970s lesbian feminism is remembered as a trans-exclusionary project. The conference attempted to solidify a lesbian cultural frame that could be shared across lesbian political pursuits. The lesbian framing that attaches to radical feminism, however, is not a commitment to the lesbian as a kind of culture or even as a kind of person. Rather, radical feminism, and its occasional commitment to lesbian separatism, was a political ideology. Though spaces, such as the Michigan Womyn's Music Festival, often call themselves separatist and, in this way, draw on the lineages of lesbian separatism, the lesbian separatism I explore in this chapter is not about a celebration of lesbian life, or even about lesbians' access to spaces of respite from the wider cultural norms of heteropatriarchy. In this chapter, I return to the 1970s to explore this memory of lesbian separatism that is mourned as lost in the current anxieties about lost lesbian space. Specifically, I return here to the specter of radical feminism that informs current anxieties and antagonisms that attach to the lesbian. I follow this figure of the lesbian separatist through a number of manifestos that are emblematic of her politics. In so doing, I reject claims that the lesbian of feminism is too dowdy or too tame for queer theory's more antisocial impulses. To the contrary, I argue that the politics of lesbian separatism are a politics of destruction that figure more violently and more literally than queer theory's antisocial negativity. Returning to the failure of race and class coalition in separatist movements that I outlined in the first chapter, I engage the Combahee River Collective's rejection of separatism in order to further define the attachment to whiteness that informs the nostalgia for this movement.

The use of the lesbian connection to discredit feminism is not a new phenomenon. In *Feeling Women's Liberation,* Victoria Hesford (2013) presents the figure of the "feminist-as-lesbian" as a spectral trope that has served to both define and discredit the "women's liberation movement." This figure, which emerged in the early 1970s, not only served to demarcate the boundary between proper and improper femininity but also was a catalyst for certain schisms and shifts within the burgeoning women's liberation movement. The lesbian, Hesford argues, "becomes the figure through which the emotive force of the attack on women's liberation is generated. . . . As a consequence, women's liberationists are marked as anterior to normal women, with the lesbian as the boundary figure through which that separation is made" (27–28). Interestingly, Lee Edelman's *No Future* proposes a very similar figure, albeit one coded as male, in the sinthomosexual. Like the feminist-as-lesbian, Edelman's sinthomosexual names the cultural fantasy of queerness as simultaneously an abject other and a defining border of the normative political subject. Taking Hesford's figure one step further, however, I engage the association between feminism and the lesbian as deployed in the separatist commitments of early radical feminist movements. Following this similarity between the feminist-as-lesbian and the sinthomosexual, this chapter reads the two figures together in order to argue that the figure of the radical feminist persists as a sinthomosexual figure. Pushing Edelman's argument further, I demonstrate that the radical feminist figures more violently than Edelman's sinthomosexual and, thus, is more closely aligned with the destructive forces of the death drive, which Edelman highlights.

Edelman's polemic takes to task an affirmative, humanistic political regime that grounds itself in an ever-deferred future that is staked on the symbolic logic of the Child, with a capital *C*. Edelman (2004, 5) names this "structuring optimism of politics" reproductive futurism. The queer, Edelman argues, figures in this logic as a negativity that "names the side of those *not* 'fighting for the children,' the side outside the consensus by which all politics confirms the absolute value of reproductive futurism" (3). *Queer,* then, for Edelman, names the constitutive outside by which reproductive futurity is defined. Put another way, the queer figure stands as the abject border of normative subjectivity in order to define the margin of the political center.

In order to make this argument, Edelman offers the neologism *sinthomosexual,* drawing together the Lacanian concept of the sinthome with the figure of the homosexual. The Lacanian sinthome, according to Edelman (2004, 35–36), is "the template of a given subject's distinctive access to *jouissance* . . . as the knot that holds the subject together, that ties or binds the subject to its constitutive libidinal career." While not meant to be literal, the sinthomosexual might be understood as follows: much of what we do and claim in politics and in our social structuring is based on the premise of improvement and forward movement. The Child is the figure most frequently interpolated as the benefactor of this future-oriented do-gooding. The sinthomosexual, by contrast, evades this commitment insisting, instead, on present pleasures. By refusing the normative logic of futurity, the sinthomosexual opens other avenues of investment and thereby threatens the cohesion of this singular structuring of the social. In this way, Edelman positions the figure of the queer, as sinthomosexual, in "the place of the social order's death drive" (3). *Sinthomosexuality* names the threat of dissolution that the queer figures in the heteronormative mandates that put genetic reproduction at the center of the social. Edelman's call to arms— though he resolutely refuses any proclamation of a prescriptive politics—is for the queer to take up that place of figural abjection, to proclaim its position as sinthomosexual, and, in this way, to disrupt the very apparatus sustained by the logic of reproductive futurism.

The feminist responses to Edelman's text have been primarily critical. Jack Halberstam (2011, 109), for example, identifies "the excessively small archive that represents queer negativity," offering, instead, an "antisocial feminism" drawn from the work of Valerie Solanas, Saidiya Hartman, and Jamaica Kincaid, among others. Similarly, Jennifer Doyle takes to task Edelman's reliance on antiabortion rhetoric. Doyle (2009) critiques Edelman for his failure to recognize both the place of the maternal body in the logic of the Child and those women for whom such kinship claims are never possible. Chris Coffman (2012) argues that *No Future* offers a critique of reproductive futurism that also, albeit tacitly, critiques Lacan's definition of "sexual difference." Contesting Edelman's own challenge to sexual difference, Coffman demonstrates that the sinthomosexual maintains the symbolic structuring of sexual difference. Others critique the nihilism evoked by Edelman's argument that the queer occupies this figural position of negativity. Most famously, José Esteban Muñoz (2009) counters Edelman's negation of futurity by figuring the queer in the utopic space of the yet to come.

I share in both the challenges and seductions that have made Edelman's text such a ubiquitous interlocutor for recent feminist and queer theory.

I want to resist the impulse to either argue against Edelman or simply contribute to the archive of the sinthomosexual. Rather, this chapter, like this book, builds on that tension. I do not add the lesbian separatist to the archive of sinthomosexuality solely to highlight gaps in Edelman's argument. Rather, I intend to push the figure of the sinthomosexual, and with it the myriad debates surrounding social negativity, further. My task here is threefold. First, drawing on Hesford's work, I demonstrate that the separatist feminist occupies a sinthomosexual structural position. Second, I argue that separatist feminism's threat to futurity figures more violently than Edelman's sinthomosexual. Third, I connect this violence not only to the destructive politics of separatist feminism but also to the material effects of some women's refusal of biological reproduction. This specter of the refusal of biological reproduction, I argue, can only figure as destruction when it is attached to white bodies. Concomitant to this, I end the chapter by thinking through the historiography that Black feminism arrived just in time to save mainstream feminism from its essentialist and whitewashed impulses. In this way, I vacillate between two focuses. First, I take seriously that the lesbian separatist figures through a sinthomosexual logic in ways that both carry through to today and that render literal Edelman's figurative negativity. Second, I move to reconsider the place of the sinthomosexual in the wake of feminism's destructive politics. Simultaneously, however, I read the project of lesbian separatism with Black and women of color feminist work in order to demonstrate that a focus on destruction, as separatism's lasting politics, cannot account for how the denial of motherhood, and even childhood, has been and continues to be one of the most destructive and instructive mechanisms of white supremacy. Moreover, I conclude the chapter by highlighting, via the Combahee River Collective, the limits of separatism as a radical politics. I do not aim here to return some value to lesbian separatism. Nevertheless, I take seriously that this strand of lesbian politics and lesbian cultural organization is central to the terms of the debates around lesbian death. I examine separatism through Edelman in order to pastoralize this argument and, in so doing, to reject the anxiety that the queer has left the lesbian behind. I return here to the pleasures of a politics of destruction while also pointing to its limitations. I will return to this pleasure and the specter of this politics today in the Conclusion.

In order to make this argument, I draw from three foundational separatist feminist texts. The first is Valerie Solanas's iconic *SCUM Manifesto*; the second is the lesser-known C.L.I.T. papers, published anonymously as numerous essays in *Off Our Backs* and *DYKE, A Quarterly* between 1974 and 1980; and the third is the call to arms "Lesbians in Revolt," an essay that articulates the central ethos of the lesbian separatist collective the Furies. The Furies are perhaps one of the better-known lesbian separatist organizations. Although the collective survived for only a year, the group's related publication, also called the *Furies,* was in print for at least another year. The C.L.I.T. papers have all but disappeared, available mostly in the archives of feminist media projects. What little is available in the secondary readings on the C.L.I.T. papers makes clear that they were highly controversial, precisely for their arguments in favor of full-scale rejection of the social through the politics of lesbian separatism. *SCUM Manifesto,* by contrast, is not typically recognized as a lesbian separatist manifesto, yet its survival as a classic feminist text cannot be separated, I argue, from the subsequent lesbian separatist movements the text influenced, including both C.L.I.T. and the Furies. The canonical status of *SCUM Manifesto* speaks to a feminist identification with a politics of destruction, even if only on the level of the figural. The failure to survive on the part of C.L.I.T. follows the post–early 1970s bifurcation of feminism away from the vitriolic tone of *SCUM Manifesto* and the controversial claims of lesbian separatism. Considering the murderousness that is implied in Edelman's discussion of the death drive, I invoke this figure of the radical feminist to demonstrate the threat of lesbian separatism as a destructive, perhaps even murderous, politics.

THE FEMINIST-AS-LESBIAN

In *Feeling Women's Liberation,* Victoria Hesford names the event of women's liberation as a switch point in the U.S. imaginary of feminist politics. Returning to the archive of 1970, and, most specifically, to the widespread media attention given to women's liberation following the publication of Kate Millett's *Sexual Politics,* Hesford (2013, 4) demonstrates that the emergence of the figure of the feminist-as-lesbian had a "defining effect on the way in which women's liberation in particular and feminism in general has been remembered and represented, in both the supracultural domain of the mass media and in the subcultural domains of popular and academic feminism and queer theory." The figure of the feminist-as-lesbian, Hesford argues, operates "as a ghost rather than an icon or symbol" due to "such over-familiarity and hypervisibility" (15). The ghostliness that Hesford names in this figure is exemplified in quick moves to disavow the relation between feminism and the lesbian. That may have once been true, they seem to say, but the persistence of this association is meant to scare rather than name. Beginning with Solanas and *SCUM Manifesto,* I turn here to consider the fright—indeed, the terror—of what I will demonstrate is the specter of destruction that the figure of the separatist feminist carries.[1]

The mark of radical feminism in the early 1970s was the refusal of femininity as conscripted by heterosexuality and the nuclear family (Echols 1989). Although mainstream feminist politics sought to reject the confines of feminine social positions through a liberal politics of assimilation, a radical, often separatist approach advocated a more violent form of feminism founded on a politics of destruction. Such feminism was enacted largely through manifestos, political writings, and direct actions (Echols 1989). The association between feminism and destruction begins with the allegations of bra burning at the 1968 Miss America Pageant.[2] The image of the burning bra has persisted as a metaphor for the violence of feminists; this image is posed in distinction to the good liberalism of feminism as an ideology of equality. Published around the same time as the infamous bra burning, Valerie Solanas's *SCUM Manifesto* has become, perhaps, the most read example of a feminist politics of destruction. Though most remembered for her advocating of a homicidal cutting-up of men, Solanas's true target was the gender system at the center of a capitalist, bourgeois state. Solanas's weapon was her words, and the vitriol of her writing became a rallying point for a radical separatist movement.

Many feminists have connected Solanas to an antisocial politics similar to the one Edelman articulates in the sinthomosexual. In responding to Edelman's limited archive, for example, Halberstam (2011, 108) offers Solanas as "an antisocial feminist extraordinaire." Similarly, Avital Ronell (2004, 2, 5, 23) highlights the manifesto's "anti-social edge" and connects Solanas to "nonplace . . . the *non* bound by the *nom,* as Lacan would say." In describing Solanas's "antisocial practices" as a kind of refusal of "the burdens of social and sexual reproduction," Hesford's analysis draws Solanas most clearly into the realm of Edelman's sinthomosexual:

> The anti-social practices of SCUM are the actions of women "too childish" and too "uncivilized" to accept the burdens of social reproduction. . . . Solanas's outlaw women are subversive because they operate from "the gutter"—the spaces of social abjection and exclusion in which figures like the street hustler and dyke come to symbolize the breakdown of the internal frontiers of the nation-state—the borders that are meant to contain the middle

class within a domain of hetero-respectability and racial orderliness. Solanas's
SCUM revolution won't happen through marches and movements—through
a protest that is also an appeal to the laws of daddy's bourgeois society—but
through the mayhem wrought by refusing to acknowledge the legitimacy of
those laws. (Hesford 2013, 102)

Laying claim to the space on the margins, in "the gutter," SCUM, Solanas's
proposed Society for Cutting Up Men, refuses bourgeois politics invested in
class ascendancy, in the political promise of social capital. The gutter represents not only a rejection of the prescriptions of heterofemininity but also
militant uprising, what Hesford labels "a Solanasesque politics of refusal"
(299). Solanas's SCUM refuses not only heterosexually scripted femininity,
a refusal that fuels the motives of radical feminism, but also a politics bent
on claiming a universal good. SCUM does not simply scoff at reproductive
futurism. Rather, it calls for a homicidal revolt whose ultimate goal is not
equality, assimilation, or recognition but the wholesale destruction of the
male sex and with it any vestiges of biology, culture, and capital that would
tie women to reproduction.

Solanas's central claim in *SCUM Manifesto* is not that men hate women
but that men hate men. The representation of women as passive and pen-
etrable, according to Solanas (2004, 37), is not a true representation but
men's projections of their hatred of their own essential femininity: "Com-
pletely egocentric, unable to relate, empathize or identify, and filled with
a vast, pervasive, diffuse sexuality, the male is physically passive. He hates
his passivity, so he projects it onto women, defines the male as active, then
sets out to prove that he is." The goal of SCUM is not simply to kill off all
men but to convince men of their complicity in their own destruction, of
the necessity of their elimination through embrace of their true femininity
("faggots" and trans women, for Solanas, provide the richest example that
such a conversion is possible). This is not to say, as the manifesto insists,
that men, and some women, will not literally die in the process. With the
end of men, both literally and figuratively, Solanas insists will come the
end of patriarchy and all its incessant baggage. As the manifesto's opening
paragraph proclaims: SCUM will "overthrow the government, eliminate
the money system, institute complete automation and destroy the male
sex" (23). To call Solanas's manifesto vitriolic is an understatement. Often
dismissed as schizophrenic rantings, many argue that Solanas is articulating
the cultural projections of feminism with extreme hyperbole.[3] Presumably,

the elimination of men would bring with it the elimination of the entire gender system, the rearticulation of sexual relations, and the complete annihilation of the family system, and with such an eradication the further elimination of the capitalist systems and class structures that work in concert with the nuclear family. One might also argue that Solanas is aptly, if pugnaciously, articulating the stated goals of a radical feminist takeover. Rather than argue for an equality politics, as has been the hallmark of liberal feminism, Solanas's Marxist approach to the gender system involves a radical destruction of all concomitant systems.

SCUM Manifesto takes radicalism as destruction to its limit. The politics of SCUM is a homicidal ideology. The bulk of the publication focuses on men's deficiency, their animalistic inferiority to women, and their self-annihilating commitment to fucking. But riddled throughout, and most pointedly in the final pages, Solanas calls on SCUM to destroy men in the most literal sense: through men's own transition to women, through a technological overtake of reproduction assuring that only females are born, or, if necessary, through murderous means. Rejecting a politics of the status quo, denying that change can happen through protest or simply opting out, Solanas calls for a kind of warfare against men, both *men* in the literal sense and all that the patriarchy has come to bolster.

The status of *SCUM Manifesto* as the harbinger of this antisocial politics gains critical speed through Solanas's figuration as a spokesperson of radical separatism.[4] *SCUM Manifesto* has been called one of the most influential works of lesbian separatist writing.[5] Many of the most acerbic, destructive, and "man-hating" writings to come out of the separatist movement attribute their influence to Solanas's *SCUM Manifesto*. Among them are the C.L.I.T. papers. The C.L.I.T. papers were first published as a series in the radical lesbian feminist publication *Off Our Backs* and were then quickly republished in the lesbian feminist journal *DYKE, A Quarterly*. Written by a group of anonymous lesbian feminists calling themselves Collective Lesbian International Terrors (C.L.I.T.), the C.L.I.T. papers took primary aim at the mainstream media, who often accused women of lesbianism in a bid to discredit and, perhaps, dismantle the movement for women's liberation (C.L.I.T. 1974a, 1974b).[6] Published as two separate statements printed in *Off Our Backs* in the May and July 1974 issues, the C.L.I.T. papers outline the forming of the collective, its goals and intentions, and the steps it would take to achieve its goals. Ultimately, C.L.I.T. sought the end of patriarchy through the destruction of heterosexuality. The means by which they sought this end, however, was with full withdrawal from the capitalist systems that were intricately bound with patriarchy and bolstered by the class-ascendant, heterosexual, nuclear family. To begin, C.L.I.T. called for a lesbian boycott of the straight press, as writers, readers, or publishers. In doing so, they argued, the radical feminist movement could control their own dissemination of information, and, even more importantly, they would thwart the cooptation of a sterilized and neutered lesbian figure being pawned by the liberal-minded, humanitarian press.

The second statement, "Statement #2," printed by C.L.I.T. in *Off Our Backs* in July 1974, identifies the various ways the straight media has colluded to co-opt the lesbian. Engaging cultural forms and figures as varied as drag queens, bisexuals, and straight women, C.L.I.T. (1974b) outlined how the co-optation of the lesbian by straight media produces this figure as simultaneously menacing and sterile. Although straight women, bisexuals, and gay camp may seem at first glance to be potentially allied with a lesbian-driven radical feminism, C.L.I.T. articulates how the media, and the liberal-minded culture's sudden acceptance of the lesbian through an avant-garde valuation of sexual liberation, seeks to placate this very figure in the maintenance of the heteropatriarchy. C.L.I.T. takes the cue from Solanas's SCUM, quoting from her manifesto and praising her shooting of Warhol, yet reverses her logic. Other women, according to C.L.I.T.— bisexual women, straight women, even lesbians who refused separatism— are not true women but men in disguise, unable to confront and exorcise the "prick within." If Solanas wanted to cut up men, chew them to bits, or remold them as women, C.L.I.T. sought to bleed them out.

The second collection of C.L.I.T. papers (1976) had a much wider circulation and prompted a frenzy of response, both positive and negative, from within the wider feminist community. Though the papers of the three original collective members were published in the July 1974 issue of *Off Our Backs,* a much wider collection was published in the burgeoning lesbian feminist publication *DYKE, A Quarterly.* The second collection, which begins with "C.L.I.T. Statement No. 3," articulates the group's investment in militancy. The opening line states it all: "In the last year C.L.I.T. has moved from the purist form of Lesbian Separatism—no contact with men—to Lesbian Militancy, to a Lesbian Militant stance of active *confrontation* with the enemy" (C.L.I.T. 1976, 41). The use of war imagery is not a metaphor but a committed stance against the "Mutual Assured Destruction (MAD its real name) of capitalist and communist cock superpowers" (41). Although

C.L.I.T. never engaged in bodily violence with men, their intent was to terrorize and eradicate "the prick within."

The sentiments expressed in the C.L.I.T. papers are mirrored in a number of other separatist writings, manifestos, and organizations at the time. The Furies Collective is perhaps one of the most well-known, or at least well-documented, intentional communities of lesbian separatists.[7] Founded in Washington, D.C., in 1971, the original Furies Collective, also known as "Those Women," included some of the most well-cited lesbian separatists, among them Rita Mae Brown and Charlotte Bunch. A year after their founding, the group began printing a monthly newspaper, also called *The Furies*, which served as a forum for lesbian separatism in the burgeoning women's liberation movement. The cover of the inaugural issue told the story of the Furies (three figures of Greek mythology described as "avengers of matricide, the protectors of women") and their relation to origin of the Furies Collective ("Furies" 1972). The Furies Collective took their name as a demonstration of their anger, of being furious at the arrogance and persistence of male supremacy. Because the Furies saw male supremacy as inextricably bound with not only sexism but racism and classism as well, it was an end to the patriarchal system that, they argued, would ultimately topple the racist imperialism of capitalism. They rejected what they saw as the feelings-driven weakness of contemporary liberal politics, most notably the more mainstream women's liberation movement. Often described as a militant organization, the Furies insisted on strategy, a uniformity of practice, and a celebrated engagement with conflict. The two residences that they shared were meant to be a kind of experiment in tactical ideology that would ultimately be able to be replicated across the movement. As the story goes, the communal residences associated with the Furies were disbanded after an escalating series of in-house disagreements over the place of children in their movement. According to Echols (1989, 235), the conversations began around the place of male children, given the all-female commitments of the group, and quickly escalated to the place of children writ large.

The inaugural issue of the *Furies* also contained the group's own manifesto, "Lesbians in Revolt" (Bunch 1972). Bylined by Charlotte Bunch, but presumably approved by the entire collective, the two-page spread elaborated on their founding claim that lesbianism is not a sexual disposition but a political commitment. To recognize and engage lesbianism as a politics, according to the manifesto, was not simply a matter of declaring one's identity or affiliation. Rather, lesbianism as political practice required a commitment to a community of women, to a rejection of male domination, and to an interrogation and repudiation of the privileges of race, class, and nationhood that were given by patriarchal lines of descent. The lesbian, according to Bunch, is the ultimate impediment to male domination. By demonstrating that women do not need men socially, economically, or sexually, the lesbian provides the foil for male supremacy's claim on women's dependence. Lesbianism, then, cannot be a symbolic gesture but requires a committed and forceful withdrawal from and rejection of all tenets and effects of heterosexuality.

The *Furies* was in print for less than two years. Even so, Echols attributes the widespread influence of the collective, at least in feminist memory, to the important writings and debates that took place within its pages. The paper carried on for another year after the end of the collective living arrangement, and its pages document the ongoing debates on the value of separatism and the thin border between lesbian ideology and man-hating. In the final issue of the *Furies* newspaper, two collective members attempt to outline the failure of the experiment. They note that the article is one of the first and only pieces published without consensus; the article also contained a bullet point list highlighting disagreement with the piece expressed by collective members. The essay makes clear that class struggles were the hurdle that the group could not surmount. The very systems of capitalist dependence on societal structures that the collective was working against were also the very structures that, as a collective, they could not overcome.

Lesbian separatism reverses the imagined individuality of sexuality. The queerness of lesbian separatism—and, to be clear, the term *queer* is used often in their texts—is not born of an individual experience of alienation within the social but, rather, seeks to alienate the very societal structures that would co-opt the individual through the domestication of identity. Put another way, sexuality in these manifestos is not an element of subjectivity but a social dynamic that creates systems of oppression. But neither is lesbianism merely a matter of gender. To be woman-identified is to refuse to participate in male-dominated structures and patriarchal practices. A refusal of the strictures of heterosexuality displaces a need to define gender or sexuality with regard to each other, if at all.

Political lesbianism is not sexuality in the identitarian or even practice-based sense. This does not mean, however, that it is simply an affiliative choice. Neither does it mean that political lesbians were not fucking or that fucking was not a part of their politics. But *fucking* may not mean sex; they were fucking off and fucking shit up. For Solanas, for example, sexuality is purely a male pursuit, a drive more closely connected to animalism than human intellect. The end of sex, for this reason, will mean the end of men. Solanas's men are zombies, driven by one thing—the pursuit of pussy: "He'll swim through a river of snot, wade nostril-deep through a mile of vomit, if he thinks there'll be a friendly pussy awaiting him" (Solanas 2004, 37). Since all sexuality, for Solanas, is constructed in a male-dominated world, all sexuality is male. As Breanne Fahs (2008, 598) argues, Solanas's endgame of a kind of radical asexuality is not predicated on a pious positioning of women in relation to sex: "Rather, asexuality is a consequence of sexuality, the logical conclusion to a lifetime of 'Suck and Fuck.'" The disarticulation of sexuality from both men and reproduction, in Solanas, will allow women to engage new levels of creativity and productivity previously unimaginable.

For C.L.I.T., they reject the image of the lesbian as an avant-garde sexual deviant. This liberal, biased attempt at social incorporation, they contend, renders the lesbian part of a palatable, even enviable, subculture. Such a move is slanderous: "They are trying to smear our name. Guilt by association" (C.L.I.T. 1974a). C.L.I.T. takes aim at faggots, bisexuals, and queers of high culture who are content to accede to this position of recognition. Liberal inclusion is "a humanitarian rat trap" that deludes social lesbians, fags, and women's libbers into complacency. C.L.I.T.'s notion of a unified femininity is not a cultural feminist embrace of a valued sexual difference. Indeed, sexual difference in any biological sense is not of interest to C.L.I.T. The "pricks" that most concern C.L.I.T. are those inside their own heads, infiltrating the forms of capitalist, imperialist, and racist systems that maintain gender subordination through the mandates of heterosexuality. Lesbians are the logical outcome of a feminist revolution. The "heterosexual farce" is a power play that straight women play into just as much as men. According to C.L.I.T., straight women are an even greater risk to the goals of lesbian separatism than any men. Men are too deluded by their own worth to recognize the threat of lesbianism. Straight women, however, can grasp just how threatening separatism is to the system from which they benefit and, for this reason, are the greatest threat to true lesbians. The straight woman's threat is twofold: she can infiltrate the separatist and she can also seduce the real lesbians back into the power play of heterodynamics.

For the Furies, lesbianism is a political choice. Lesbianism is not simply a rejection of heterosexuality, of male–female relations; it is also a rejection of the societal norms of women and femininity. Lesbianism is political because sexuality is political, gender is political, and rejecting the social demands to be legible within these categories is also political. The radical lesbianism to which the Furies aspire rejects any notion of the political as an individual pursuit. The radical separatist politics that they espouse must be based first and foremost on a centering of necessity of relations and of the interconnectedness of multiple forms of oppression.

Some might attribute the seemingly brief heyday of radical separatist politics to its inefficacy. And yet, the cultural association between separatism and feminism remains strong, perhaps even more than any other radical movement. The extremism associated with separatist politics, now largely heralded as "man-hating," serves as fodder to dismiss feminism wholesale. But even in many feminist or feminist-affiliated circles, radical separatism is rejected as an aberrant past. In this next section, I turn to consider how we might read these lesbian separatist moments through the logic of the sinthomosexual.

SEPARATIST FEMINISM AND THE SINTHOMOSEXUAL

The polemicizing force of Edelman's *No Future* is grounded in what has been called a suicidal politics, one that in refusing futurity refuses survival. The jouissance that Edelman claims as queer is associated with a kind of excessive, orgasm-driven sexuality measured mostly through practice.[8] And yet, the figures that Edelman draws on are marked not by sexual excess in the way one might imagine but by a kind of callous and depraved disregard for an appropriate humanistic investment in the other that itself results in a kind of perverse pleasure.[9] The queer uptake of this spectral position of nonreproductive sexuality, as Edelman advocates, tracks differently than radical feminism's mandated rejection and vehement refusal of the reproductive mandate. Nevertheless, the terror of the death drive as a kind of murderous, annihilative force tracks well with the stated aims of lesbian separatism. In order to consider the sinthomosexual potential of radical lesbian separatism, I want to first consider the most salient and pointed articulation of Edelman's polemic:

> Fuck the social order and the Child in whose name we're collectively terrorized; fuck Annie; fuck the waif from *Les Mis*; fuck the poor, innocent kid on

the Net; fuck laws both with capital ls and small; fuck the whole network of Symbolic relations and the future that serves as its prop. (Edelman 2004, 29)

It is clear here that the "fucking" imagined to define the sinthomosexual is not simply or merely *fucking* in its most banal, copulative sense but also in giving the proverbial finger to any demand that such fucking be made to have meaning in the "structuring optimism of politics" (5). The gesture given in the "fuck" is a dismissal, a refusal, rather than an outward or aggressive attack. In this way, the sinthomosexual sidesteps the question of children as the bearers of futurity and turns elsewhere. The sinthomosexual, thus, figures not as an active destroyer of children or even the future but rather as simply brushing such questions to the side in favor of other kinds of pleasures and indulgences. The radical separatist feminist, by contrast, continues to figure as a destructive, terrifying, even murderous threat to the cohesion of the social, to the family, to men, and, most pointedly, to male children.

In the first chapter of her book on motherhood, *Of Woman Born*, Adrienne Rich (1995) shares the following anecdote:

> In a living room in 1975, I spent an evening with a group of women poets, some of whom had children. . . . We talked of poetry, and also of infanticide, of the case of a local woman, the mother of eight, who had been in severe depression since the birth of her third child, and who had recently murdered and decapitated her two youngest, on her suburban front lawn. . . . Every woman in that room who had children, every poet, could identify with her. (24)

That anyone, let alone a mother, would murder a child remains unthinkable today. Unthinkable to most, that is, except for mothers. Recounting this anecdote, Jane Gallop (1988, 2) reminds us: "*Of Woman Born* not only speaks to the secret of common maternal anger but treats that anger as a surface eruption of an even darker, deeper violence that systematically constitutes motherhood as a patriarchal institution." The Child, for these feminists, cannot be simply rejected or refused; the Child itself is already the figuration of a thwarted future. As Jennifer Doyle (2009) argues, Edelman's reliance on the Child—particularly the Child as figured in one of Edelman's anecdotes as the larger-than-life fetus—elides the maternal body that is always connected to that child. Edelman (2004) addresses this elision tangentially in a footnote. He notes: "The overwhelming presence of male *sinthomosexuals* in cultural representation reflects, no doubt, a gender bias that continues to view women as 'naturally' bound more closely to sociality, reproduction, and domesticating emotion" (165). Edelman goes on to admit that there may be some female sinthomosexuals, particularly in Hitchcock's characters, though these figures are marked through an excess of "'love'—rather than a refusal of sociality and desire" (165). It is this connection of women to the emotional and domesticating spheres that both motivates the destructive impulses of radical feminism and makes such impulses so terroristically threatening. Furthermore, Edelman might insist that his sinthomosexual has no literal relation to any actual persons. And yet, I argue, it is precisely the literal feminist refusal of reproduction—the threat to the actual, biological end of generations—that marks this feminist figure as dangerous.

The Child as the bearer of the future's potentiality is not a signifier that is available to women. Gayle Rubin's (2011) groundbreaking essay "The Traffic in Women" makes this argument by connecting Engels's work on kinship systems and Marx's analysis of the reproduction of labor in the service of capital to oedipal drama via Freud and Lacan. The kinship system, reinforced through heterosexuality, Rubin argues, is structured to assure the persistence of wealth and social capital for the patriarchal lineage. Articulated in Lacanian parlance through the symbol of the phallus, this inheritance is given through the exchange of the phallus in the oedipal drama. As Rubin reminds us, "The girl never gets the phallus. It passes through her, and in its passage is transformed into a child" (54). The Child, then, does not promise a political or social future for all; rather, the Child becomes the instantiation of the father's future via the phallus. The Child is always the proto-father. We might also argue, by this oedipal logic, that the girl is both always a child (i.e., "women and children") and never a child. She fails to overcome the oedipal drama because she is never able to become other than a woman, specifically a mother, and thus never able to be or have the phallus.

The lack of discussion of the oedipal crisis in *No Future* is a curious omission. By being against children, refusing the mandates of reproduction, the sinthomosexual also refuses the oedipal inheritance of the phallus. Without the oedipal drama and its concomitant threat of castration, the law of the father, the motor of the symbolic, fails to inaugurate meaning. The figuring of the sinthomosexual as the excessive force of jouissance—

figuring as it does as "insisting on access to *jouissance* in the place of access to sense"—derives from the sinthomosexual's threat to the logic of the oedipal drama that would serve to contain the sinthome (Edelman 2004, 37). The trouble here, however, is that this negation of the oedipal does nothing to dismantle the privileged place of the phallus in the symbolic order. Refusing the promise of the phallus—that is to say, refusing reproductive futurity—inaugurated, as Rubin argues, in its passage from father to son, does not necessarily collapse its value. We might find here the kind of hopeful promise of a symbolic structured otherwise that Edelman so resolutely refuses to claim. By withholding the phallus and its promise of heterosexuality, the son-father imagines he can rescript the symbolic otherwise. Of course, the figural child in Edelman's argument is also the white child figured as the inheritor of the nation. As Juana María Rodríguez (2014, 36) notes, "The child as political symbol, legal subject, or social player in psychoanalytic dramas is . . . always already constituted by race."

If Edelman reads the political promise of the future in the sentimental attachment to the Child—and, we might add, with the political investment in the phallic promise of the oedipal drama—the project of lesbian separatism takes aim at the structural position of Daddy. Both SCUM and C.L.I.T. want to kill Daddy. This murderous attack on Daddy pushes the reader to consider the limits of oedipalization. The destruction of the oedipal triangle would dismantle not only heterosexuality but, with it, gender difference. SCUM and C.L.I.T. are the most resolutely oedipal, taking aim at the father, oriented toward the destruction of femininity through the cessation of reproduction. It is Daddy that keeps women barefoot and pregnant, consigned and confined to the burdens of reproduction. Or, again following Rodríguez, Daddy is the state, demanding docility. Daddy as the state also demarcates whose reproduction is seen as serving the state and whose is rendered a threat to the coherence of the nation. By claiming lesbianism as a structural position, rather than simply a personal identity or sexual practice, lesbian separatism names the threat that women's refusal of reproduction poses to the patriarchal machine inaugurated and reinforced through the law of the family.

The destruction of the symbolic is also the target of C.L.I.T. Tackling the symbolic as language, C.L.I.T. called for a refusal of all cultural discourse that would seek to define and contain the lesbian. The liberal attempt at social incorporation—an incorporation enacted, as they argue, by a media more invested in the promotion of the avant-garde sexual deviant—they contend, renders the lesbian part of a palatable, even enviable, subculture. It is not just mainstream media that would co-opt the significatory force of the lesbian but women's liberation and gay liberation as well. Rejecting the heterosexual "artifice" that ascribes gender difference, C.L.I.T. (1974b, 11) proclaims: "Daddy is a piece of shit who demands respect." C.L.I.T. takes aim at drag culture: "Males can afford to keep on laughing at momma, having no heart, no ability to empathize with momma who is the real victim of family life" (4). The family here is the maker of the rules of both heterosexuality and patriarchy, enforced through the law of the father. Rather than offering a refined image of the lesbian that might bring her into the confines of the familial, that might make her an identifiable subject of the properly social, C.L.I.T. proclaims: "It is far more important to become unintelligible" (16). Like the sinthomosexual, C.L.I.T. rejects "futurism's logic of intelligibility," moving instead to "insist on the unintelligible's unintelligibility" (Edelman 2004, 106–7). Refusing not only intelligibility, C.L.I.T.'s goal is, simultaneously, to become alienated from the intelligibility of the mainstream.

Beyond challenging the bounds of proper femininity, separatist feminism challenged the bounds of the properly political. It is here that we might find the most traction with Edelman's overarching analysis of the modalities of social change. Edelman falls short of insisting on the murderous elimination of children, opting instead for a kind of passive approach, one Heather Love (2007, 130) describes as "looking to throw out as many babies as possible with his bathwater." Edelman's approach to politics is, in fact, not to approach it at all. The politics that Edelman eschews is governed by a logic of opposition that always promises a better tomorrow. This opposition, which relies on what Wendy Brown (1995) calls "wounded attachments," seeks legitimation through the state by means of a politics of identity. Part of what the sinthomosexual's acquiescence rejects is not only a politics formulated on a linear narrative of progress but also a politics staked on empirical and tangible outcomes. If we are not fighting for rights, for the future, then what *are* we fighting for? This sense of hopelessness in the rejection of empirical, futural politics has been labeled by one of *No Future*'s reviewers as "political suicide" (Fontenot 2006). Though the sinthomosexual never takes the plunge, the feminist separatist just might. There is something nihilistic about feminist separatism; it is not entirely clear what happens after society has been destroyed. The cultural memory of a specifically lesbian separatism tends to align this movement with a utopic politics of elsewhere. A 2009 *New York Times* article, for example, laments the loss of "lesbian land" that was so central to certain kinds of separatist movements of the 1970s (Kershaw 2009). Although the cultural nostalgia for separatism, perhaps mostly from within the women's movement, invokes a kind of rural utopia, the ongoing association between feminism and a nihilistic politics of destruction rests on the figure of the radical separatist feminist. Returning to Edelman's litany of those childish figures to whom the sinthomosexual offers a resolute "fuck you," we might imagine the feminist rejoinder as follows: Kill the patriarchy and the Man in whose name we are collectively terrorized; kill Daddy Warbucks; kill Jean Valjean; kill the predatory rapist; kill pricks both in your pants and in your head; kill the whole network of capitalist relations and the future that serves as its prop.

The association between feminism and the refusal of the conscriptions of heteropatriarchy—namely, through a refusal of reproduction—I argue, has had the effect of shifting the plane on which the futural logics of liberal humanism are staked. Put another way, the centrality of the Child, which Edelman so astutely argues, is made possible because radical feminism has decentered the nuclear family as the central mandate of the "structuring optimism of politics." Part of what queer refusal of futurity offers, per the sinthomosexual's acquiescence to his assigned social position, is a collapse in the internal logic of the social. Such a collapse does not, however, guarantee its cessation. The future will march forward, though perhaps it will be spun to a different horizon. Indeed, what I have attempted to show here is that we cannot measure the outcomes of social refusal through the logics in which they are embedded. By all accounts, patriarchy survives, as does capitalism, racism, and classism.

SEPARATISM'S FAILURES

By the end of the 1970s, separatism had fallen out of favor, to put it mildly, as the political imperative of lesbian feminism. In the stories that feminist theory tells about itself, as Clare Hemmings (2011) notes, feminism was rescued from the essentializing, whitewashed politics of lesbian separatism by Black and women of color feminism. Most narratives name the Combahee River Collective's "A Black Feminist Statement" as the fomenting point of rescue and also as the refusal of separatism as lesbian's political ethos. The statement articulates a Black feminist politics that is rooted in both identity politics—namely, the collective's experience as "Black

feminists and Lesbians"—and coalition politics that "realize that the liberation of all oppressed peoples necessitates the destruction of the political-
economic systems of capitalism and imperialism as well as patriarchy"
(Combahee River Collective 1983, 218, 213). The founding of Kitchen Table:
Women of Color Press was central to Black feminist work after Combahee's statement. Kitchen Table is most known for their anthology *This
Bridge Called My Back,* which is canonical in women's studies and women
of color feminism specifically for how its contributors responded to the
presumed whiteness of the women's liberation movements of the 1970s.
These critiques of white feminism are staked, among other modes, on the
failures of separatism to address race and class disparities and coalitions
within the women's movement. An interview with Barbara and Beverly
Smith, sisters who were central to both the collective and the press, asks:
"Is a lesbian separatist position inherently racist?" Barbara responds: "So
seldom is separatism involved in making real political change, affecting
institutions in the society in any direct way." Beverly echoes: "One of the
problems of separatism is that I can't see it as a philosophy that explains
and analyzes the roots of all oppression and is going toward solving it"
(Smith and Smith 1983, 120–21). Their critique of separatism stems from its
narrow political focus, as well as the unacknowledged class privilege necessary to opt out, so to speak, of society.

This is not to say that lesbianism as a mode of critique or a politics of
destruction is absent from *This Bridge Called My Back.* Pat Parker's speech,
"Revolution: It's Not Neat or Pretty or Quick," is a call to arms, in some
ways literally. Parker recognizes revolution as "a long and dirty process"
(Parker 1983, 241). Under revolution, according to Parker, "we will be faced
with decisions that are not easy. We will have to consider the deaths of
friends and family. We will be faced with the decisions of killing members
of our own race" (241). Parker's conception of revolution, that it is not
neat or pretty, resonates with the destructive impulses of separatism. Elsewhere, Cheryl Clarke, whose words provide the epigraph to this chapter,
emphasizes the absolute necessity of lesbian politics to resist heteropatri-
archal imperatives. This politics, however, is expansive—she states, "I, for
one, identify a woman as a lesbian who says she is"—and does not rely on
separatism as the goal. Rather, for Clarke, lesbian politics can be a site of
cross-racial and coalitional work that refuses the mandates of alliance to
either race or gender (Clarke 1983, 128). As a political claim, the lesbian in

this frame is capacious because it centers its claim not in an alliance with but rather in an alliance against.

This Bridge Called My Back does not offer a neat corrective to the racism of white women or a sanitized model of a unified feminist movement. Rather, it models coalition-building that does not require a sameness of identity or oppression but that engages relationships to power as the grounds for shared political commitments. Gloria Anzaldúa names this shared relation to power as "queer." She notes, "We are the queer groups. . . . The over-whelming oppression is the collective fact that we do not fit, and because we do not fit *we are a threat*" (Anzaldúa 1983, 209). The queer threat that Anzaldúa names mirrors the threat that lesbian separatism attempts to harness. The threat of lesbian separatism, however, tended to collapse inward, to reify a group over and against its outsiders. This collapsing inward is especially clear in the construction of lesbian spaces that I out-lined in chapter 1. The queer threat that informs *This Bridge Called My Back,* however, moves out into the world. In her preface to the volume, Cherríe Moraga (1983, xiv) notes that the feminist movement, especially in its use of the lesbian as a political claim, "grew to be exclusive and reactionary." The threat—that is, the danger—that the coalition work that the anthol-ogy demonstrates is not the nihilistic politics of lesbian separatism. By contrast, the writers and activists take up the banner of "radical"—with the subtitle *Writings by Radical Women of Color*—as a commitment to the messy work of revolution. This is a revolutionary commitment that moves outward, that seeks to change the conditions of the world rather than retreat from it.

I end here with *This Bridge Called My Back* because its work is rarely taken up within the same threads as the polemical texts of radical femi-nism and lesbian separatism. When Kitchen Table Press or the Combahee River Collective, the founding collective of the text, are brought into con-versation with lesbian separatism, it is usually as a necessary corrective to the limits of separatism (Rudy 2001). In this move, *lesbian* appends to *sepa-ratism* and is evacuated from Black and Third World feminism. What is more, this distancing from the failures of specific lesbian separatist groups demands a distancing from both *lesbian* and *separatism*. But, as Julie Enszer (2016) argues, separatism is not only or even necessarily about a separate space or separate movement for lesbian feminists. Anxieties today about the loss of lesbian separatist space or the need for lesbian-serving marketplaces eschew the political commitments of lesbian separatism. And yet, it is this strand of feminism—that is, lesbian separatism as a specter of man-hating, vitriol bent on destruction—that, as Hesford (2013) demonstrates, continues to haunt feminism today. Rather than disavow this figuration of feminism, however, I want to take seriously the pleasure that can be had in encountering and even engaging this form of feminist politics. More directly, many of us who might refuse the label of "lesbian" also embrace, and perhaps even relish, encounters with these forms of feminist vitriol. But, as Parker and Clarke demonstrate, a commitment to a lesbian politics—a politics that, in Clarke's (1983, 130) words, refuses the mandates of heteropatriarchy through which "women are kept, maintained, and contained through terror, violence, and a spray of semen"—is not about a unified lesbian ideal or lesbian community. Rather, it is a commitment to the messy work of revolution, of refusing to work within given frameworks, and demanding different worlds. Moreover, if we follow the lesbian to this moment, a focus on the lesbian feminist commitments of Combahee, *This Bridge Called My Back,* and other salient markers of this time, the lesbian disrupts the narrow and singular focus on separatism.

Of course, what I have not addressed in this chapter is how contemporary commitments to lesbian separatism, and even just to the lesbian as a unifying framework, are grounded in trans exclusion—or more specifically, trans-antagonistic panic—while also claiming the mantra of radical feminism. This movement has created a false narrative of radical feminism as both historically and necessarily essentialist and trans exclusionary.[10] In many ways, I want to reclaim the banner of radical feminism as a political commitment to radical politics against and away from its distortions in trans exclusion. I opened this chapter with the West Coast Lesbian Conference and the debates that began there about trans women's place within lesbian space. But here I want to highlight that lesbian politics is not only and not always about space. Attachments to the histories of separatism as a political commitment are easily misplaced as attachments to spaces and places.[11] When these attachments persist in places and spaces, they lose the political stakes and political commitments that were germane to these histories. I hope I can offer a redirection of attachment to the politics of lesbian feminism. When we follow these attachments, we must take seriously that our commitments will often fail in practice. Current anxieties over lesbian death reflect attachments to failed practices. We can release these attachments without releasing commitments to the political paradigms that the lesbian offers.

Radical feminism's separatist politics mark feminists as dangerous. That is, feminist refusals of heterosexuality, marked through lesbian separatism, pose a real and literal threat to reproductive futurity. The danger of feminist refusals of and resistances to the heteropatriarchy is different from the danger of sexual violence that marked the feminist sex wars of the early 1980s, though the articulation of both may have related effects. I turn in the next chapter to examine the danger to women's sexuality marked by the feminist sex wars in relation to an emergent politics of sexuality marked by the AIDS crisis.

4 Lesbian Bed Death

Danger, Desire, and Killjoy Feminism

The end of male dominance would mean—in the understanding of such a man—the end of sex.

—ANDREA DWORKIN, *Intercourse*

On a blustery October Sunday in 1987, hundreds of thousands of people gathered in Washington, D.C., for the Second National March on Washington for Lesbian and Gay Rights. Following the first march in 1979, this march took on new directions and a new sense of urgency against the backdrop of the AIDS crisis. By many counts, 1987 was a milestone year in the first decade of the AIDS crisis. Early that year, ACT UP (AIDS Coalition to Unleash Power) was founded in New York City. For the first time, then president Ronald Reagan publicly acknowledged the epidemic. The demands of the march reflected the growing public awareness of AIDS and, specifically, an attention to the government's slow response to the crisis. Among the demands of the protestors were: civil protections for people with AIDS, increases to AIDS funding for research and care, a gay and lesbian civil rights bill, legal recognition for gay and lesbian relationships, and the repeal of anti-sodomy laws. The march's organizing principles also reflected a coalitional commitment to issues of race, class, and gender. Among the organizers were Eleanor Smeal, then president of the National Organization for Women; Cesar Chavez, labor organizer; and Jesse Jackson, at the time a candidate for the Democratic presidential nomination. The group's platform also included demands for reproductive freedom and the end to sexist and racist oppressions.

I begin with the 1987 march because it was, according to many accounts, where Jade McGleughlin, activist and organizer, made political the words *lesbian bed death* (D'Emilio 2014, 17; Przybylo 2019). Today, the phrase *lesbian bed death* travels as a commonsense joke about lesbian sexuality. Of course, the reigning joke about lesbian sexuality remains: What does a lesbian bring on a second date? (Answer: A U-Haul.) The U-Haul joke names the perception that lesbians' commitment to the domestic bliss of monogamous coupling is so strong that they often bypass the typical timelines of courtship and jump headfirst into cohabitation. The trope of lesbian bed death, similarly, associates lesbian sexuality with domesticity and the quiet comforts of pair bonding. *Lesbian bed death,* here, names the perception that lesbian couples, more so than other domestic, monogamous, or cohabitating couples, experience a precipitous drop in sexual activity once they have settled into the routines of monogamous coupling. The phrase itself gained traction in the late 1980s and early 1990s in both lesbian cultural circles and in academic debates on lesbian sexuality (Iasenza 2000, 2002). There are mixed genealogies for the origin of the phrase, specifically its connection to ideas about waning sex practices in lesbian couples. There is no debate, however, that lesbian bed death was central to the concerns Jade McGleughlin brought to her speech at the 1987 march.

Contra the commonsense understanding of lesbian bed death as an empirical decline in discrete sexual acts between a couple, McGleughlin's speech centered her concerns that the contemporary sexual politics, in both feminist and mainstream gay and lesbian movements, risked dangerously privatizing sex as an individual choice over and against sex as a community-building practice, as well as community as the context for sexual desire. While McGleughlin agreed that there was a challenge to lesbian sexuality, a challenge she named "lesbian bed death," she located this challenge not in the individual or couple but in the waning of politically driven lesbian publics.[1] In her proposal to Sue Hyde and John D'Emilio, the organizers of the Sex and Politics Forum at the 1987 march, McGleughlin (1987) argued that in any response to lesbian bed death "we have to be talking about a revitalized movement that moves sexuality from the couple back into the community." McGleughlin's commitment to rejecting the normativizing pull of mainstream gay and lesbian politics in favor of a sexual public mirrors Leo Bersani's (2009) call, in his now canonical essay "Is the Rectum a Grave?," to embrace gay male sexual formations that turn away from a political mandate that sex can be good, that it is valuable, only in the sanitized realm of the private and toward a sex politics that embraces abjection by refusing a sex that is redemptive. Both McGleughlin and Bersani, in their commitments to sexual publics, were responding to the moralizing and normalizing liberal convergence of antipornography feminism and early equality-driven gay rights.

In the previous chapter, I explored the destructive politics of lesbian separatism and the literal dangers of a feminist refusal of heterosexual reproduction. Here I move to examine how lesbian sex or, more specifically, the two genealogies of lesbian bed death describe a different attachment to the political potentials of lesbian social formations that refuse gender and sexual norms. In this chapter, I stage an encounter between the radical feminist theories of Andrea Dworkin and the desubjectivating, antifoundationalist queer theories of Leo Bersani's "Is the Rectum a Grave?" through the lens of lesbian bed death. I bring together the work of Dworkin and Bersani, against the backdrop of the emergence of the phrase *lesbian bed death,* for two reasons. First, Bersani accuses feminist and/or lesbian sexuality (and, as I show, they become one and the same) as bent toward a normative good, and he does so in direct response to Dworkin's undercited text *Intercourse.* Second, I follow Bersani to Janet Halley's *Split Decisions: How and Why to Take a Break from Feminism,* wherein she offers Bersani as a corrective to the moralizing demands of a feminism, a demand often traced to Dworkin, too rooted in saving women from the violences of heteropatriarchy. I map this framing of feminism to the commonsense understanding of lesbian sex as equalitarian. In line with my read of McGleughlin's use of *lesbian bed death,* specifically that feminist activism and feminist spaces in the first decades of the women's liberation movement offered the possibility for lesbian sexuality and lesbian relationally that rejected the structuring logics of heterosexuality, I argue that lesbian bed death refuses the moralizing demands that Halley accuses feminism of while highlighting the overreliance of heteronormative logics of sexuality in feminist and gay and lesbian politics of the time. More importantly, I thread my argument from chapter 3—namely, that the lesbian in both separatist and antiseparatist frameworks offered a political commitment to destruction that moved away from the individual to the structures and logics of the social—by reading Andrea Dworkin as refusing pastoralizing, to use Bersani's accusation, or softening feminist politics that return to liberal incorporation into an existing social structure.

LESBIAN BED DEATH AND FEMINIST ANXIETIES

In the sexological lineage of lesbian bed death, many attribute this phrase to the early work of feminist sociologist Pepper Schwartz.[2] In 1983, Pepper Schwartz and Phillip Blumstein published their now infamous study *American Couples: Money, Work, Sex*. Schwartz and Blumstein quickly rose to the national stage, with guest appearances on a variety of daytime talks shows, to discuss the book's controversial subjects (Allison 1983).[3] Schwartz and Blumstein's study focused on four types of couples—married heterosexual, cohabitating heterosexual, cohabitating lesbian, and cohabitating gay, all of them overwhelmingly white—in order to explore a variety of relational negotiations and everyday habits of American couples in the second half of the twentieth century. Combining extensive survey data with over three hundred in-depth interviews, *American Couples* focused specifically on "money, work, and sex" as points of both intimacy and contention for enduring relationships. Much of the critical acclaim of the book came from the authors' frank explorations of nonheterosexual, nonmarital pairings in the wake of both the sexual revolution and the women's liberation movement.[4] Indeed, within the text, Schwartz and Blumstein rely on the terms *new man* and *new woman* to demonstrate the ways that the political upheavals of the 1960s and early 1970s, regarding both gender and sexuality, fundamentally reshaped relationship dynamics.[5] Although the words *lesbian bed death* are nowhere to be found in the pages of the book, one can trace the association between lesbian bed death and *American Couples* to Schwartz and Blumstein's data-driven assertion that lesbian couples have less sex than the other three types of pairings and experience an even greater drop-off in sexual encounters as their relationships progress.[6]

One of the primary reasons Schwartz and Blumstein offer for the dearth of lesbian sex in long-term monogamous couples is the influence of feminist critiques of sexuality. According to Schwartz and Blumstein, feminist consciousness—that is, the political awareness that feminism has brought to individual women's lives—has negatively affected lesbians' willingness to engage in certain sexual behaviors: "Since lesbians have grown up learning society's restrictive guidelines governing female sexuality, we feel their sex lives may be affected in many unconscious ways" (Blumstein and Schwartz 1983, 239). Schwartz and Blumstein attribute lesbians' hesitancy around sex, specifically oral sex, to a socialized taboo surrounding female sexuality. Further bolstering their implication about the effects of feminism, they note that younger women, empowered through feminist movements, are likely to demonstrate even more resistance to such social norms. While Schwartz and Blumstein focus on the perceived persistence of feminine shame surrounding sexuality, the authors suggest elsewhere that sexual initiation is more fraught for lesbian couples both because their dual-female dyad is not governed by the same rules that expect and emphasize male initiation in sex and because of their own hesitancies around desire and coercion.[7] In other words, if there is no male libido driving the sexual needs of the couple, there is no predetermined sexual initiator. In diagnosing these problems of lesbian sexuality, Schwartz and Blumstein are quick to remind readers that these are measurements of genital sexuality, whereas they "have learned that lesbians prize nongenital physical contact—cuddling, touching, hugging—probably more than other couples do" (197). Put another way, Schwartz and Blumstein recognize that they are diagnosing a problem of lesbian sexuality through the metrics of genitality. They are quick, then, to assure readers that lesbians may, indeed, experience sexual satisfaction, though primarily through "nongenital physical contact." This emphasis away from genital sexuality has a neutering effect on the figure of the lesbian, marking her as drawn to more supposedly feminine, perhaps even more childish, modes of physical relating such as "cuddling, touching, [and] hugging." I highlight this point because much of the attention to lesbian sexuality in the wake of *American Couples* focused on the question of genitality and the phallocentrism that defines measurable sexual practices.[8] Furthermore, for the purposes of the argument here, I think it is important to note the ways in which lesbian sexuality as depicted in *American Couples* is thought to be associated with less dangerous, perhaps less threatening, forms of sexuality because of the insistence that lesbians refuse penetration. In this way, the public perception of lesbian sexuality as excessively feminine marks lesbians as less dangerous than gay male sexuality, a point I will return to below.

Feminism, as Schwartz and Blumstein discuss it, shifts the relational dynamics between men and women as well as heralds an age of more freedom of sexual expression and sexual pairing. In their frame, feminism produced the conditions of possibility for married or cohabitating heterosexual couples to experience more sexual freedom and more egalitarian roles in their domestic lives. Nevertheless, according to Schwartz and Blumstein, for lesbians, feminism becomes less liberatory and more restrictive of certain kinds of sexual expression and experience. The argument becomes,

then, that lesbians, owing to their socialization as women, suffer simultaneously from a feminized shame around sexuality and a reluctance to be
the sexual initiator. Sexologist Suzanne Iasenza (2000) argues that this kind
of "gender socialization theory" is itself a product of the rise of feminist
consciousness and the uneasy displacement of biological essentialism to a
kind of social essentialism. The myth of lesbian bed death, according to
Iasenza, is imbricated with other early 1980s theories of lesbian sexuality,
most notably the concept of lesbian fusion. *Lesbian fusion* is a term that
began to circulate in sexology circles as interest in documenting and describing lesbian sexuality increased after the publication of *American Couples*.[9]
As the name suggests, the theory of lesbian fusion claims that "lesbian
couples, because they contain two women who are socialized to be more
relational, achieve a greater degree of sustained intimacy" (Iasenza 2000, 60).
In other words, lesbians experience the "urge to merge," like good women,
generally valuing intimacy over desire, stability over passion. Such gender
coding fails to read lesbian sexuality as complex in its own right or lesbian
coupling as anything other than a feminized impulse to domestication.
The concept of lesbian fusion, therefore, serves to reinforce a perception
of lesbian relationships and lesbian sexuality as both hyperfeminine and
childish—that is, presexual—in nature.

Feminist responses to *American Couples* and the lesbian fusion panic contested any heteronormative framing of lesbian sex. JoAnn Loulan's 1984
book *Lesbian Sex*, for example, highlights the numerous differences in lesbian lives that may contribute to their differential sexual activity, as compared to heterosexual counterparts, and notes the various ways in which
lesbians engage in sexual intimacy that may be outside of the purview of
normative sexuality. Similarly, Marilyn Frye's (1990) polemic response to
the desexualization of lesbian sex—aptly titled "Lesbian 'Sex'"—hinged on
refuting a definition of *sex* based on male orgasm. Frye's "Lesbian 'Sex'"
centers on her contestation of the definition of *sex* used to measure lesbian
sexuality. Much like earlier feminist arguments—for example, Anne Koedt's
"The Myth of the Vaginal Orgasm" (1970)—Frye argues that the definition
of *sex* used by Schwartz and Blumstein relies on a phallocentric emphasis
on both penetration and orgasm as the defining parameters of sex proper.
Frye strongly contests Schwartz and Blumstein's claims regarding the dearth
of lesbian sex based on their failure to define what it means to have sex when
defining the "times" per week, month, and year that couples copulated.
Frye's critique is both methodological—"How did the lesbians figure out

how to answer the questions 'How frequently?' or 'How many times?'"—
and a critique of the wider impetus to measure and define female sexuality
(Frye 1990, 73). Within the latter emphasis, Frye goes so far as to state: "I'm
willing to draw the conclusion that heterosexual women don't have sex
either; that what they report is the frequency with which their partners had
sex" (73). For both Loulan and Frye, the problem is not that lesbians lose
their sex drive. Rather, the problem is that metrics for measuring sexuality
rely on understanding sex as a discrete event whose parameters are marked
by measurable genital change—namely, erections—and discrete orgasms,
typically measured through penile ejaculation.

While Frye contests the empirical framing of lesbian sex, she also
pushes back on the multitudes of sexological studies that followed, and
continue to follow, Schwartz and Blumstein.[10] Whereas many in the socio-
psycho-sexual realm reimagine the empirical side of the debate—whether
measuring lesbian sex differently or simply offering new and different data—
Frye questions why lesbians even want to be counted in the first place.
Naming the phallocentrism of sex is not new to Frye and, indeed, part of
what worries her is a shift away from lesbian feminist concerns about the
phallocentrism of sex in the 1970s and toward the 1980s demand for lesbian
sex to "count" within this phallocentric frame. Lesbian sex, then, is not
only a challenge of measurement but also a challenge of meaning. Following earlier feminist arguments about the inability of phallocentric language
to capture women's experiences, Frye (1990, 75) contrasts lesbian sex to gay
men's sex, noting the latter to be "articulate," consisting of "a huge lexicon
of *words*: words for acts and activities, their sub-acts, preludes, and denoue-
ments, their stylistic variation, their sequences." Lesbian sex, by contrast,
is "inarticulate," unable to be mapped to current structures of meaning.
Frye's argument asks the question: What does *lesbian sex* mean? Or, more
specifically, what did the supposed loss of lesbian sex mean for feminist
and queer politics in the 1980s?

Lesbian sexologist Michele O'Mara's doctoral work offers a different
genealogy for the origins of the term *lesbian bed death*. In her dissertation,
O'Mara (2012) follows the trails of *lesbian bed death* to an activist community of lesbians in and around Boston in the mid-1980s from whom the
phrase emerged as both parody and portent. O'Mara ultimately gets the
story from Jade McGleughlin, who situates the origin of *lesbian bed death*
in contemporaneous discussions about the waning and shifting of lesbian
communities and lesbian sexualities. More than a naming of the empirical

decline of lesbian sex, McGleughlin, as summarized by O'Mara, recalls that the phrase *lesbian bed death* "captured the larger loss of a sexual community where women had grown accustomed to having a public space for sexual discussions, and the excitement of the sexually charged women's movement" (83). In other words, the loss of a "sexually charged women's movement" was shifting the role of community and activism in lesbian desire.

The question of the place of sex in national gay and lesbian politics was central to the Sex and Politics Forum at the 1987 march, organized by Sue Hyde, director of the Privacy Project at the National Gay and Lesbian Task Force (NGLTF), and moderated by historian and academic John D'Emilio. In 1986, in the wake of the Supreme Court's decision in *Bowers v. Hardwick*, a ruling that refused constitutional protections for consensual sodomy, the NGLTF started the Privacy Project as a grassroots effort to mobilize activists in states where anti-sodomy laws remained.[11] The Sex and Politics Forum was among their first major organizing actions. The forum deliberately staged a conversation between the sanitizing of gay male sexuality in the AIDS crisis and the panic attached to lesbian sexuality in the pornography debates. What is more, the panel was meant to both provoke and resist the embrace of liberal mandates that render queer sexuality a protectable private choice over and against centering queer sexuality as politics. The guiding questions for the panel included: How do we refuse defining gay sex only through the lens of a public health issue? How do we reckon a diminishing lesbian sexuality amid feminist debates on sexuality, violence, and power? What can gay men and lesbians learn from each other as they forge a politics of sex (NGLTF 1987)?

The forum took place on the Saturday night before Sunday's massive march. More than five hundred people gathered in an auditorium on the campus of the George Washington University. In addition to McGleughlin, panelists included scholar Margaret Cerullo and sex-positive lesbian activist and writer Amber Hollibaugh. As one journalist reported, "If there was a central theme to the meeting it was that our sexuality—the actual lusts, passions and activities we engage in with each other's bodies and minds— has to be central to the politics of lesbian and gay liberation" (Kinsman 1987). Across the evening, panelists insisted on a refusal of assimilation and an emphasis on the necessity of sexual cultures and sexual politics.

When writing to D'Emilio and Hyde to propose a paper for the Sex and Politics Forum, McGleughlin (1987) offered "to address the contradictions between a rigorous discussion of sexuality within feminism and the continuing reality of lesbian bed death." Bridging the feminist insistence on an analytic of gender with her own observations of the disappearance of sexually charged feminist spaces, McGleughlin posited that it was the question of lesbian desire that propelled both intragroup and extragroup anxieties about lesbian sexuality. More specifically, McGleughlin (2021) worried that the mainstream gay and lesbian insistence on a right to sexual privacy, both in the wake of the *Bowers v. Hardwick* ruling and in response to the sex panic of the New Right, failed to recognize the ways that sexuality, and specifically queer sexuality, was part of a wider community structure and not simply a private engagement between two individuals. Within the women's movement, she recalls, women were able to claim a kind of sexual agency and subjectivity of their own. McGleughlin connects the sexual potentiality of these spaces not to an overly sanitized claim on women's inherent relationality but to the sexually and erotically charged impulses of radicalism and collective work. Moreover, McGleughlin notes that "without men to establish the value of women, their work and their sexuality, women within this movement became subjects with the power to recognize each other" (213). To this end, McGleughlin's (1987) rallying cry for her speech was: "In a dialogue that seeks to transform a discussion of sexuality largely focused on danger to one that can encompass, explore, and create new ways of articulating women's pleasure, we have to be talking about a revitalized movement that moves sexuality from the couple back into the community." Channeling a lesbian political ethos of the 1970s, McGleughlin refused a gay and lesbian politics that would simply reproduce the heterosexual nuclear family as its central organizing principle. In other words, if we follow *lesbian bed death* to the 1987 Sex and Politics Forum, we find at its root the promise of lesbian sexual politics that refuses the normative demands of the nuclear family and insists instead on collective and community formations that, as panelist Margaret Cerullo notes, foreground "rebellious identities and communities" (quoted in Kinsman 1987).

SEX WARS AND THE FEMINIST–QUEER SPLIT

The influences of the feminist sex wars are clear in the interpretive machinery of the *American Couples* study, as well as in the continued uptake of *lesbian bed death* in popular and academic sexology.[12] The feminist sex wars mark the time from the late 1970s to the early 1990s wherein feminist politics bifurcated along the lines of pro-sex sex radicals and antipornography, proregulation feminists. Among the central debates of the sex wars was how to best remedy sexual violence and its relationship to law and culture. The antipornography side argued that pornography literalizes sexual violence and leads to increased violence against women in their personal and public lives. Following this commitment, antipornography feminists sought to regulate the production and distribution of pornography and other so-called obscene or offensive materials. The pro-sex faction, however, argued that any regulation of sexuality was a violation of the sexual freedoms that feminists and lesbians had fought for over the previous twenty-plus years. This reorientation of feminist politics also splintered the many attempts at a unified lesbian politics (Duggan and Hunter 2006, 12). One effect of the feminist sex wars was the resulting image of feminists, and feminism, as antisex.

In the memories of feminist theory, much of the antisex sentiment of the time is attributed dually to Catharine MacKinnon and Andrea Dworkin. While both were scholars in their own right, in the early 1980s they collaborated to influence the passage of the Minneapolis Anti-pornography Ordinance and they continued to collaborate on scholarship and legislation across the 1980s and 1990s.[13] For mainstream feminism, the time around the sex wars marks a shift away from a post–civil rights, liberties-based legislative agenda—the Equal Rights Amendment and *Roe v. Wade* being two hallmarks of liberal feminism of this time—to a more punitive legislative agenda as exemplified by the antipornography ordinances that are associated with the work of MacKinnon and Dworkin.[14] In recent reflections of that time, McGleughlin (2021, 217) sums up this shift as moving away from early abortion debates that framed reproductive rights as a right to sex to a regulatory regime, one that included mainstream gay and lesbian politics, that rendered sex a private choice.

While the sex wars mark a dividing line in feminist politics—with the pro-sex lesbian sadomasochists on one side and the antipornography lesbian killjoys on the other—they also provide one of the many origin stories for queer theory's refusal of feminism and, thus, its concomitant refusal of the lesbian. Janet Halley's *Split Decisions: How and Why to Take a Break from Feminism* makes this split clear and argues forcefully for the necessity of this fissure. In arguing for a theory of sexuality that "takes a break from feminism," Halley (2006) diagnoses feminism, in all its forms, as a reductive, moralizing project in search of rescue for a subordinated subject, mostly women, away from the totalizing power of the subordinating other, mostly men. The feminist quest to save women, Halley argues, results in a moralizing claim that must always foreground women's subjectivity, what Halley calls "carrying a brief" (5). In her taking a break, Halley embraces queer approaches to sexuality, largely those that fall under the banner of the antisocial thesis. This approach to theorizing sexuality refuses to affirm a good sex that might be accessed if only power did not get in the way. As one critic notes, Halley sets up a firm opposition between "the presumed good of undifferentiated, decontextualized, and dehistoricized bodily pleasures, and . . . the allegedly pleasure-killing, paranoid, and moralizing power of feminism" (Franks 2007, 257). In other words, in Halley's formation, the queer offers the open promise of a sexual politics that embraces sexuality in its myriad forms over and against a feminist politics that insists only on the dangers of sex.[15]

Halley finds most tract with the moralizing imperatives of cultural feminism. According to Halley (2006, 61), the cultural feminist project relies on the narrative that "female values have been depressed and male values elevated in a profound moral error that can be corrected only by feminism." One of the many limits of cultural feminism's approach, for Halley, is that it insists that "virtuous sexuality is *feminine* sexuality" (64). This feminine sexuality, according to Halley, "has a decidedly infantile, lesbian, and caring shape," a kind of soft sexuality that Halley aligns with "lesbian sensibility" (64, 66). By pairing "lesbian sensibility" with a moralizing and redemptive mode of feminist sexual politics, Halley mirrors that commonsense understanding of lesbian bed death—namely, that lesbian sex represents the promises of an egalitarian sex outside of the violences of masculinity and heteropatriarchy and that therein we, in fact, find no sex at all. More importantly, for my argument here, Halley aligns "lesbian sensibility" with that from which we must take a break in order to confront sexuality's nonredemptive, aggressive, and potentiality violating vicissitudes. As an example of what the possibilities this taking a break would allow, Halley offers the work of Leo Bersani.

Leo Bersani's 1987 essay "Is the Rectum a Grave?" mirrors concerns about the loss of sexual publics in the mainstream gay and lesbian movement's drive to identity-based liberalism that were central to the conversations at the Sex and Politics Forum (Kinsman 1987). In addition to insisting on the pleasures of expansive sexual publics, Bersani takes to task the "pastoralizing, redemptive intentions" of a feminist insistence on attention to the violences of power in the structuring logics of sexuality. Instead, Bersani (2009, 22) offers "the inestimable value of sex as . . . anticommunal, antiegalitarian, antinurturing, antiloving." In order to make this argument, Bersani unpacks the specter of gay male anal receptivity that, as he diagnoses, feeds the homophobic terror that the AIDS crisis unleashed. Bersani connects this terror not to the virus itself but to the specter of an "insatiable desire, with unstoppable sex" that is more readily associated with normative ideas about female sexuality that some feminists, represented in Bersani by MacKinnon and Dworkin, seek to undo (16). As Halley (2006) notes, what concerns Bersani most is the risk that in resisting a cultural imperative against promiscuous sexuality, the gay liberals have gone the way of cultural feminists.[16]

While Bersani lumps Dworkin and MacKinnon together as emblematic of the feminist insistence on access to good and redeeming sex, reading Dworkin alone—and with an attention to the presumption, very much alive in the commonsense story of lesbian bed death, that lesbian sex promises a pastoral and redemptive site of sexuality—opens us to a different read of lesbian bed death that might offer pleasures similar to those that Halley finds in Bersani. I focus here on the one solo-authored Dworkin text with which Bersani engages in his essay. In her 1987 text *Intercourse*, Dworkin builds on her previous work on pornography to expand her analysis to reveal the rampant cultural associations between heterosexual intercourse and male pleasures in female submission. The central objects of Dworkin's analysis are famous literary texts from *Madame Bovary* to James Baldwin's *Another Country*. The central claim of Dworkin's polemic is that literary and artistic depictions of heterosexual intercourse center on men's violent occupation of the female body, which then becomes woman's central condition. The text builds stepwise through increasingly violent depictions of heterosexual intercourse by drawing the connection between women's abjection in intercourse and violence as constitutive of the female condition in heterosexuality. In the concluding section, Dworkin draws the cultural analysis of the previous two sections into the realm of the law. In doing so, she aptly demonstrates how the numerous regulators of sexuality—religion, education, the state—work in concert to assure who is violated and who is not as a normative framework for regulating sexuality. Herein, Dworkin argues not only for the primacy of gender in any analysis of sexuality but, even more so, that regulations on sexuality in fact produce the gender system as we know it.

Dworkin takes sodomy law as one site of regulation that promotes and perpetuates women's sexual, and thus social, subordination. Regulating what bodies are able to engage in specific sexual practices—which, according to Dworkin, is what sodomy laws do—both relies on and perpetuates a sense of naturalness connected to a sexual act. With regard to sodomy laws, she states: "Men being fucked like women moves in an opposite direction; so there is a rule against men being fucked like women" (Dworkin 2006, 192). In other words, the criminalization of sodomy is not simply a homophobic measure against male–male sex; it stands to enforce who should rightfully—that is, "naturally"—be in the position of submission and who in the position of domination. To loosen these assignments, Dworkin parodies, would be "a lessening of differences between the sexes, the conflation of male and female natures into one human nature" (192). Dworkin, thus, reads sodomy statutes not as a protection against rape—as they are often invoked today—but as legislating who is rapeable and who is not. In other words, according to Dworkin, sodomy laws are not based in fears of male anal receptivity but in shoring up the gendered logics of heterosexuality.

The great traction of Bersani's essay is his engagement with the cultural repulsion of gay male anal receptivity. Bersani recounts the story of a young Florida family run out of town after their three hemophiliac sons were diagnosed with HIV. The fear engendered by the specter of AIDS in this family, Bersani (2009, 18) argues, is intimately connected to the unconscious representation of "the infinitely more seductive and intolerable image of a grown man, legs high in the air, unable to refuse the suicidal ecstasy of being a woman." What is articulated in the bottom figure is a kind of unexpected transgression that allows for this pleasure. It is not only with his legs high in the air that this figure becomes woman but also in his deep pleasure in the act of submission. Rather than refuse the cultural panic that to be sexually submissive is to be abjected, Bersani calls for a willful embrace of this abjection, for an embrace of the specters of violation and shame that this abjection engenders. For Dworkin, this is the rub, so to speak. The abjection of submission is not something that women can cast off so easily or experience so selectively. For certain subjects—and this formulation for Dworkin may, in fact, include gay men—the eroticization of this submission is something prescribed to them, forced and reinforced through nearly all modes of social relation.[17] She argues: "It is a radical critique of the elements of social life that maintain intercourse as a right, as a duty, as pleasure, no matter what the cost of intercourse as such, no matter to whom. . . . Intercourse distorts and ultimately destroys any potential human equality between men and women by turning women into objects and men into exploiters" (Dworkin 2006, 12). Part of what Dworkin's text considers is what the limits of pleasure are. It is one thing to experience another's desire for your subordination in the controlled confines of a sexual scene. It is another entirely to have your everyday existence saturated with that desire.[18]

Though not responding to Bersani's essay, Dworkin asks a question I have often found myself asking in relation to this suicidal figure, particularly in the context of understanding the rectum as a grave: Given the metaphorical association between rectum and grave, what is dead or buried there? To which Bersani would answer, "Proud male subjectivity." But when we think this question in terms of the numerous specters of death that are attached to this rectum / grave, I cannot help but wonder how we imagine the phallic and penetrative force that catalyzes this shattering ascesis. Dworkin (2006, 80) observes:

> Remarkably, it is not the man who is considered possessed in intercourse, even though he (his penis) is buried inside another human being . . . disappeared inside someone else, enveloped, smothered, in the muscled lining of flesh that he never sees, only feels, gripping, releasing, gripping, tighter, harder, firmer, then pushing out: and *can he get out alive?*

It seems clear that in this phallic economy, only men can actively choose to identify with the nonphallic. This is not to imply that homosexuality is a choice but that the celebration of male penetration depicted here is valued precisely as this kind of choosing.[19] There is, of course, still a phallic, or at least penetrative, interaction at the center. Part of what makes this figure so intolerable is not simply that it brings us face-to-face with men's penetrability but that it forces us to confront men's rapeability. Of course, one way we are able to understand this context is through work like Dworkin's *Intercourse.* Dworkin is in agreement with Bersani that for men and women, tops and bottoms, the abnegation of self in this paradigm of power is pleasurable. She is not, though some may accuse her of this, arguing for a kind of false consciousness on behalf of women. Rather, she thinks we should be wholly concerned with this pleasure in submission.

Dworkin implies the question: Would we desire abjection if it were not formed through sexual logics that restrict who has access to abjection, who is to be properly abjected? This is where lesbian bed death is instructive. In the dominant genealogy, lesbian bed death is common sense. In this framing, a feminist insistence on the violence of sex, that same insistence that Halley asks us to take a break from, follows lesbians, because they are feminists, to the private space of the bedroom, where they are unable to shed the public structuring of sexuality as domination and power—that is, as binarized gender logics of active and passive. And because they are feminists, they cannot, or will not, be rapists. And because feminism has refused to read the power dynamics of sex as anything but rape, or potential rape, lesbians are left with a libidinal economy wherein there is no sex because there is no rape. This logic is most evident in the responses to a genealogy of lesbian bed death that starts with *American Couples*. These responses, which continue today, go one of two ways. The first response is empirical and seeks to disprove the report that lesbians have less sex. The second is theoretical and seeks to define lesbian sexuality away from heterophallic structures, such as penetration and orgasm. Both responses, however, return us to the couple and the private sphere.

Feminists have long dismissed Dworkin as a vitriolic extremist. Indeed, much of the disavowal of Dworkin has come from avowed feminists.[20] This disavowal is made as a defense against being labeled a prude or antisex—an anxiety that is readily apparent in the tropes surrounding lesbian bed death, a theme to which I will return shortly, and that animates Halley's insistence that theories of sexuality must take a break from feminism. Part of the misrepresentation of Dworkin as claiming "all sex is rape" hinges on a misplaced interpretation of women's position as always already victims. Even more so, this misunderstanding requires that Dworkin's claims regarding intercourse be read literally rather than as a descriptive account of how meanings are assumed naturalized through recourse to the body. To leave with the impression that all sex is rape is to distill sex to the binary opposition of domination and submission, yes and no.[21] In this way, sex is something good and pleasurable or bad and violating. Rather than simply relegating to sex to such binarisms, however, Dworkin forces us to confront the messy, violent underside of the pleasures of abjection. In her concluding chapter, Dworkin connects the violent connotations of intercourse to both women's depictions as filth and sexuality's explicit connections to death. In her characteristic tenor, Dworkin (2006, 241) states: "Sadism and death, under male supremacy, converge at the vagina: to open the woman up, go inside her, penis or knife. The poor little penis kills before it dies." Drawing together these connections, Dworkin argues for the absolute ordinariness of the sexual abjection of women. She extrapolates from the embodied positions of intercourse through a whole host of cultural associations between submission, abjection, filth, and death.

The image Bersani presents in "Is the Rectum a Grave?" relies on the kinds of associations Dworkin draws out of the heterosexual imaginary. Dworkin, however, offers Bersani's association in reverse. Reading Freud's assertion of the subject's early association of the penis and the fecal material held in the rectum, Dworkin asserts the easy association between the vagina and the rectum. She states, "The mucous membrane that the man touches in intercourse with his penis, the vagina, is dirty like the rectum. . . . The vagina of the woman is not phenomenologically distinct from the mucous membrane of the rectum" (Dworkin 2006, 238). For Dworkin, however, this association is not the seat of pleasure in abjection but the constitutive association: "Being excremental is the dimension of inferiority that legitimates and makes appropriate sadistic sexual acts that pass as simple sex, a cruelty in sex, the brutal domination through sexual subjugation of a worthless, essentially scatological thing" (238). According to Dworkin, what makes anal penetration both so seductive and so repulsive in the cultural imaginary is its likeness to vaginal rape. The pleasure in abjection that Bersani advocates for refuses, by embracing, the shame of sexual receptivity but does little to engage the structuring logics of that shame. What is more, despite its rhetoric as radicalism and its refusal of a mainstream gay liberalism, Bersani's commitment to abjection implies an ability to choose—to lean into, if you will—such desires. While this is a politics of refusal, in that it refuses the mandate to make sex meaningful for good, it stops short of the radicalism of destruction that lesbian politics promises in its return to the world.

While feminist critiques of the turn to the legal sphere to address sexual violence often pair Dworkin with MacKinnon, *Intercourse* makes clear that Dworkin finds the emphasis on the criminalization of sexual violence dangerous, especially if it is not accompanied by a critical interrogation of the cultural meaning of intercourse.[22] Rather, and especially when paired with Bersani, Dworkin forces us to confront the limits of a politics of pleasure that cannot interrogate its context. For Bersani, intercourse is pleasurable because it is dangerous; for Dworkin, intercourse is dangerous because it is pleasurable. Embedded within the question of the relationship between pleasure and danger is that question of violation. In Bersani, sex is too much connected to practice. Dworkin, however, shows that sexual practice bleeds out into the cultural foray, ultimately informing a whole host of relational possibilities. Like Bersani, Dworkin is interested in the ways in which we all participate in systems that are also the root of our oppression. In "Is the Rectum a Grave?" Bersani names the ways that white, class-privileged gay men found themselves shocked by the discrimination they experienced during the AIDS crisis even while they failed to be able to confront the systems of racism, classism, and sexism that led to such discrimination. Similarly, Dworkin pushes her readers to understand the multiple ways in which we all participate in a system that allows for sexual violence. Rather than name and address the ways in which sexual violence both produces and relies on the gender system, dominant logics continue to imagine sexual violence as aberrant, traumatizing, and criminal over and against a pure sexuality that is productive and communing.

Lesbian bed death becomes a commonsense explanation of lesbian sexuality when sexuality is understood as always already imbued with specters of power and violence—that is, when sexuality's primary frame of reference is heterosexuality. This is not to say that there is some pure form of sexuality that is available outside of its social context. Both Bersani and Dworkin agree that moves to regulate sex through the liberal state assume that there is a pure form of sexuality, a sexuality for good that can be found under the right conditions. No one knows better than feminists, perhaps than women, however, how exhausting and almost impossible the drive for a communitarian sex can be. Indeed, it is the promise of a pure communitarian sex that is the context for sexual violence and that perpetuates a system of remedy that can only respond to such violence through carceral logics.[23] If such conditions were possible—that is, the conditions of a sexuality not marred by power—however, lesbian sex appears to offer the perfect route to such pure sexuality. If Bersani is interested in penetration as the thing that defines sex, at least at the level of culture, then lesbian sex might promise an escape from the top/bottom dynamics of penetrator and penetrated that Bersani so forcefully embraces. If the power dynamics of sexuality are violent and if that power is understood as the effect of a top/bottom dynamic, then lesbian sex, with its failure to fit phallic formations, would offer a sexuality free from power and violence. That lesbian bed death is understood as a common, and commonsense, experience of lesbian sexuality, however, points to the inability to understand sexuality outside of these frames of reference. Again, this is not an empirical claim about lesbian sex. Nor am I arguing for some form of sexuality that can be understood outside of power. Rather, the commonsense understanding of lesbian bed death names the assumptions that, without these specific power dynamics, there is no sex.

THE LESBIAN PLEASURES OF KILLJOY POLITICS

When Halley (2006, 155) reads Bersani for what is possible when we bracket feminism, she also notes that "one of the pleasures of reading [Bersani], for me, is imagining the indignation and offense it probably arouses in cultural-feminist readers." What makes Bersani's formulation so seductive, then, is not only that it escapes an insistence on a project of sexuality that saves us from its violences but also, perhaps even more so, that it offends, it shocks, it fights back. I cannot help but find mirrors in these pleasures of fighting back in the kind of vulgarity and vitriol that Dworkin insists on in *Intercourse*. Like Halley's pleasures in reading Bersani, I must admit my own pleasures in reading Dworkin. I find Dworkin's insistence on the violences of heterosexuality as a social system, and the effects of that social system in the everyday sexual and social practices of those outside of hegemonic masculinity, very seductive. And it is this seduction, this pleasure, that allows me to find myself in her text. Moreover, I find her language thrilling. The history of the feminist sex wars often aligns Dworkin with a reductive insistence on danger. But, as Leah Claire Allen (2016, 49) notes: "Dworkin was also deeply invested in pleasure ... particularly in the pleasures of diagnosing the worst dangers of our culture and its record." Bersani offers a kind of pleasure in embracing the debasement that marks receptive sexuality. It is an in-your-face analysis that seduces with its very bluntness. The same is true for Dworkin. Far from offering a vision of sex that is redemptive, loving, and nurturing, Dworkin makes the madness of heteropatri-archal sexual norms its own kind of pornography. Dworkin's thrill is in her refusal to pretty up her commitment to utterly filleting the world as it is given in her insistence that the world could be otherwise.

Contrary to any commitment to make sex good, Dworkin leans into sex as bad, really bad, even worse than bad. Sex for Dworkin, especially when demarcated as penetration, is grotesque, repulsive, revolting. Like Solanas, Dworkin's is a politics of destruction. In this, Dworkin brings the radicalism, the vitriol, the refusal of the kind of lesbian politics I explored in the previous chapter, to the sex wars. Far from fighting violences with the promise of a redemptive sexuality, Dworkin insists we burn the whole thing down. The brutality of her politics is also the brutality that made a radical feminist insistence on lesbianism as a political imperative so seductive. By repudiating intercourse, Dworkin does not promise some softer, more palatable, less violent version of sex as we know it. Rather, she makes libidinous the commitment to annihilation not of the subject but of the system. Whereas Bersani leans into the abnegation of self in the individual surrender, even when taken by force, of abjected sexuality, Dworkin advocates a violent abandonment of any structuring logic of the sexual.

The commitment to destruction that Solanas and Dworkin promise in their feminist extremism is also, as it informs and builds on lesbian feminist politics of the 1970s, the context for new ways of engaging sexuality that some facets of the women's liberation movement made possible. We might follow this commitment forward to the lesbian sexual publics that emerge amid and in response to reinvigorated conversation on lesbian sexuality in the wake of the sex wars. These lesbian publics, as Ann Cvetkovich (2003) demonstrates, offer both an engagement with the everyday, the absolute ordinariness of sexual trauma, and a commitment to refusing an individualizing pathology in response. Far from softening sex, Cvetkovich argues, queer feminists metabolize the everyday of sexual traumas into lesbian publics. Cvetkovich also engages Bersani's argument for the value of abjection as perpetuating a logic of "sexuality as fundamentally traumatic" (51). Lesbian sexuality, especially butch and femme narratives, in Cvetkovich's read, refuses to bifurcate sex as good or bad, pain or pleasure, even as dominant or submissive.[24] Rather, lesbian sexuality offers a different context for engaging, negotiating, and making meaning of sexual practices in a wider social context. In other words, lesbian sexuality can be a site of "unpredictable relations between gender, sexual, and bodily presentations . . . [that] are both material and constructed" (51). The structuring logics of lesbian sexuality—and their refusals, refutations, and reworkings—exceed the site of an individual sex act. Thus, encounters and engagements with the refusals, refutations, and reworkings are the context of lesbian sexual publics. Put more simply, it is entirely possible for the abnegated self of Bersani's suicidal bottom to pick up, dust off, and return to the everyday as a coherent masculine self.[25] The lesbian, and especially butches and femmes, by contrast, must negotiate the multiple selves that are differently interpolated in social contexts.

Sara Ahmed's feminist killjoy is also instructive here. The killjoy is that feminist figure who, in her insistence that the world as it is given is a site of violence, disrupts the happiness of others. In her disruption, the killjoy becomes the cause of violence and the one who refuses the pleasure of others. Part of Bersani's argument, and by extension Halley's, is that eliminating a sex–gender system predicated on the violences of domination would also eliminate the pleasures of subverting that system. Such a world would be a world of no pleasure at all. But, as Ahmed argues, the killjoy brings her own pleasures; and here is where Cvetkovich's lesbian counterpublics refute the assumption that any interrogation of violence requires a sanitary response. If we follow Ahmed (2017, 255), "to be willing to kill joy is to transform a judgment into a project." The promise of lesbian sexual publics, for Cvetkovich and others, is that they are erotically generative sites that refuse and rework the violences of heterosexuality without pretending to escape those violences.

Following lesbian bed death to Ahmed, Cvetkovich, and others refutes the commonsense story of lesbian bed death—namely, that feminist politics kills sex. To the contrary, I argue that the killjoy politics of lesbian feminism, as exemplified here by Andrea Dworkin, is the context for a lesbian sexuality that refuses liberal individualism in favor of collective action. Part of Halley's complaint is that feminists throw the boys out with the bathwater. Indeed, late in the project she notes that the promise of lesbian feminism failed precisely because lesbians, she argues, all have attachments to real men (fathers, sons, uncles, brothers) in their lives (Halley 2006, 110–11). Halley wants there to be a political and theoretical world of sexuality in which the very enactments and expressions of sexuality that some feminists find problematic, especially male masculine heterosexuality, serve as the object ground of that politics and analysis. Again, this framing of feminism relies on an equation of feminism with a liberal project of good. Reading Dworkin with the multiple genealogies of lesbian bed death, as I have done here, points to a feminism, perhaps a specifically lesbian feminism, that is predicated not so much on desire for the same as on a politics that engages the violences of heterosexuality, maybe even a politics that hates men. Here lesbian identity is not so much happenstance as it is both an understanding and outright rejection of heterosexual mandates.[26] This is a lesbian feminism that does not seek comfort or to eradicate violence in order to get to a true and good sexuality. Rather, this brand of lesbian queer feminism promises an engagement with power, destruction, and annihilation that does not turn inward on the subject but instead turns outward to the subject's context. If we follow my argument from the previous chapter, part of what lesbian feminist politics, even in the most everyday practices, promised was an embrace of these destructive impulses. Taken as part of this genealogy, lesbian bed death becomes a warning against the sanitizing impulses of a gay and lesbian politics that relies on the privacy claims of a liberal subject.

The legislative initiatives of the early 1980s imagined that if men stopped viewing pornography, they would stop asking for blowjobs from their secretaries. And that if men stopped asking for blowjobs from their secretaries, they might start seeing their wives as humans and not objects of their domination. None of these logics address the very structure of both the nuclear family and the liberal individualism that produces men's position of domination, whether or not they have access to pornography. This is the power dynamic at play. In other words, if we could simply legislate sex enough, we could guarantee everyone's rightful access to good sex and only good sex. Responses to the #MeToo movement, for example, focus largely on increased representation of women and people of color in the entertainment industry and beyond. If sexual harassment is the structuring framework for understanding sexual violence in the wake of #MeToo, then the power dynamics of the workplace translate to the bedroom. In this way, I mean to reverse consent logic as being rooted in a contemporary structuring of sex as transactional and pivot, instead, to the way that sexual harassment informs said logic. By this I mean that our understanding of why and how some intimate sex goes bad, so to speak, is based on our understanding of individual frameworks for both harm and intimacy. Following lesbian bed death, by contrast, can point us to a more collective—I am deliberately not saying *communal*—understanding of the context of both sexual violence and sexuality writ large. The development of the term *lesbian bed death* has historical significance in that it names a very specific nexus of feminist and queer concerns regarding both the relationship of sex and politics and, even more so, the place of violence—sexual violence, political violence, the violence of heterosexuality—therein. I have told the story of lesbian bed death to highlight how the lesbian emerges as a warning figure of the killjoy effect of feminist concerns with sexual violence. Schwartz and Blumstein situate a lesbian lack of sexual desire within the wider context of the feminist sex wars and the cultural equation of feminism with an antisex stance. Lesbian bed death, then, becomes evidence that feminist concerns with sexual violence will thwart one's ability to actively engage with sexual desire. Jade McGleughlin's use of the term shifts this narrative, naming instead an erasure of lesbian sexual publics against the backdrop of both the feminist sex wars and the AIDS crisis and the increased liberalization of mainstream LGB politics.

Moreover, responses to the panic about lesbian bed death in the wake of *American Couples* mirror many of the responses to anxieties about the death of lesbian identity today. Just as scholars and activists sought to refute lesbian bed death through recourse to the empirical—that is, by either proving the numbers wrong or questioning the assumptions that led the counting—so too is the response to perceptions of a decline in lesbian identity. In chapter 3 and in this chapter, I have disentangled the lesbian from identity to explore how the lesbian points to certain destructive impulses in feminist politics, impulses that I argue are akin to but not easily aligned with queer theory's antisocial thesis. In the next chapter, I return to the empirical—that is, to "actual" lesbians—to ask after the use and limits of mapping the lesbian with aggression.

The basic premise of the Sex and Politics Forum at the 1987 march was that gay men and lesbians have something to learn from each other in understanding and engaging a politics of sex. As McGleughlin (2021, 219) recalls: "AIDS activism, and the pleasures of collective movement-building, provided new ways to become politically involved in public conversation about sexuality and mirrored the transformative possibilities of the Women's Movement's intersubjective space." Indeed, by the early 1990s, a queer politics had taken hold. Such is the context for the emergence of a more queerly driven lesbian politics as enacted by the Lesbian Avengers.

5 Killer Lesbians

*Reading Aggression from the
Lesbian Avengers to the New Jersey 4*

On the first day of school in the fall of 1992, the Lesbian Avengers set out for Public School 87, in Middle Village, Queens, a predominantly Irish working-class neighborhood in District 24, with a helium tank and hundreds of lavender balloons printed with the words "Ask about lesbian lives." As a marching band, dressed in kilts reminiscent of Catholic schoolgirl uniforms, played a rendition of "You Are My Sunshine," lesbians greeted schoolchildren and their parents, handed out balloons, and demanded the reinstatement of a recent public education push to include diversity in the curriculum (Baus and Friedrich 1993). Other Avengers held a banner proclaiming "Teach About Lesbians" and smaller posters that listed names of major women in history known or thought to be lesbian. Against the backdrop of District 24's outright rejection of the Rainbow Curriculum, the Avengers protest has two goals: the reinstatement of the curriculum and a protest of the curriculum for not including wider conversations on lesbian representation. This first major action was controversial even in the most radical lesbian spaces. In the months leading up to the action, as the group attempted to bolster their numbers, they lost a number of members in response to the choice to picket at a middle school rather than at the school board, for example. While some left, others found the aggressive and shocking tactics of the Avengers to be a draw to the group (Schulman 1994, 280–81).

The lesbian, as a cultural figuration, has long been associated with aggression. In chapter 3, I showed how the separatist politics of the 1970s marked *lesbian* as a nihilistic and murderous project committed to the end of men. In chapter 4, I argued that the commonsense understanding of lesbian bed death points to assumptions that the lesbian's killjoy politics lead to an inevitable death of sex. In both of these chapters, I highlighted how lesbian figurations are associated with an angry and even "extreme" feminist politics. While this claim of lesbian anger and extremeness persists today, it is only one facet of what Lynda Hart (1994) calls the lesbian mark of aggression. Since the end of the nineteenth century, the figure of the lesbian has been marked by an aggression that mirrors how women's violence is marked as lesbian. These associations are not without context. Lisa Duggan (2001, 3) argues, "The black beast rapist and the homicidal lesbian both appeared in new cultural narratives at the end of the nineteenth century, as threats to white masculinity and the stability of the white home as fulcrum of political and economic hierarchies." Both Duggan and Hart connect the roots of lesbian aggression archetypes to the invert model of sexuality that posited lesbian sexuality as a kind of masculine corruption. In this way, the lesbian is equated with a drive for violence that is assumed endemic to her masculinity. The association of aggression, specifically as a kind of masculinized violence, continues to circulate today. However, as I take on here, the context of that circulation can have real and grave material consequences.

Aggression itself deserves our attention. Aggression is imagined as anger made physical but not quite violent. Aggression can be an affective stance that is both distancing and acute. Aggression is felt as antagonism that may provoke new aggressions or may occasion retreat. Aggression itself is not violent, though it may announce violence to come and make a threat of violence, and in this way it cannot be separated from threats of physical violation. Aggression is also imagined as excessive. When others accuse feminists or queers of being aggressive with their politics, they often are naming their experience of the very existence of such politics as being too much. We can think here, again, of the feminist killjoy. This kind of aggression is a misreading of the existence of that which makes us uncomfortable as being the root cause of our discomfort. Most markedly, aggression is hostile. As a hostility, aggression becomes the event that precipitates a claim of violation. Feminist aggression, of the kind that lesbian separatism figures in chapter 3, is rooted in rage logics that, Jack Halberstam (1993, 191) notes, "[resist] the moral imperative to not fight violence with violence." Halberstam connects representations of feminist violence to both lesbian aggression and a specific form of lesbian empowerment.

The specificity of lesbian aggression relies on reading the lesbian as outside of the bounds of proper femininity and, as I outlined in chapters 3 and 4, aligning the lesbian with a feminist project of destruction. In a U.S. context, the former took root in the late nineteenth century. Duggan (2001) traces the arrival of the lesbian in the U.S. popular imagination, as masculine invert, to a late nineteenth-century anxiety about threats to white men's dominance, most readily articulated in the widespread media, social, and media attention to and circulation of the story of Alice Mitchell's murder of her lover Freda Ward. Similarly, Lynda Hart demonstrates that women's violence has been coded as lesbian since at least the Victorian era, in frameworks ranging from criminality to literary representation. According to Hart (1994, 9), it is the deep imbrication of violence with the lesbian that marks the lesbian as deviant, not that she has lesbian lovers. More recently, feminist aggression has been thought in psychoanalytic terms. In *Gut Feminism,* for example, Elizabeth A. Wilson (2015) examines feminism's intolerance for its own aggressive impulses. Like the negativity that is central to queer theory's antisocial thesis, lesbian aggression has the potential to unsettle any slide into a politics of optimism that promises the good feeling of recognition and assimilation.

In this chapter, I consider lesbian aggression through three case studies: the legacy of the Lesbian Avengers, the case of the New Jersey 4—a group of young Black women incarcerated in the early 2000s after defending themselves against street harassment—and more recent direct action activities carried out by antitrans feminists, also known as TERFs (trans-exclusionary radical feminists), in the name of the lesbian. In other words, I turn here to examine three ways that aggression attaches to the lesbian: aggression as a political tool, lesbian identity as a self-evident mark of violent aggression, and accusations of in-group aggression that belie material harms. I bring together these three modes of lesbian aggression to demonstrate that the lesbian is evoked differently in relation to aggression in different contexts and to different ends. My aim here is to take seriously the ways that lesbian aggression can produce different consequences, life or death consequences, in different contexts. In examining the Lesbian Avengers, I argue that lesbian aggression can be mobilized for political purposes only in specific contexts. In examining the New Jersey 4, I demonstrate how the racialization of lesbian aggression reproduces violent hegemonies. In examining the claim that to be called transphobic is itself an act of aggression, and to do so in defense of the lesbian, I argue that this has the effect of removing the lesbian from a political interest in and engagement with transmisogyny and trans death. In the previous two chapters, I explored the pleasures in and promises of a politics of destruction that germinated in lesbian feminisms of the 1970s. Here, I map that politics of destruction to lesbian aggression. In this chapter, and across these three cases, I ask the question "What use is lesbian aggression now?"

THE LESBIAN AVENGERS

The Lesbian Avengers were founded in 1992 by lesbian activists Anne-christine d'Adesky, Marie Honan, Anne Maguire, Sarah Schulman, Ana María Simo, and Maxine Wolfe. Each of the founding members had a long history in feminist and gay and lesbian organizing, and most members had been involved in ACT UP and Queer Nation. When they began, the Avengers were responding to the sense that lesbian issues were being left out of prominent feminist and queer causes. By 1992, the landscape of queer direct action was shifting. In the wake of splintering factions and leadership struggles of ACT UP, new groups were forming. The Lesbian Avengers sought to, as founder Sarah Schulman (1994, 282) reports, "set a new tone for lesbian politics—a post–ACT UP lesbian movement." Much like related groups at the time, including Queer Nation and ACT UP, the Lesbian Avengers employed direct action protest and in-your-face street actions. Though the group began in New York, chapters rapidly popped up in other cities across the United States and United Kingdom. The founding of the Avengers came on the tail end of the Reagan–Bush years and on the eve of Giuliani's New York City. The early 1990s was also marked by claims of postfeminism. As I discussed in chapter 2, this specific historical nexus produced a ripe moment for claims of lesbian specificity. While in retrospect this time may be marked the emergence of a specific lesbian political subject, as Ann Cvetkovich (2001) and others argue, the early 1990s was also a time of heightened anxiety around lesbian visibility. Unsurprisingly, anxieties around lesbian invisibility produced new kinds of lesbian visibility.

The Avengers' first major action, a response to the perceived lack of lesbian representation in New York City's Rainbow Curriculum, a diversity-driven education initiative, was controversial even in the most radical of lesbian spaces. Across 1992, New York City was alight with controversy over the inclusion of gay and lesbian references in the city's newly mandated Rainbow Curriculum. The curriculum was developed after a number of racist incidents in the late 1980s in order to offer elementary schoolteachers tools for recognizing and celebrating cultural difference in their classrooms. At the same time, the New York Public School system had recently approved a plan to offer condoms and AIDS education in select high schools (Lee, Murphy, and North 1994). In the Rainbow Curriculum, a section on family structures referenced gay and lesbian familial arrangements and made suggestions for books that celebrated gay parents. Although the references to gay families were scant in the 443-page document, the Catholic–driven religious right immediately attacked the curriculum and built a citywide campaign to block its implementation. Following on this backlash, District 24, in Queens, refused to adopt the curriculum. When the Avengers first formed, they set the Rainbow Curriculum ban in District 24 as the target for their first action (Schulman 1994). They spent the summer months wheatpasting flyers around New York and recruiting upward of thirty dykes to join the action.

While this first action was controversial, the Avengers quickly gained both local and national attention. In the weeks and months that followed this action, the Avengers staged a number of zaps in protest of antigay ordinances popping up around the country, especially Colorado's Amendment 2. Amendment 2 was one of many ballot initiatives across the country seeking to block or outright ban civil protections for gays and lesbians. In response to Colorado's ballot initiative, which would prohibit any law that would allow for civil protections, national gay and lesbian organizations called for a ban on tourism and travel to Colorado. So, when the mayor of Denver came to New York to promote Colorado tourism, the Avengers were everywhere he was, all the while chanting: "We're here, we're queer, we're not going skiing" (Schulman 1994, 283). When *Self* magazine scheduled an employee ski retreat to Colorado, the Avengers invaded the offices of their publisher, Condé Nast (284). Within days, *Self* canceled the ski weekend. Across the 1992–93 academic year, the Avengers continued to protest in support of the Rainbow Curriculum. In the wake of Clinton's landslide election and ongoing debates about gays in the military, 1993 saw another surge in antigay measures on state and municipal ballot initiatives. Building on their rising national platform, the New York Avengers mobilized to support chapters across the United States and elsewhere. The programs of the Avengers were trifold. First, they engaged in a politics of visibility primarily through direct action protest and guerrilla-style wheatpasting and flyering campaigns. Second, they undertook a number of ballot box initiatives, especially in response to state-level proposals. Most notably, they were instrumental in mobilizing gays and lesbians in Lewiston, Maine, to register to vote and push back against a Christian Right–based campaign to repeal Lewiston's nondiscrimination ordinance. Finally, and built on the model of their Maine initiative, one of the primary actions of the Avengers was development of the Lesbian Avengers Civil Rights Organizing Project (LACROP). LACROP not only fought ballot initiatives around the country but also wrote and produced *Out against the Right: An Organizing Handbook* as a guide for organizing and mobilizing under the rubric of *lesbian* and in distinction to more conservative gay and lesbian movements.

The sustained cultural and media attention to what has been dubbed "lesbian chic" across 1993 vexed the Lesbian Avengers' commitment to a politics of visibility (Cvetkovich 2001; Rand 2013). I say "vexed" because the Avengers' platform was built on both combating lesbian erasure and the subsequent demand for lesbian visibility. And yet, 1993 marked a time of cultural shifts with regard to lesbian visibility. Across 1993, a number of mainstream publications featured cover stories on lesbian icons or lesbian lifestyles. Following *New York Magazine*'s May 1993 cover story "Lesbian Chic: The Bold, Brave New World of Gay Women," featuring k. d. lang, critics dubbed the emerging trend "lesbian chic" (Ciasullo 2001). Lesbian chic presented gay women as a stylish new market interested more in fashion and suburban respectability than feminist politics. As Erin J. Rand (2013, 122) argues, the Avengers' "efforts to increase lesbian visibility were both constrained and enabled by their articulation to the lesbian chic phenomenon and by their circulation within a capitalist and heteronormative economy of desire." On the one hand, the emergence of lesbian chic stymied the Avengers' claim of lesbian invisibility. On the other hand, the aggressiveness of their politics was made all the more visible in contrast to the palatable normativity of the lesbian darlings of the media. For Rand, "their performance of lesbianism interrupts the very expectations and effects of visibility politics itself" (128).

Even though 1993 was the year of lesbian chic, the early 1990s were a moment of cultural anxiety about lesbian murderousness. The Avengers were at the vanguard in a year when anxieties about lesbian killers were at an apex. Across 1991 and 1992, the very public arrest and trial of Aileen Wuornos, the so-called lesbian serial killer, were front and center in news media. The year 1992 also saw the release of the films *Single White Female* and *Basic Instinct*. Both films align the lesbian with a kind of calculated and murderous psychosis. In both name and action, the Lesbian Avengers drew on stereotypes of lesbians as violent, man-hating, political-baiting radicals. A central rallying cry of the Avengers was "We recruit." The claim to recruit is rooted in the public fear that lesbianism is a contagion. Rejecting mainstream models of gay and lesbian respectability, the Avengers played up the cultural anxieties that lesbians produced and against which the lesbian was posited as chic.

Like other groups of their time, the Avengers used graphics in creative and attention-grabbing ways. The Avengers' most recognizable logo is a Looney Tunes–style bomb, a solid black sphere with a lit fuse. The cartoonishness of the Avengers' bomb evokes mass murder and a retro military milieu while also winking at the viewer. Similarly, the Avengers repurposed an advertisement of 1950s waitresses holding the cartoon bomb, as well as the famous Aleksandr Rodchenko "Read Books" poster from the Russian Revolution. These images have the effect of both pushing against pacifying images of women and tying the Avengers to communist revolutions. Elsewhere, the Avengers used the iconic image of Pam Grier as Coffy, the murderous avenger in the eponymous blaxploitation film. The Avengers' use of Grier and blaxploitation drew on imaginaries of revolutionary moments of the 1960s, specifically of the Black Panther Party.[1] The marrying of the absurdist art of the bomb with the excitement of revolution and the playfulness of the images' paradoxical juxtapositions were all a part of the draw of the Avengers. The moniker "Lesbian Avengers" invokes associations with Marvel's comic series *The Avengers,* a group of superheroes made famous across the mid-twentieth century that includes the Hulk, Ant-Man, and Captain America. In this way, they evoke both a status of working for the good and against the patriarchy, as well as the stylized violence of the midcentury superhero aesthetic.

If one of the concerns of late 1980s lesbian organizing was the loss of lesbian activist spaces, the Avengers sought to reignite those spaces. While the group was explicitly political, that politics was not restricted to protests and actions. As many Avengers recall, their biggest draw was the parties. Perhaps the Avengers' longest-lasting legacy was the creation of the Dyke March, first produced at the April 1993 March on Washington for Lesbian, Gay, and Bi Equal Rights and Liberation. Founding member Sarah Schulman had been on a book tour in early 1993, seeding Avenger chapters in cities across the United States. In the days leading up to the April march, a number of Avengers hit the streets in D.C. promoting a "dyke march to the White House" (Schulman 1994, 285). Schulman estimates that nearly twenty thousand people showed up and marched from Dupont Circle down Pennsylvania Avenue. In the wake of that first Dyke March, even more chapters of the Avengers sprang up across the United States and globally. The Washington march was followed that June by the first official NYC Dyke March in tandem with a local Pride event held in Bryant Park. As I discussed in chapter 1, Dyke Marches remain a fixture in countering the mainstreaming and corporatizing of Pride festivals in many U.S. cities. As the first D.C. Dyke March approached Pennsylvania Avenue, the group paused in front of the White House. With lit torches, similar to a carnival-style sideshow, a line of lesbians, wearing Avengers shirts with the iconic cartoon bomb logo, brought the flames to their mouths and proceeded to eat fire.

Eating fire was a hallmark of New York Lesbian Avengers' actions (Baus and Friedrich 1993; Cogswell 2014). The fire breathing began as a direct pro-test response to the arson and murder of Black lesbian Hattie Mae Cohens and white gay man Brian Mock, in Salem, Oregon. After months of racist and homophobic taunting by a group of neo-Nazis, Cohens and Mock were attacked with a Molotov cocktail through the window of their apart-ment in the middle of the night. The murder of Cohens and Mock by a self-proclaimed group of skinheads was the most violent incident in a number of arsons and vandalism leading up to Oregon's Ballot Measure 9, which would have classified homosexuality as morally corrupt and in line with pedophilia and sadism. On Halloween of 1992, a little over one month after the murder, the Avengers, in tandem with the Anti-Violence Project's annual Halloween Take Back the Night march, held vigil to draw atten-tion to violence against gay and lesbian people. In Greenwich Village, the Avengers erected a shrine to Cohens and Mock. In ritual, the Avengers ate fire, an adaptation of a circus performance, as a symbolic refusal to allow the fire-bombing deaths to consume the lesbian and gay community in fear. As the Avengers marched through the streets, they carried their torches high and chanted, "The fire will not consume us, we take it and make it our own" (Baus and Friedrich 1993). The shrine to Cohens and Mock was topped with hand-drawn flames and the statement: "Burned to death for being who they are" (Baus and Friedrich 1993). The fire-eating response follows the Avengers' tactics for shocking and performance-based street action re-sponses. However, the images of white lesbians—as Kelly Cogswell (2014) relays, it was primarily white members of the group who sought out the fire eating—marching in the street with torches aflame cannot but elicit images of lynch mobs. Indeed, much of the Avengers' literature and archive fails to address the racial motivations for the murder. The murderers were tried and convicted under hate crime laws because of the clear racist motivations of the attack. Taking on Cohens and Mock as representatives of antigay violence without attending to the racist logics of the murders erases race from the equation.

In many ways, the lesbian organizing of the Avengers mirrors the organizing strategies of liberal white feminists in the 1970s. The focus on "civil rights" reflects a particularly liberal strategy of inclusion even as the Avengers' tactics are avowedly radical. In this case, *radical* describes more their tactics and methods than their political endgames. The Avengers utilize the language of race-based civil rights movements of the 1960s, a common tactic of gay and lesbian movements of the past thirty years. In their focus on civil rights, the Avengers make a tacit delineation of race-based civil rights projects as having achieved their goals. That is to say, by claiming that the time is now for lesbian and gay civil rights, the Avengers imply that the civil rights movements of the 1960s were successful and completed. Specifically, as reflected in Schulman's (2004) call for a "Freedom Summer" and her organizing of a "Freedom Ride," the Avengers put forth a platform of lesbian solidarity that was predicated on a shared lesbian experience that would create a solidarity over and against differences. Schulman argues: "No matter how we differ from each other, most lesbians and gays have been shamefully treated at some point, and many of us have been abandoned by our families" (21). In this way, the shame and stigma of homophobia are imagined to be universal and experienced in the same ways across demographic groups. What is more, the drive to organize around shared experiences of homophobia imagines that homophobia is the primary violence affecting gay and lesbian people. As Schulman herself notes, against the backdrop of the 1993 debates on gays in the military, white men were overrepresented in the media even while Black women were discharged at higher rates under the ban. The demand for more representative attention to Black lesbians in the military belies the greater question of the role of the military in providing marginalized and impoverished communities with access to resources and promises of class mobility with great risk to their lives.

The Avengers' failure to build sustainable coalitions with other groups, specifically with leaders in movements for racial, class, and immigrant justice, ultimately led to the fracturing of the New York chapter across 1995 and 1996. The group decided to ignore the requests of Barbara Smith and other Black lesbian feminist leaders to not use the language of "Freedom Rides" in their multistate tour in the lead-up to Lewiston's vote in 1993. When the Avengers announced their Freedom Ride route, they received a letter from Smith and other lesbians of color asking them to change their branding and warning that their use of "Freedom Rides," a central organizing strategy of Black civil rights movements, would be, at a minimum, offensive and appropriative and, at a maximum, cause further ruptures in antihomophobic organizing happening within communities of color. As Schulman (1994) reports, despite Smith's request, the group pushed forward with the use of "Freedom Rides." The justification, Schulman argues, was that Avengers of color had liked the use of the term and, she implies, a truly antiracist campaign would allow for dissent among women of color (313–18).[2] Smith (1999) herself took up the issue in a number of speeches, ultimately published in her essay "Blacks and Gays: Healing the Great Divide." As Smith makes clear, her request was not only about a simple disagreement over who gets to use the term but also about the value of coalition politics versus the single-issue—in this case, the lesbian as a unifying framework—politics that the Avengers were espousing. The Avengers' use of "Freedom Rides" had the effect of branding them as a primarily white, single-issue group. As Kelly Cogswell (2014) remembers, in the years that followed, the group continued to struggle with overcoming the sense that the group was informed by white needs and unable to address the racial injustices that their members faced.

In the Introduction and second chapter of this book, I argued that the lesbian lost its feminist political claim somewhere between the sex wars and the dawn of lesbian chic. The Avengers provide a perfect foil to that narrative. Indeed, Dyke Marches persist as some of the most inclusive, expansive, and radical sites of lesbian politics and lesbian possibility (Currans 2012). The Avengers trafficked in a lesbianness that drew on a framework of lesbians as rabid feminists and sexually adventurous, a notable departure from the commonsense story of lesbian feminism as antisex. As Rand (2013) demonstrates, while the Avengers' methods followed the radical direct action work of groups like ACT UP and Queer Nation, their political goals were largely civil rights–based and, thus, liberal in their aims. Like many of the separatist groups of the 1970s, the Avengers, at least the New York chapter, ultimately fell apart over the inability of the white group leadership to take seriously the needs and demands of lesbians of color (Cogswell 2014). What made the Avengers' work so seductive, and what continues to draw many to their work today, is their specific brand of lesbian aggression. Rand (2013) argues that the group trafficked in excessive lesbianism. This excessive lesbianism, I argue, is enacted as a kind of aggression. Aggression, and lesbian aggression specifically, is only available as political tool for certain, largely white, subjects. I turn here to explore how commonsense understandings of lesbian aggression fare differently for lesbians of color. Far from mobilizing aggression for its political thrill, associations between lesbian identity and aggression can be dangerously racialized as a signal of criminal intent.

THE NEW JERSEY 4

The specter of lesbian aggression takes on a different valence in the case of the New Jersey 4.[3] On August 18, 2006, a group of young Black lesbians traveled from Newark, New Jersey, to Greenwich Village in Manhattan for a night on the town. After leaving the bars around 1:30 a.m., the group of seven was walking past the IFC movie theater when a loitering stranger began hitting on the youngest of the group. As Patreese Johnson, one of the women, reports, Dwayne Buckle smacked, "Let me get some of that."[4] Confused by what Buckle was requesting, Venice Brown asked for clarification. At which point, Buckle pointed to Johnson's crotch. When Johnson dismissed his advance by stating she was gay, Buckle reportedly told the group he "would 'fuck' them and 'turn you all straight'" (18). Verbal sparring ensued and Buckle spat in the face of Johnson's friend Renata Hill. Buckle continued to engage the group both physically and verbally. He called Venice Brown a "fat elephant" and proclaimed Hill to be a man (19). He threw his cigarette at the group and punched Hill in the face. Over the next few minutes, a physical fight broke out between the group and Buckle. As the confrontation escalated, Buckle tore three locs from one woman's head. A number of men from the street joined in and variously attempted to scare Buckle into retreat or came to his defense. At one point, Buckle had Hill in a stranglehold. Johnson came at Buckle with a dull kitchen knife, slashing at his arm and backpack. When the groups dispersed, Buckle realized he was bleeding and requested that someone call an ambulance. Shaken from the fight and fearing for their own safety, the group retreated to a nearby McDonald's before again moving on toward the train. When police arrived, they set out after the group and quickly found them within blocks of the incident. All seven women were arrested and taken to central booking. The seven were charged with "gang assault" in the second degree and booked into Rikers Island.

By the next day, the case of the alleged "girls gone wilding" attack was all over the New York papers (Belenkaya et al. 2006). In the *New York Times* article "Man Is Stabbed in Attack After Admiring a Stranger," two white women reporters crafted a narrative wherein Buckle—whom they portrayed as a respectable up-and-coming filmmaker—was attacked unprovoked (Buckley and Hammer 2006). The *Times* reporting is based entirely on a statement given by Buckle from his hospital bed. The *New York Daily News* ran the headline "Girls Gone Wilding: Lesbians Locked Up in W. Village Beating" (Belenkaya et al. 2006). And the *New York Post* proclaimed: "Girl Gang Stabs Would-Be Romeo" (John Doyle 2006). Across the media, the women were called a "lesbian" gang and depicted as though they were out looking for men to beat up and Buckle had simply been in the wrong place at the wrong time. The use of *wilding* conjured immediate connections to the Central Park jogger case seventeen years prior.[5] In this way, and with the accompanying photos of a young, butch Terrain Dandridge, the media evoked stereotypes of Black masculinity and sexual aggression. Across all accounts, Buckle is depicted as an innocent bystander, simply admiring a beautiful woman. Three of the seven women pleaded guilty and served six-month sentences followed by probationary release. The other four, who remained at Rikers, went to trial the following April. Each of the four was convicted of felony gang assault in the second degree and sentenced to between three and eleven years in prison. At the time of sentencing, all four of the women had been incarcerated since their arrest on August 18.

In the week of trial sentencing, New York's dailies rang out with celebrations of the group's convictions. "Attack of the Killer Lesbians" was the hook for the *New York Post*'s reporting (Italiano 2007). Reports portrayed the group as animalistic, calling the attack "wilding," the women a "wolf pack." When the trials began, the case was profiled by the *New York Daily News* with the headline "The Case of the Lesbian Beatdown" (Ross and Connor 2007). In the blurb, the group is described as "a posse of lesbians," whereas Buckle is elevated as an aspiring filmmaker who was simply insulted by the implication, made through a comment by one of the women, that his shoes were cheap. After their conviction, the *New York Daily News* proclaimed, "Lesbian Wolf Pack Guilty." The article opens by stating: "Four tough lesbians from New Jersey were transformed into cry-ing convicts yesterday" (Martinez 2007). The case prompted Bill O'Reilly, at the time of Fox News fame, to run a segment titled "Violent Lesbian Gangs a Growing Problem" (Wheeler 2007). In this episode, O'Reilly de-scribes an increase in lesbian gangs in major metropolitan areas. These gangs, he opines, come together with one motive: to attack men and rape and recruit young girls. O'Reilly's exposé features supposedly expert testi-mony detailing the rise of an underground network of pink-pistol-toting dykes. Across the report, O'Reilly asserts that this growing problem is fueled in "lower socio-economic crew[s]" and that these groups have similitude with "ethnic gangs." Central to O'Reilly's concerns are both the recruit-ment tactics of these alleged gangs and their extreme violence. Though sarcastic in tone, even the scant gay news coverage picked up on the titil-lating title of a killer lesbian gang: "Killer Lesbians Mauled by Killer Court, Media Wolf Pack" read the title in *Gay City News* (Day 2007).

The metaphor of a wolf pack is telling because it implies a kind of cal-culated and coordinated attack, with specifically racialized implications. By calling the group a "wolf pack," reporters dismiss, if not erase, the vio-lence of the catcall that prompted the fight.[6] Across reports, Buckle's actions were downplayed as the innocent attempts of a straight man to engage a woman. That Buckle made a sexually aggressive advance on the women is never in question. Indeed, court documents repeatedly use Buckle's claim to be interested in conversing with the group to paint Buckle as an inno-cent and unprovoking victim. Whereas the early *New York Times* reporting relayed that Buckle was admiring a stranger, in the trial and in subsequent media reports, Buckle backs off this tone, stating instead his interest in the "slightly pretty one" while doubling down on his calling Brown "an elephant" and Hill "a man" (Italiano 2007). By dismissing Johnson as only "slightly pretty," Buckle denounces his own culpability. In this way, he is saying that since Johnson is only slightly pretty, he could not have been aggressively coming on to the group in the way the women argue. From the media to the courtroom, Buckle's come-on is portrayed as entirely inno-cent. While the group is moored only as "lesbian," Buckle is given more specificity in the world when he is identified in relationship to his pro-fession, variously described as a "sound mixer," an aspiring filmmaker, and local student. During the trial and conviction, the judge repeatedly admonished the defendants, reminding them that words do not carry the same violence as fists and knives (Day 2007). In his comments on their sentencing, the judge justified the abnormally harsh prison terms with a commitment to making the streets of New York, specifically the rapidly gentrifying Greenwich Village, safer for both residents and tourists (Harto-collis 2007).

That the group was tried under gang laws—an indictment justified by the city prosecutor on the basis of number (two or more makes a gang)—cannot be separated from the ways that gang rhetoric in the United States is used to justify racialized criminalization. As Lisa Marie Cacho (2012, 63) reminds us, "Gang-related crime is even classified as belonging to a dif-ferent class and caliber of violence than the very same crimes committed by nongang members." Even if New York's threshold for gang charges is strictly quantitative—that is, according to the law any offense committed by two or more people constitutes gang assault—the rhetorical heft of *gang* already paints a different picture of the group's motives and intentions. As Cacho demonstrates, the implication of gang-like behavior relies on racial-ized ideas of "urban" masculinity that is presumed always already criminal. While the law already mandates greater sentencing charges for offenses deemed gang level assault, the social meaning attached to *gang* when cou-pled with specific bodies—that is, with the bodies of people of color—makes juries more likely to convict. This bias confirmation renders defendants guilty before they are even tried. The media reporting and jury conviction shared one important element that made their assessments all the more credible to a general public: the vast majority of writers and jurors were women, specifically white women. Convictions by a primarily white, pri-marily female jury fails the claim of feminist solidarity that women are suspected to be committed to, especially in the face of male violence. To be sure, woman identification has never provided enough of a common ground to assure alliances. Even so, the ability of white women to distance themselves from the young women of the New Jersey 4 helps to high-light the specifically racialized combination of the lesbian and aggression in this case. As Beth E. Richie (2012) argues, the experience of the New Jersey 4 does not follow the dominant framework for responding to vio-lence against women. Since the early 1990s, most notably on the heels of the Violence Against Women Act, mainstream feminist responses to male violence against women have focused largely on legislative initiatives and government funding for support services. These shifting frameworks have tracked with the rise of both the nonprofit-industrial complex and the prison-industrial complex. That is to say, both the protection of women and the concomitant criminalization of racialized and impoverished communities of color have found a space in the logics of neoliberal capitalism (Richie 2012).

The plight of the New Jersey 4 cannot be separated from the place of the attack. For the New Jersey 4, being lesbian is what made their aggression real, is what made it violent. Lesbianism is what made them a gang rather than a gaggle. But this use of the lesbian cannot be disentangled from their position as Black outsiders in the persistently gentrifying Greenwich Village. Since the last decade of the twentieth century, the neighborhood had been experiencing increasing gentrification and so-called quality-of-life laws meant to push the young queers of color whose social scene marked the area as a queer space out of the newly developing community. The Christopher Street Pier, made famous as the site of public sex in the 1970s and 1980s and as the practice ground for New York's burgeoning ball scene in the 1980s and 1990s, was effectively razed at the turn of the century and replaced with tower apartment complexes and manicured parks and jogging trails (Manalansan 2005). The changes in Greenwich Village at this time were driven largely by a mainstream gay politics focused on consumerism and privatization (Hanhardt 2013). The homonormative paradigm of class-ascendant white gays in Greenwich Village was part of a wider shift in the geopolitics of the area at the time. The early 2000s were marked by numerous community meetings and actions aimed at promoting community safety through increased policing and surveillance of those deemed outsiders. As Christina B. Hanhardt (2013) demonstrates, the results of such actions were the easy equating of youth of color and trans women of all ages, those very communities that made the Village a gay enclave in the first place, with threats to community safety and coherence. Put more directly, in the name of safety, white property-owning residents sought increased surveillance and policing of Black and Brown queers who were racialized as outsiders.

It was young, queer of color neighborhood activists in Greenwich Village that began to push for attention to the group and the horror of their trial and incarceration. Despite widespread coverage in local news, there was almost no coverage of the plight of the New Jersey 4 in either national gay news or national feminist news (Carney 2012; Richie 2012). Fabulous Independent Educated Radicals for Community Empowerment (FIERCE), a community group born in the late 1990s in direct response to the increase in community and police aggression against queer and trans youth of color in the area, had a mission to empower and develop queer youth of color as leaders in movements for racial, sexual, and economic justice. From the beginning, FIERCE worked to challenge who had rights to the public space of Greenwich Village by fighting against development near the piers and for the rights of queer youth to the public spaces that have been made valuable by their culture. FIERCE mobilized almost immediately to raise funds for the group's defense, as well as to provide updates to the community and start letter-writing campaigns while the women were incarcerated. One week after their sentencing, Imani Henry (2007) wrote about the group's plight in *Workers World* and directed readers to the FIERCE website. FIERCE's campaign to get their story out resulted in a broader community response. Over the coming year, Dyke Marches in New York, San Francisco, and Boston (and likely many others) worked to raise funds and awareness.

Outside of Dyke Marches and FIERCE's activism, the New Jersey 4 did not garner significant lesbian media or activist attention. Indeed, across their years of incarceration, huge amounts of money and people power was spent on marriage initiatives. Lesbian, as it attached to the New Jersey 4 and outside of politically engaged lesbian and antiracist communities, became a commonsense claim of criminality and malicious intent in the media narratives of the New Jersey 4. Most interestingly, for this project, the New Jersey 4 have not become the face of lesbian feminism's murderous impulses. Whereas cult figures like Valerie Solanas and Aileen Wuornos are lauded as the literalization of feminism's aggression, specifically toward men, their whiteness allows them to take up such status without addressing the ways in which their whiteness also protects them from certain forms of criminalization. Though both Solanas and Wuornos were imprisoned, notably for crimes they most certainly committed, the context of their incarceration is markedly different. Indeed, while both were imprisoned, neither were read as criminal in the same manner as the New Jersey 4.

The case of the New Jersey 4 highlights a deep racialization of the lesbian that follows aggression to criminalization rather than to a celebrated punk politics.[7] In the case of the Lesbian Avengers, their use of direct action protests and commitment to an avowedly lesbian movement takes advantage of the rhetorical coupling of the lesbian and radical feminism, read as aggression, as a threat to the cohesion of a heterosexual social order. And yet, their most effective actions returned to lesbians as specific kinds of people rather than the lesbian as a political commitment that might destabilize, even destroy, existing structural norms. By contrast, the media coverage of the New Jersey 4 links the women's lesbian identity to assumed violent impulses that seek to attack—specifically, that seek violent attacks on men. Though most of the coverage does not name the women's race in its headlines, race becomes the hinge point that literalizes the imagined violent impulses of the lesbian. Here, aggression attaches to lesbian identity in ways that mirror longer histories of the imbrication of racialization and the construction of homosexuality. As Estelle Freedman (2006) demonstrates, early twentieth-century concerns with lesbian relations in the context of prisons produce the figure of the "prison lesbian." In this figuration, Black women, accused in this context of seducing white women, become the true lesbians through a racialized association with "'male' sexual aggression" (144). When this figuration follows the cultural association of radical feminism as a threat against men, the earlier figuration of sexual aggression that targets white women gets turned outward as enacting real violence against men. This longer racialized history of reading lesbian figures as harbingers of violence and aggression is not easily commodified for political gain. Indeed, we are in the present day again mired in a sex panic that relies on pathologizing social identity and practices to violent, often sexually violent, intent. The shift today, however, is that this panic claims to work for the protection of lesbians.

TERF IDEOLOGY AND ANTITRANS AGGRESSIONS

In 2018, a group calling itself Get the L Out, as in out of LGBT, staged a zap-style action at the start of the London Pride parade (Gabbatiss 2018). The protesters, numbering about eight, carried signs that read "Lesbian not queer," "Lesbian = Female homosexual," and "Trans activism erases lesbian." Despite not being registered for formal participation in the parade, the group demanded to march with the sanctioned parade. When organizers refused to allow the group to join, the group was allowed to march ahead of the official delegations. Thus, despite being formally banned from the parade, the protesters marched with an air of leading the parade. The condemnation from organizers and the wider LGBT community was swift. Nevertheless, the action made international news, bringing the rhetoric of trans-exclusionary radical feminism to a broader audience.

Ten years prior to the action at London Pride, the term *TERF* was coined by Viv Smythe, a journalist with the *Guardian*. Smythe (2008) used the term on her personal "Feminism 101 FAQ blog" in reaction to rising public trans-phobia being spread under the rubric of radical feminism. In its early per-mutation, *TERF* was used to delineate those who were using the banner of radical feminism to question and police trans people's identities and experiences, with the effect of equating radical feminism with trans exclu-sion, from those who were avowed radical feminists and whose radical feminism was adamantly trans inclusive. *TERF* is now shorthand for any form of transphobia enacted in the name of feminism, women, or lesbi-ans. As movements for trans inclusion and trans acceptance have become more widespread, antitrans feminists have upped their strategies for trans exclusion. Antitrans feminists, according to Veronica Ivy (2018), have devel-oped three forms of propaganda to make their movement seem to be com-mon sense. First, they argue that trans women's access to "women-only" spaces constitutes rape. Second, they claim victim status, arguing that the use of the term *TERF* is itself a slur and a violent attack. Third, they argue and advocate for the pathologization of trans experiences as mental health disorders that both medical and political establishments have a duty to treat through barring trans people access to medically appropriate care. In each of these points of propaganda, but most especially the claims to sex-ual violence, the lesbian is the fulcrum on which this campaign is waged. TERF rhetoric claims the lesbian in three ways: that lesbians are being erased, that lesbian spaces are under attack, and most perniciously, to put it mildly, that trans women claim both lesbian identity and lesbian space in order to sexually assault lesbians.

The platform of Get the L Out presents a prime example of the TERF logic that Ivy outlines. In a flyer distributed at London Pride, and other Pride celebrations across the United Kingdom in 2019, they accuse trans politics, a framework that goes beyond individual trans people to any pro-gram or platform that accepts and supports trans people, of enacting vio-lence against lesbians in three ways. First, they accuse any allowance of medical transition for trans men as being a form of conversion therapy away from lesbian identity and toward heterosexuality. Second, they argue that early access to gender-affirming medical technology, specifically for transmasculine adolescents, amounts to medical abuse against lesbians. And third, they accuse mainstream gay and lesbian acceptance of trans women as lesbians as perpetuating a rape culture in which "true" lesbians are coerced into sex with "males who 'identify' as women" (Get the L Out 2019). Here, trans people's existence becomes the very site of violence against lesbians.

While Get the L Out is only one example of TERF ideology, their organizing points are echoed in many arenas and seep into wider cultural anxieties
about the death of the lesbian.

The framework utilized by Get the L Out is in sync with another small
but vocal group of academics who claim a so-called gender critical stance
to what they term "the transgender question." The gender critical stance, in
its most pared down form, asserts "woman" as a political condition that is
immutable under the persistence of patriarchy. They then use this stance
to question the legitimacy of trans identities—specifically, trans women's
claims on womanhood—under the guise of legitimate academic debate.
In its most vitriolic forms, the gender critical stance has made claims that
trans people's existence is itself violent, often described as rape, and is an
occupation of women and lesbian identity. As a prime example, Sheila Jeffreys's 2014 book *Gender Hurts* presents as its thesis that allowing for social
and medical transition has materially harmful effects on both trans people
and their communities. There has always been a fierce and often majoritar-
ian acceptance, if not insistence, of trans women's right to claim "lesbian"
as a social and political identity. In recent years, however, as trans politics
and trans experiences have become a part of wider cultural conversations,
there has been increased attention to a vocal minority of activists and academics who have made questioning trans lives central to their platforms.
Often, if not always, these conversations are staged as a claim for protecting
lesbians and for protecting the sanctity of lesbian space and lesbian politics.

Critical engagements with TERF ideologies largely, and necessarily,
focus on either the essentialized and biologically reductive definition of
woman used by antitrans feminists or, and really concomitantly, the dis-
torted version of feminism that allows for such essentialized reductions.
Julia Serano's *Whipping Girl* (2016), for example, locates transphobia, especially transphobia that seeks to exclude trans women from the category
"women," in a wider cultural narrative of "effemimania"—that is, a fear of
male femininity—that is rooted in traditional misogyny. Serano notes this
expansion of misogyny, and resultant valorization of masculinity, in the
fact that is it trans women, and not always trans men, who are most violently excluded from movements and spaces that root themselves in the
category "women." More recent work has sought to locate trans women
in the histories of lesbian and radical feminism. Emma Heaney (2016) centers trans women in the histories of lesbian feminism in order to counter
trans-exclusionary impulses today. Similarly, Finn Enke (2018, 12) rejects the

easy association of the "1970s" with the violent exclusion of trans women, which was certainly happening, to "naturalize the separation of trans women from feminism." These arguments, and myriad more, are necessary counters to a trans-exclusionary ideology that takes feminism as its justifying claim.

In this project, I take as axiomatic that trans women are women, that trans lesbians are lesbians, that trans women belong in lesbian space, and that expansive modes of doing gender, even when perceived as falling into traditional presentations, are lived feminist practices. I am less interested here in making the case for trans women's inclusion in the categories of "lesbian" or "feminist"—a case that has been and continues to be made by trans women themselves—than I am in examining the mobilization of the lesbian in TERF ideology. As I outlined in chapter 1, "lesbian," even more so than "woman," was the defining ground on which Michfest staked its trans exclusion. The exclusion of trans women at Michfest mirrored anxieties over the inclusion of trans women in lesbian separatist space that date at least as far back as the 1973 West Coast Lesbian Conference. While many of these arguments are the seeds for contemporary TERF ideology, they focused primarily on arguing that trans women did not count in their political understanding of "women," though largely left unquestioned that trans women did exist. Indeed, even in their attempts to separate trans women from the category "lesbian," these movements made clear that they believed lesbians also existed. In other words, trans women's demands for inclusion in lesbian space were not viewed as a threat to lesbian identity or lesbians as persons. By the late 1990s, fears about butch lesbians "defecting" to manhood via gender-affirming medical transition sparked their own anxieties about the durability of lesbian identity (Halberstam 1998). More recent antitrans sentiment, a sentiment most readily captured through the acronym *TERF*, however, accuses trans people of committing violence, usually narrated as sexual violence, against both the category "lesbian" and individual lesbians. This mobilization of the lesbian is different from earlier instantiations of trans exclusion that argued that trans women were not rightful lesbians. Rather, this new brand of trans exclusion argues that trans women, as well as trans men, genderqueer folks, and anyone who questions the gender binary, are actively and willfully attacking lesbians and lesbian identity.

In other words, trans-exclusionary feminists mobilize lesbian identity and lesbian spaces in order to legitimize their exclusionary practices. Most notably, these strategies cross both activist and academic bounds. For example, the reddit subgroup r/gendercritical, which was largely devoted to antitrans boundary-marking in the name of lesbian feminism, had over fifty thousand subscribers. The *New Yorker* profiled a group calling itself Radfems Respond, which had many of its meetings and conferences shut down by protesters (Goldberg 2014). Many who fall in the antitrans and gender critical camps assert that being called a TERF is, itself, a form of hate speech—that is to say, a form of violence. Threats of real violence, it seems to me, are categorically different from using the term to name a true antitrans threat. That *TERF* has become an umbrella term names the ways that more insidious forms of antitrans rhetoric are mobilized. In this way, TERF rhetoric is much like the Westboro Baptist Church. The church, which holds less than one hundred members, most of whom are related to each other, is a small minority. Nevertheless, the targeted picketing of the group has taken on widespread cultural meaning and come to stand in for a whole host of religious antagonisms against the LGBT community.

More pernicious, and with more provocations of actual violence, is the quick equation of trans women's presence in lesbian space with sexual violence. Historically, "women's space" has meant lesbian space, even if heterosexual women were in the space, and in this capacity the exclusion of trans women has been a lesbian issue (Heaney 2016; Enke 2018). More recently, however, antitrans activists, under the guise of radical feminism, have been making claims that trans women's rightful claim to lesbian identity is extinguishing lesbian identity. As Ivy observes, a significant response critiquing TERF ideologies is from cisgender radical feminists. Nevertheless, antitrans rhetoric posits that trans women are leading a kind of infiltration of lesbian space, lesbian ideologies, and lesbian sexual practices.[8] Whereas in previous decades, transphobia manifested in actively barring trans women from "women's space"—a practice that persists, to be sure—more recent antitrans rhetoric has taken on the claim that trans subjectivities, trans politics, and trans visibility are forms of active violence against lesbian lives and lesbian identity. Curiously, this follows the same recruitment and contagion logic that the Lesbian Avengers harnessed. For example, journalist Abigail Shrier's highly criticized 2020 book *Irreversible Damage: The Transgender Craze Seducing Our Daughters* argues that the number of teenagers who identify as trans men has risen in direct correlation to an infiltration of trans activism in popular culture discourse. The author attributes this rise of trans identities to a political affront to women and girls and as a calculated attack on lesbian identity. The author implies that adolescents are forgoing lesbian identification, which she equates with a real and true identity, in favor or trans and genderqueer identities, which she equates with a false promise of escaping the stressors of femininity in a misogynist society. Shrier attributes this false promise of trans identification to increasing peer pressure and the quick availability of medical support. Here, the reliance on pathologization and the specter of sexual violence mirrors the pathologization and sex panics that have long targeted gays and lesbians.

Antitrans activists accuse trans women of rape by equating trans women in lesbian space as enacting a violent assault. Similarly, and with most immediate and potentially lethal consequences for trans people, antitrans activists accuse trans women of seeking medical and social transition for the primary goal of gaining sexual access to cisgender women. The accusations of rape expand beyond the idea that individual trans women are out to rape cisgender women, a heinous proposal in itself, to the idea that trans women's very existence is a violation of a sacred central feature of femaleness. These claims mirror Janice Raymond's (1994, 104) famous assertion that "transsexuals rape women's bodies by reducing the real female form to an artifact." In more recent years, this ideology has traveled to the mainstream, potentially all the way to the Supreme Court, in a series of antitrans "bathroom bills" and legislation that criminalizes trans kids' access to gender-affirming medical care. This narrative of violence against lesbians—which I am reticent to even dignify with a response, but I must assert that no such violence occurs—is especially pernicious in the face of increased understandings of the immense violence that trans women, especially trans women of color, face every day. The Human Rights Campaign began tracking violence against trans people in 2013. As this book heads to press, they have just documented 2020 as the worst year yet for murders of trans people in the United States (HRC Foundation 2021).

Trans-exclusionary ideology recasts the lesbian as a passive victim. Herein, the lesbian no longer figures as a feminist threat. Rather, the lesbian accuses others of threat. Curiously, this threat that trans-exclusionary feminism lobs at trans people, and trans women specifically, in the name of the lesbian mirrors the claims of "lesbian menace" that foregrounded so much lesbian feminist response in the early women's liberation movement. Simultaneously, the lesbian signifies away from aggression. Indeed, when trans-exclusionary feminists accuse trans people of violence, they recast the lesbian as a passive and protected mode of white femininity, one that was previously used to pathologize Black lesbians, via racialized logics, as sexually aggressive. From the Lavender Menace to the Lesbian Avengers, lesbian activists have reworked accusations of sexual aggression, read as a kind of violence, to question the heterosexual logics and normative gender frameworks that lead to these accusations. That trans-exclusionary ideology now claims the lesbian for the opposite side of this framing, thereby separating the lesbian from earlier political modalities. What is more, antitrans ideology has harnessed the very accusations—specifically, of aggression and sexual deviance—to engage with and fuel a dangerous narrative of trans people as, to use Talia Mae Bettcher's (2007) term, "evil deceivers."

REJECTING TERFS' CLAIM ON THE LESBIAN

Across the past three chapters, I have traced lesbian figurations that announce or engage feminism's threats to heteronormative social order. In these figurations, the lesbian marks the dangers of feminism. This association between the lesbian and danger, a danger the figures feminism as a politics of destruction, is, I argue, one of the most enduring attachments to the political promise of the lesbian. Moreover, many of these sites of danger point us to deep pleasures in lesbian identity and lesbian political promise. Indeed, the aggression that the Lesbian Avengers harness is about mobilizing the pleasures that can be had in naming the lesbian as dangerous. In chapter 1, I argued that attachments to spaces, places, and mobilizations of lesbian identity are, in fact, attachments to modes of lesbian political promise that are rooted in a radical feminism, one that engages destruction. Much of the affect of radical feminism—think here of Solanas or Dworkin—is rooted in meeting the violences of heteropatriarchy with equally violent and antagonistic response. It is this affective history of radical feminism, which I outlined here as also central to those attachments that inform anxieties over lesbian death, that trans-exclusionary groups claim when they call themselves radical feminists. And yet, as I argue here, in so doing, antitrans ideologies recast the lesbian's role as that of victim.

Many people have strong attachments to lesbian identity and also reject the claims made by antitrans activists in the name of the lesbian. If not, we could easily let the lesbian go to the clutches of that small minority. Rather than rescue this analytic from the clutches of TERFdom, rejections of antitrans activisms might follow the wedge the lesbian pries at to explore how the lesbian continues to disrupt. By arguing for the lesbian as disruption, I risk valuing the ways in which the lesbian has been mobilized by antitrans ideology. This, to be sure, is not my intention. Rather, the ways in which queers, trans women, and trans and cis lesbians claim, name, make, produce, and inhabit lesbian politics and lesbian publics continues to contest the assumed meaning and boundary-making of lesbian as a supposedly radical feminist identity. What antitrans ideology fails to grasp is that if, indeed, people are disidentifying with the lesbian, this disidentification is not directly the result of an antagonism to the lesbian housed within the trans. Rather, the disidentification with the lesbian is more clearly linked to a disidentification with antitrans logics that have kidnapped the lesbian for their own exclusionary terms.

It is no surprise, however, that antitrans activists have mobilized around the claim of the lesbian. The lesbian that antitrans activists claim is not always the same but bears a striking resemblance to the lesbian that is imagined as dead and dying. As I have shown across this project, these attachments often point to failed projects of white feminism. Antitrans mobilizations of the lesbian reflect separatist imaginaries, as discussed in chapter 3, wherein withdrawal from and rejection of a gender system are the key to its destruction. Such imaginaries, however, fail to account for how that gender system is central to the project of white supremacy and racial capitalism. When Shelia Jeffreys (2014), for example, defines *woman* through a sex caste system, woman's place in that system is the white homemaker. To centralize this figure fails to account for how the white home, the home of the homemaker, is the product of a violent, racialized caste system. Though not all antitrans activists lament the loss of the lesbian and not all who lament the loss of the lesbian are antitrans, the overlap between the attachments of antitrans activists and those who lament the lesbian losses I outlined in chapter 1 is stark. Those who worry about lesbian death, who narrate the lesbian's pasts as political promise, must necessarily disavow, in the strongest possible terms, the use of lesbian identity and lesbian politics as justification for antitrans violence. Moreover, such worriers must reclaim the lesbian as a capacious project in which trans women, and trans lesbians, are central.

The lesbian has an axe to grind. In this way, the project of the lesbian is perceived and mobilized as one of destruction, and so responses to perceived aggression exceed the effects of that aggression and reflect, instead, fantasies of destruction. I began this chapter with the work of the Lesbian

Avengers in order to demonstrate how projects built on mobilizing lesbian aggression rely on the protections of whiteness. To be sure, in their many iterations, the Lesbian Avengers were a multiracial, multigenerational, and multigendered group of activists.[9] Indeed, following the ACT UP model, many regional and municipal chapters took on their own flavor, so to speak. Nevertheless, the short history of New York's Lesbian Avengers helps to illuminate how a politics of aggression is limited when it cannot engage classed, racialized, and other forms of aggression. For the New Jersey 4, lesbian signaled aggression in ways that were not politically useful but instead rendered the group criminal and justified incarceration. The Avengers utilize the ways that the lesbian is aligned with aggression, but their project remains safe because it follows lesbian chic and normative whiteness. The New Jersey 4 are accused of aggression because when racialized the lesbian becomes violently criminal. Antitrans activists off-load lesbian aggression onto trans subjects to accuse trans politics of a masculine project of sexual violence while justifying their own project of gender violence. Curiously, the project of antitrans activism basically repeats the ways in which the queer and the trans are imagined as aggressing the lesbian to the point of destruction.

Across the text, I have shown both the uses and failures of lesbian in different political and social climates. I have tracked the ways in which anxiety around lesbian death often fails to account for the capaciousness of lesbian as a political claim as well as the shifting context and contents of lesbian identity across time and space. Much of the contemporary anxiety about the lesbian's death is narrated as a kind of violence. And yet, what is longed for in these anxieties are often moments or movements that have been critiqued for their violence, especially with regard to race and gender identity. The lesbian remains a rich ground for political and theoretical commitments not despite the lesbian's racist and essentialist pasts but because those pasts have never been as monolithic as the anxiety makes them appear. To say that the lesbian is too white or too essentialist is not to dismiss the lesbian. Rather, such an investment in the lesbian opens the lesbian up. And yet, for the lesbian to remain as viable as its defenders desire, it will have to relinquish some attachments.

Lesbian, whether lesbian identity or lesbian politics, has always signaled danger, but now we find the lesbian in danger. When we find the lesbian on this side of the divide, as articulated in antitrans ideology, the lesbian loses political potency. Without political potency, the lesbian becomes that which has to be abandoned. But this is not the version of lesbian identity or lesbian politics that produces anxiety about lesbian death. Indeed, as I have traced the lesbian to various sites of political engagement, the lesbian promises danger, even when those promises fail. This danger is not to be mistaken as a political "good." The lesbian projects I trace here have failed in many ways. And while lesbian spaces, and concomitantly lesbian identities, have been sites of struggle, that struggle can, and often does, return us to the project of building different worlds.

Conclusion

We Are Not Post-Lesbian

On May 26, 2015, the Instagram account @h_e_r_s_t_o_r_y posted a picture of singer-songwriter Alix Dobkin wearing a t-shirt emblazoned with the words "The Future Is Female."[1] The original shirt was made as an advertisement for Labrys Books, New York's first feminist and avowedly lesbian bookstore. The post was one of the first for the @h_e_r_s_t_o_r_y account, an account dedicated to lost lesbian cultures, but it quickly launched the account and its curator, Kelly Rakowski, to national and international recognition. Soon thereafter, Rakowski collaborated with Los Angeles–based feminist boutique Otherwild to produce a new run of the now iconic "The Future Is Female" t-shirts. By the end of 2015, and at the dawn of the 2016 U.S. election cycle, "The future is female" became the rallying cry for a burgeoning new wave of liberal feminism in the wake of both the #MeToo movement and Hillary Clinton's presidential campaign and devastating loss. On January 17, 2017, the day after Donald Trump's inauguration, millions of people around the world took to the streets under the banner of the Women's March. In addition to pussy hats, a ready response to Trump's (2016) vulgar claim to grab women "by the pussy," there were thousands of shirts, posters, tote bags, and other such items that proclaimed, "The Future Is Female." The dawn of the #MeToo movement and the concomitant election of Donald Trump had undoubtedly brought this brand of feminism back to mainstream conversation and attention.

I am finishing this book in the early days of the Biden presidency, over a year into the coronavirus pandemic, and amid the ongoing crisis of systemic racism and white supremacist violence. On the morning of March 4, 2021, I opened my Twitter feed to furious chatter over corporations tweeting their

support for "womxn's history month." On March 1, for example, Twitch, a
streaming platform for gamers and a subsidiary of the global conglomer-
ate Amazon, announced a new initiative to feature more women gamers
as its kickoff to "womxn's history month" (@Twitch, March 1, 2021). The
backlash was swift. Many accused Twitch of actively erasing the specificity
of women by adding the *x*. This pushback echoed trans-exclusionary logic
that such attempts at inclusion are predicated on the erasure of cisgender
women. Others, however, noted that "womxn" rang similar to "womyn,"
language that has historically been used to signal trans exclusion in lesbian
and separatist spaces. It is hard to fault Twitch for the failed use of this language. In 2019, Dictionary.com included "womxn" among the more than
three hundred words it added to its official lexicon.[2] The official entry defines *womxn* as both trans inclusive and central to "intersectional feminism."
This definition, however, fails to note that such language—notably, *womxn*
but also *womyn, wimmin,* and *womon*—is rooted in radical, often lesbian
and separatist, politics of the 1970s. That the language of radical feminism
would find home in corporate diversity speak five years after the resurgence of "The Future Is Female" is a fitting cap to a feminist revival that
has been aestheticized in relation to lesbian histories and politics.

I open here with "The Future Is Female" because this iconic slogan is now
widely recognizable, though seldom identified through its lesbian feminist
roots. This slogan is not the only marker of lesbian feminist aesthetics in
the current feminist moment. Indeed, Otherwild, which first produced
and marketed the shirts in 2015, has become one of the biggest producers
of lesbian feminist nostalgia wear. This resurgence of lesbian ephemera, as
Cait McKinney (2020) notes, is inseparable from new forms of information
sharing and the saturation of visual culture in the wake of social media,
especially sites like Instagram and Tumblr. McKinney argues, "This aesthetic emerges from an affective and commercial economy in which a wide
range of primary source materials are reblogged, scanned, copied, and circulated through social media" (208). But these reproductions rarely engage
with the histories of lesbian feminism or with the politics that these actors,
slogans, and other ephemera espoused. Precisely because this ephemeral
uptake arrives without a clear articulation of the history that it signifies,
this current moment of lesbian aestheticism does not engage a "temporal
drag," as Elizabeth Freeman (2010) articulates.

There is a curious paradox: on the one hand, the last five years of the
decade saw a precipitous uptick in the use of language and aesthetics long

associated with lesbian feminism. On the other hand, as I noted in chapter 1, fears over the loss of the lesbian have persisted and, indeed, grown over these same five years. I do not mean to suggest that the return to lesbian feminist aesthetics offers evidence for the lesbian's persistence. To the opposite, I worry that this lesbian aestheticization actually works to incorporate lesbian feminist politics into regimes of consumerism in much the same way that the 1990s' emphasis on lesbian chic constructed the lesbian as both an object for consumption and a new marketplace for diversity-minded liberal consumers. It is easy to read this aestheticization of lesbian feminism as symptomatic of a wider nostalgia for a past revolutionary moment. In this way, the recent uptake of lesbian feminist aesthetics is not surprising. As I have charted across this project, especially in chapters 3 and 4, current attachments to lesbian figurations of the 1970s are attachments to lesbian feminism's revolutionary promise. The recent return to lesbian feminist aesthetics can be read, as McKinney (2020) offers, as a form of political nostalgia. But these aesthetics reference certain modes of lesbian feminism without an attachment to the political ideology or goals of that movement. This attachment to modes of lesbian feminism, absent a radical political commitment, mirrors how the attachments to the lesbian that I outlined in chapter 1 are attachments to the methods or modalities of lesbian feminism without a deeper interrogation of the use or usefulness of lesbian feminist politics today.

The attachment to modes of political organizing—separatism, for example—over and against the ideologies that informed such organizing resonates with Wendy Brown's (1999) diagnosis of left melancholy. Drawing on the work of Stuart Hall and Walter Benjamin, Brown argues that "left melancholy represents not only a refusal to come to terms with the particular character of the present . . . it signifies, as well, a certain narcissism with regard to one's past political attachments and identity that exceeds any contemporary investment in political mobilization" (20). Here I want to suggest that anxieties about the lesbian's persistence are also a "refusal to come to terms with the particular character of the present." I do not mean that as a flat condemnation. Rather, I offer this formulation as an invitation. Heather Love (2009, 149), in her text *Feeling Backward: Loss and the Politics of Queer History,* follows Brown to offer an interpretation: "Melancholic leftists cling to the lost objects because of actual feelings of love, actual desire for radical social change: the problem with their politics is not the attachment but rather the paralyzing effects of melancholic incorporation and disavowal." In my own experience, I have found the claims that "no one wants to be a lesbian" to produce dizzying effects. I see all around me political movements and identity structures that center lesbian life, especially in the radical work of trans lesbians. The juxtaposition of this work with the insistence that the lesbian has fallen out of favor produces my loss of equilibrium. In many ways, I hope that this text can unfreeze some of this "melancholic incorporation and disavowal."

Sara Ahmed (2017) ends her book *Living a Feminist Life* with a call for a return or a revival, to use her words, of lesbian feminism. Ahmed calls for this revival "precisely because lesbian feminism posed feminism as a life question" (213). Similarly, in 1978, Barbara Smith made a case for reading Black women's literature as lesbian literature even in the absence of homosexual bonds. In her reading of Toni Morrison's *Sula,* Smith (1978, 24) notes: "Sula's presence in her community functions much like the presence of lesbians everywhere to expose the contradictions of supposedly 'normal' life." Ahmed mirrors Smith. Lesbianism, Ahmed (2017, 226) argues, "stands for what is unacceptable." This refusal to accept what is unacceptable drives the lesbian's project. Ahmed grounds her insistence on the political viability of lesbian feminism as a project of willfulness, one that moves from the individual into the world. This lesbian project is about changing the world.

Ahmed's lesbian feminist revival reflects a renewed interest in the "lesbian potentiality," to use Rox Samer's (2022) term, of the 1970s. Much of this work has sought to grapple with the promises and pitfalls of lesbian feminism by, as Kate Eichhorn (2015) argues, rejecting a nostalgic turning back, one that risks the melancholic freeze Brown warns against, in favor to new modes of reading these moments. In examining the vexed relationship between contemporary investments in past lesbian feminist projects and a postmodern critique of nostalgia, Eichhorn argues, "What makes feminist nostalgia unique, then, is that it is not nostalgia for something tangible but rather for the conditions under where there was nothing for a feminist to be nostalgic about" (259). Many of us came of age in the twenty years after the first decade of the women's liberation movement, as Eichhorn notes, during a time in which the promises and institution of this moment were in decline, if not under attack. As I have mapped herein, this also coincides with events of the lesbian's consolidation away from feminist political claims, most readily marked in the 1990s turn to "lesbian chic."

These events also mark the lesbian's crossover to mainstream acceptance though a whitewashed legibility of homonormativity.

If, as I trace in the Introduction, the lesbian's status as besieged emerges in the fallout of the feminist sex wars and the uptake of lesbian chic, today's anxieties about the lesbian's persistence arrive at a moment in which, as I argue in chapter 5, the lesbian has been weaponized by projects of trans exclusion and antitrans violence. Across the latter half of this project, I trace the lesbian's potentiality to a feminist politics of destruction. This is not a project of violence for violence's sake but rather a commitment to a world-building project that actively works against, rather than within, existing social structures. Herein, we might trace the nostalgia that Eichhorn names in current returns to 1970s lesbian feminism as an engagement with the pleasures that the affects of this political commitment produce. As I map in chapter 5, it is also this affective pleasure that trans-exclusionary projects harness in their claims that lesbians and lesbian identity are under attack. Moreover, an engagement with these pleasures that stops at the individual—that is, at questions of who is or is not a lesbian—but does not move out into the world, guided by lesbian feminism as a project, falls short of the political promise that the lesbian offers.

Recent anxieties about lesbian loss that map to trans-exclusionary ideologies mirror earlier, and contemporary, claims that the queer has killed the lesbian. The difference, however, is that the inaugurating moments of queer theory seemed, at least in some instantiations, to enact a forgetting of lesbian and feminist radical potentials (Walters 1996). This moment of trans-exclusionary rhetoric and antitrans violence, however, claims to be an enactment of the very lesbian feminist projects that queer theory left behind. Despite widespread disagreement with the claims and central tenets of trans-exclusionary radical feminism, this small but vocal minority has come to dominate our discussions by preying on earlier fears of the lesbian's erasure. To this end, I have offered the preceding engagements with the lesbian's political potential to wrest the lesbian away from the clutches of trans exclusion. Indeed, I hope the greatest takeaway from this book is that anyone who worries about the lesbian's political and identarian future must necessarily repudiate, in the strongest possible terms, the capture of the lesbian for inherently conservative means that shore up the lesbian as a project of violence against women and other marginalized groups through the normative frames of gender and sexuality. By reading the lesbian as disruption, a disruption that we can trace to the lesbian's vexed positioning between feminist and queer political commitments, I have offered the lesbian as a middle term, one that refuses to stabilize as either feminist or queer but exerts necessary pressure in both directions.

It is no surprise in our current moment, wherein a resurgence of the New Right and its focus on supposed family values has produced, or reproduced, sex panics that target trans and gender-variant folks, wherein reproductive rights are under attack, and wherein the language of white supremacy has become the political platform of the right, that we would find a return to the pleasures and promises, most marked in the aesthetics of feminist responses to both #MeToo and the Trump administration, of lesbian feminism. I worry, however, that such returns, including my own herein, continue to mark the lesbian as a project of white feminism. When disavowals of lesbian identity mark the lesbian as stagnated in the essentialist and white-washed failures of 1970s feminism, this has the inverted effect of naming the lesbian as both white and essentialist. The lesbian, as I have argued here, has always been a site of contestation. And while these contestations have often been sites of failure, and even sites of harm, the lesbian's ability to wade through fraught terrain has always held out promise. This promise, however, is not the promise of a unified or solidified lesbian identity or even lesbian politics. Rather, this is a promise of the lesbian as a capacious world-building project.

We might find the lesbian's political promise in spaces and places where the nostalgia for lesbian feminism's past is not as obvious. For example, one is less likely to see a "The Future Is Female" shirt at a Black Lives Matter march, which is not to say that there will not be some. This is not to imply that the Movement for Black Lives has not inspired its own aesthetic commitments. Indeed, at a Black Lives Matter march one is likely to see the "goddess shirt" and its variations. The "goddess shirt" is designed and produced by Bay Area designer Thugz Maison. This shirt is a simple black tee with white block lettering that lists the first names of iconic Black and Third World feminists—Audre (Lorde), Gloria (Anzaldúa), Angela (Davis), and bell (hooks)—in a left-justified column on the front. While these two shirts have become readily recognizable symbols and political fashion statements, their contexts and implications differ. "The Future Is Female" was a campaign and a rallying cry rooted in a lesbian feminist movement that is largely remembered for its essentialist failures. In its return today, it offers a kind of nostalgia for the heady days of lesbian separatism. The past that the shirt names arrives as a trace without an engagement in its politics. The goddess shirt, by contrast, offers a citation. The use of only first names on the shirt suggests the wearer's intimate familiarity with the authors and requires an equally familiar recognition to be legible to others. In this way, wearers of the shirt root themselves in the foundational work of Black and Third World feminisms. The familiarity that the shirt claims situates its wearer in this genealogy. When we follow the genealogies of these scholar-activists, however, we find lesbian feminist commitments.

Black Lives Matter is an avowed queer, feminist, trans-affirming movement for social change that centers Black experiences and Black lives in the fight for transformation and racial justice. In many ways, Black Lives Matter marks a new era of social activism made possible by social media, the ready availability of video-recording devices, and the rapid spread of information. Black Lives Matter began as a social media hashtag and has expanded to an international scale with chapters and meetings in nearly every major city in the United States and other places around the globe. On its website and throughout its media presence, the leading founders of Black Lives Matter connect their work to the histories of feminist, queer, and, mostly importantly, Black revolutionary politics. As Cathy J. Cohen notes in conversation with Sarah J. Jackson, the importance of queer women's leadership in Black Lives Matter cannot be understated (Cohen and Jackson 2015). And yet, she also warns that the media's attention to this queer feminist leadership as a new movement risks erasing the histories of Black, lesbian, feminist, and queer leadership and action. Rather, it is of note that Black Lives Matter identifies themselves in citation to early queer, lesbian, feminist, and Black and Third World revolutionary activists and movements. Is Black Lives Matter not also a lesbian movement? While neither the three primary organizers nor the organizational literature identify the people or principles of the movement with the word *lesbian,* if the lesbian names a bridge between feminist and queer commitments, commitments that move outward to build new worlds, then lesbian politics are everywhere present in the movement. What is more, the absence of the lesbian signifier in this femme-centric, feminist, queer movement may signify a new relation between the feminist and the queer, a relation that no longer requires the lesbian as a middle term.

If we follow *nostalgia*'s original meaning as "a longing for home," then this return to the aesthetics of lesbian feminism can tell us something about the need for this home today. Following Eichhorn, we might read this as a nostalgia not for a specific or myopic lesbian identity or lesbian moment but for the feminist potential that the lesbian signified in the emergent feminist movement of the 1970s. Moreover, there is something in this current political milieu that makes this lesbian feminist aesthetics both meaningful and pleasurable. Rather than mark this time as a forgetting of lesbian feminist pasts, we can read these events as calling forth the social and political commitments of multiple lesbian feminist pasts while also allowing these commitments to be changed and reworked toward the needs of the present. By releasing the lesbian from a singular framework of identity, one that is rooted in exclusion, we can open the lesbian to a capacious political project of world-building. Perhaps, then, we can all rejoice: Long live the lesbian!

Acknowledgments

All the flaws in this project are mine and mine alone. But the fact that it is in your hands (or on your screen) is because I have been surrounded by amazing and wonderful people who have loved me, supported me, and challenged me. I hope my words here can convey my immense gratitude.

This project started in the fall of 2001. At 9 a.m. (EST) on September 11, I took a seat in my first women's studies class, where we watched *But I'm a Cheerleader* as the world we knew changed forever. I was grateful to have that feminist space as I came into my own queer consciousness in the days and weeks after 9/11. I am even more grateful to my professor in the class, Patricia Bizzell, who gave me both the confidence to pursue this work and the warning that I was a terrible writer (and subsequent permission to enroll in her first-year writing course). Jim Nickoloff, Ed Thomson, and Jennifer Knust were also formative mentors in my undergraduate years and have been my biggest cheerleaders since. I hope you will see a bit of our work together here. I began the thinking that became chapter 2 as a project manager for Women's Wellbeing Studies at Boston University. I am forever grateful for the mentorship of Uli Boehmer and Emily Rothman.

In a more real sense, this book began as a dissertation project. Elizabeth Wilson shepherded me and this project through many an existential crisis. Elizabeth is uniquely skilled at responding to my panicked emails with a cool rationality that is both calming and encouraging. I appreciate the time and patience she has given me, especially the counsel to listen to my gut. Michael Moon was a mentor and guide even before I arrived at Emory. I am especially grateful for his encouragement to stay with the difficult conceptual work of the project and even more so for his animating stories that give me delightful access to some of the most exciting moments of queer theory's histories. Lynne Huffer asked difficult questions, and this project, and my sense of myself as a scholar, are better for it. I am indebted to her for her insistence that I define my terms and for pushing me to remain with my argument.

I remain grateful for the wonderful collegiality and friendship of the faculty, staff, and graduate students in the Department of Women's, Gender, and Sexuality Studies at Emory University where I completed my doctoral work. I am especially grateful for the friendship and mentorship of Rosemarie Garland-Thomson, Jonathan Goldberg, and Deboleena Roy. I am forever grateful for having known the incomparable Berky Abreu. And extra special thanks to my graduate cohort: Samantha Allen, Sarah Stein, Natalie Turrin, and Lauran Whitworth.

At Loyola Marymount University, I have the best of colleagues. Thank you, Marne Campbell, Andrew Dilts, Elizabeth Drummond, Anna Muraco, Eliza Rodriguez y Gibson, Claudia Sandoval, and Amy Woodson-Boulton. I have received immense support from my dean, Robbin Crabtree, and (former) associate dean Jonathan Rothchild. My department is a model of feminist collegiality, and I am grateful for colleagues who make our working conditions not only bearable but enjoyable. Thank you, Amanda Apgar, Sandibel Borges, Danielle Borgia, Ronjaunee Chatterjee, Sina Kramer, Jessica Martinez-Tebbel, Jennifer Moorman, Stella Oh, and Traci Voyles. We enjoy the support of the very best administrative coordinators. Thank you, Kayla Begg, Liz Faulkner, and Dean Messinger. My faculty cohort has been a source of endless support and laughs. Thank you, Karen Enriquez, Thomas Herndon, Brett Marroquín, Kai Okada, and Sylvia Zamora. Since 2020, I have been especially lucky to work with the Teaching Toward Justice faculty team. Thank you, Arnab Banerji, Jen Ferguson, Linh Hua, Julia Lee, Christopher Murillo, Tara Pixley, Julian Saint Clair, and Brendan Smith. Extra special thanks to my co-conspirator Jennifer Williams.

Academic life can be particularly isolating. I am grateful, however, for the academic comrades who make the work fun. Thank you, H. Rakes, Omari Weekes, and Mary Zaborskis for being my conference buddies. Thank you, Linda Garber, who became a friend and mentor in the final days of this book. Carly Thomsen provided much-needed eleventh-hour encouragement as I crossed the writing finish line, and I am forever grateful. Emily Owens is my partner in all things lesbian studies. I am so grateful for our collaborations, for our friendship, and especially for the many Zoom hours we shared in the depths of pandemic isolation.

In 2016, I participated in the Lesbian Studies in Queer Times Symposium at the University of Michigan. I am forever grateful for Valerie Traub and Sue Lanser for making the space and for generously holding us in the conversations that emerged. That meeting fomented much of my thinking in this project, and I hope what I offer here fits the desires of that gathering.

My work in this project was funded through a number of grants. Many thanks to the Mary Lily Research Grant at the Sallie Bingham Center for Women's History and Culture at Duke University, the Bellarmine College of Liberal Arts Faculty Research Grant at Loyola Marymount University, and the Bellarmine College of Liberal Arts Faculty Summer Writing Grant at Loyola Marymount University.

Thanks to my editorial team at the University of Minnesota Press. I have the utmost respect and gratitude for the three anonymous reviewers who provided generous, constructive, and generative feedback on this project.

Across the seven years that this project has been ruining my weekends, I have been lucky to share life with the very best of friends. In Los Angeles, I am grateful for the love and support of my coffee club/pandemic pod: Jay Barbor, Andrew Dilts, Sid Hansen, Sina Kramer, Jesse Ricker, and Tara Stewart. Thank you, Ashley Berryhill, Miles Friesen, and Crystal Murphy. When I arrived in Los Angeles, friends from all stages of life welcomed me with open arms. Thank you, Sarah Arthur, Ronjaunee Chatterjee, Laura Gillespie, Tyler Law, Sunitha Menon, and Maureen Murphy. Marie Draz helped me to fall in love with Southern California. Sasha Klupchak and Rachel Weitzenkorn joined me on the West Coast and proved, as always, that dreams really do come true.

In Atlanta, I found frequent escape, whether to Taco Tuesdays, Whiskey Wednesdays, or Queer Fit Saturdays. Thank you, Ashley Coleman Taylor, Melissa Creary, Shannan Hayes, Marta Jimenez, Taryn Jordan, Christina León, Stu Marvel, Shae Mosely-Robinson, T. M. Mosely-Robinson, Jen Sarrett, Omari Weekes, and Lizzy Venell. Also in Atlanta, I finally found the older brother I have always longed for—Ben Girard. The Girard family, Ben, Aimee, Justin, and Jason, continues to remind me to put down the writing and seek out adventure. Aaron Goldsman is forever my mirror and lost other half. Joc Coleman Taylor makes clear that best friendship knows no distance. Natalie Turrin made Gibson Street a home.

My family of origin and extended family structures have always been a source of support and sustenance. Though he might disagree, my father, Bill, taught me what it means to be a feminist. My mother, Suzanne, modeled it for me every day. She was also my first teacher and is the model I bring with me to my own classroom. I am grateful for their friendship and encouragement, even and especially when they might be a bit befuddled by my pursuits. The same goes for my siblings: Maureen, Emmet, and Michael. It is a great joy to find us getting even closer as we age. When I return to Chicago, my aunts, uncles, and cousins make me feel like a veritable celebrity. My cousin Madeleine Durkin has been my closest confidant and greatest cheerleader since before we could walk. She should never forgive me for how mean I was in grade school, but I am so glad that she has. I am grateful, too, for the family I have joined and that has welcomed me heartily. Thank you, Meagan, Tristan, Dean, Kim, and Jonathan.

J, I hope you find in this book a promise for your own feminist commitments in this world. Witnessing your developing feminist consciousness is a great joy, and I hope you continue to be surrounded by lesbian and queer visions of world-building.

A, words cannot capture the depth of joy that is sharing this life with you. If lesbian offers a promise of living otherwise, it started in that hallway. Thank you for your unyielding love and support in the hell that has been finishing this project.

Everything I know about queer community and feminist world-building is rooted in my most enduring familial and social bonds. For more than twenty years, I have been part of the most life-giving, world-sustaining friend group, known affectionately as the Mardoonis. Abby, Claire, Kathryn, Katie, Kevin, Lauren, Mary, and Shawna, this book is for you.

Notes

1. For a brilliant take on *Work in Progress*'s "butch middlebrow," see Kessler 2021.

INTRODUCTION

1. Anxieties about the death of the lesbian at the borders of feminist and queer emerged in the early 1990s. See, for example, Martin 1994. More recently, *Feminist Theory* dedicated an entire issue to the question of lesbian haunting (Eloit and Hemmings 2019) and in late 2020 the *Journal of Lesbian Studies* compiled a special issue under the provocation "Is lesbian identity obsolete?" (Hagai and Seymour 2022). There are innumerable references to the end of the lesbian in the intervening years.

2. *FTM* here refers to the identity associated with female-to-male transexuals, an identity that today is captured under the name *trans men*.

3. For a succinct narrative of the challenges of lesbian separatism, see Rudy 2001.

4. For more on the sex wars, see Duggan and Hunter 2006; Bronstein 2011; Cossman 2021; Bracewell 2021.

5. For more on lesbians and AIDS activism, specifically in ACT UP, see Cvetkovich 2003; Brier 2007.

6. For more on the shifting terrains of third wave feminism, see Heywood and Drake 1997; Walker 1995.

7. In 1993, the lesbian hit the mainstream with three prominent magazine covers. First, in May of that year, *New York Magazine* ran a cover featuring butch icon k. d. lang with the title "Lesbian Chic: The Bold, Brave New World of Gay Women." The following month, *Newsweek* released a Pride issue that featured two normatively feminine white women in a lovers' embrace with the title "Lesbians: Coming Out Strong; What Are the Limits of Tolerance?" (Salholz and Glick 1993). Finally, in August, *Vanity Fair* ran the infamous cover featuring a photo of lang in a three-piece suit, tipped back in a barber's chair, being shaved by a bathing-suit-clad Cindy Crawford (the early 1990s' most famous model/cover girl) with the title "k.d. lang's Edge: Crossing Over, Catching Fire" (Bennetts 1993).

8. For more on *dyke* as related to and distinct from *lesbian,* see Willey 2016, 2017.

9. For more on the anxieties of lesbian loss in this time, see Stein 1997.

10. For even more examples of the lesbian's besieged status as the precursor to any work on the lesbian, see Eloit and Hemmings 2019; Stein 2010; Noss 2013.

11. Since at least Arlene Stein's work in the early 1990s, if not sooner, worries about the durability and viability, the disavowals, and even lovingly humorous engagements route the lesbian's limits through the 1970s. While not exhaustive, see, for example, Stein 1993; Stein 1997; Musser 2015; Enke 2018; Eloit and Hemmings 2019; Kubala 2020.

12. Oftentimes the generational conflicts that invoke the lesbian are mapped along the lines of who was there when X happened. Earlier articulations of this generational conflict mark the border as the pre- and post-Stonewall generations (Escoffir 1990). Borders are drawn almost neatly along decade lines: there during and after 1970s lesbian feminism, there during and after the 1980s crisis years of the AIDS epidemic, there during and after the culture wars of the 1990s. In the opening paragraphs of *Identity Poetics,* for example, Linda Garber relays a familiar scene. Garber (2001, 2), who describes herself as straddling the generational divide between Generation X and baby boomers, finds herself at a conference where "a white lesbian academic or political activist who is older than I am begins to discuss the 'generation gap' in lesbian theory, bemoaning the derision and/or erasure of lesbian feminism in queer theory." As Jaime Harker (2018, 12) recalls in *The Lesbian South,* "When I was coming out in the early 1990s, lesbian feminism was already a throwback." While claims of lesbian erasure often fall along generational lines, the one thing that sustains across generations is a claim of lesbian erasure.

The lesbian's generational anxieties mirror and attach to dominate frameworks of feminist theoretical and political progress narratives. As Hemmings argues, this is most readily apparent in the waves narratives and the neat dividing of feminist timelines into distinct decades each with their own critical problem and attention. Even more so, as Hemmings and others demonstrate, narratives of feminist generational conflicts (and I would argue that lesbian generational conflict mirrors these) are rife with metaphors and expectations that generational conflict is a kind of familial conflict. In this way, Hemmings (2011, 148) asserts, "feminism is locked into a psychoanalytic dynamic of vigorous supersession (by the younger) and melancholic nostalgia (of the older), and figures both mothers and daughters as themselves always bound in antagonistic relation . . . (relations that) can only be hostile." This is best reflected in narratives of generational difference that assume both loss and conflict. For example, in 2013 *Feminist Studies* put out a special issue titled "Categorizing Sexualities" that included a forum under the rubric "Lesbian Generations," which had grown out of a panel of the same name at the 2011 Berkshire Conference on the History of Women (Rupp 2013).

13. See, for example, Huffer 2013.

14. For two of the inaugurating demonstrations of queer of color critique's roots in Black, women of color, and Third World feminism, see Ferguson 2003; Muñoz 1999. See also Eng, Halberstam, and Muñoz 2005.

15. For more on the violence of trans-exclusionary radical feminism, see Ahmed 2016; Pearce, Erikainen, and Vincent 2020.

16. I am thinking here of Huffer 2013; Willey 2016; Hesford 2013; Traub 2016; Luis 2018; Musser 2018; Harker 2018; Hogan 2016; McKinney 2020; Gieseking 2020; Samer 2022.

1. LESBIANS KILLED THE LESBIAN BAR

1. See, for example, Clinton 2016; Cauterucci 2016.

2. To be clear, there are a number of prominent lesbian bars whose closing has generated such anxiety. I am thinking here specifically of the Lexington Club in San Francisco, Phase 1 in Washington, D.C., Sisters in Philadelphia, and Rubyfruit Jungle in New Orleans. I focus here on the Lex because its location in San Francisco marks it as a particular harbinger of lesbian death. For more on San Francisco as a site of displacement for "nonconformist gays" in relationship to the incorporation of mainstream gays and lesbians, see Mattson 2015.

3. In Stein's (1997) account of the closing of Amelia's, it is not that lesbians were losing numbers but that lesbian diversification meant that there was no longer a need for a homogenous gathering space. Following a quote from the owner, who lamented the bars closing as being "'a victim of the lesbian community becoming more diverse,'" Stein states, "Paradoxically, it was the growth and diversification of lesbian communities, rather than their decline, that destroyed the neighborhood bar" (184–85).

4. For more on San Francisco's transformation from queer destination to tech playground, see Sycamore 2013.

5. For a detailed history of feminist bookstores, with specific attention to both racism and the shifting arena of bookstores in publishing across the 1990s, see Hogan 2016.

6. For more on the history and importance of lesbian spaces and places, see Retter, Bouthillette, and Ingram 1997; Enke 2007; Brown-Saracino 2017; Gieseking 2020.

7. According to economists, the median life span of all restaurants is about four years (Luo and Stark 2014).

8. One of the central lamentations of the anxiety around lesbian death is that lesbians have become domesticated. Rarely are the ways in which socializing, specifically nightlife, shift across the aging process included in these conversations. In this way, it is often imagined that younger people do not want gay bars. While Wild Side West's reputation as an old school dyke hangout may imply a kind of generational split, it may also be that this long-standing hold is what attracts young queers looking for connections to lesbian space.

9. Gieseking's (2020) research echoes this point in the context of New York.

10. For histories of the gentrification of San Francisco's Mission District and the attendant gay politics, see Ramirez 2003; Hanhardt 2013.

11. "The land," for participants of the Michigan Womyn's Music Festival, refers both to the literal land on which the festival is held and the way in which notions of "the land" or "our land" come to define the spirit and ethos of the festival.

12. For a history of the women's land movements, see Luis 2018. For a history of women's music festivals, see Morris 1999.

13. For a succinct collection of publications related to the conversation around trans inclusion at Michfest in the late 1990s and early 2000s, see Koyama 2003.

14. I take up the histories of lesbian separatism more thoroughly in chapter 3.

15. For more on Michfest and the S/M debates, see Cvetkovich 2003.

16. I rely on Nancy Burkholder's (1993) own recollections of the 1991 Michfest.

17. I am especially grateful to Emi Koyama's (n.d.) steadfast documentation of the history of Camp Trans and of trans women's exclusion at Michfest. While most of the narrative I share here is drawn from the stories shared in *TransSisters: The Journal of Transsexual Feminism,* those of us seeking to understand this history in the last decade of Michfest are indebted to Koyama's documentation.

18. The use of girlhood as the unifying frame of the definition of *women* also assumes a singular notion of girlhood. This framing fails to account for the ways that race and place inform the meanings and mechanisms of girlhood socialization.

19. For a history of the centrality of women's music festivals to Black feminist consciousness, see Hayes 2010.

20. While I focus here on the publicly available descriptions of the seminars and published reports from Traub, I must also note that I was a participant in the second seminar.

21. Admittedly, this proclamation leaves me to wonder where this scholarship finds its home if not in these fields.

22. Indeed, Traub (2016, 268) cites such lineage.

23. I am thinking here of Cvetkovich 2003; H. Love 2009; Freeman 2010.

24. To be clear, while I question the static claim that queer theory dispenses with the lesbian, *lesbian* has certainly been a pressurized term since the consolidation of queer theory in the early 1990s. Even so, this lesbian framework is not static. Biddy Martin's (1994) "Sexualities without Genders and Other Queer Utopias" carries the heaviest weight in claims of the lesbian's expulsion from queer theorizing and queer politicizing in the early 1990s. Central to Martin's concern is the way that *queer* cleaves sexuality from gender in a way that renders gender, and its assumed connection to feminism as a project, both static and stagnant. This stagnation, according to Martin, provincializes and, in many ways, depoliticizes femininity and concomitantly the female body through an assumed fixity of gender in feminist projects. As she argues, "The result is that lesbians, or women in general, become interesting by making cross-gender identification or an identification with sexuality, now implicitly . . . associated with men, over against gender, and, by extension, feminism and women" (107).

The lesbian takes on a different role in Susan Gubar and Robyn Wiegman's 1998–1999 exchange in *Critical Inquiry.* In the summer of 1998, Gubar, then a distinguished professor of English and women's studies at Indiana University, published a revised version of her talk "Who Killed Feminist Criticism?," retitled "What Ails Feminist Criticism?," in the summer issue of *Critical Inquiry.* Gubar states her thesis in this essay as such: "Prominent advocates of racialized identity politics and of poststructuralist theories have framed their arguments in such a way as to divide feminists, casting suspicion on a common undertaking that remains in dispute at the turn of the twentieth century" (880). Gubar finds evidence for her claim in what she identifies as "a barrage of diatribes directed against white feminists" across the 1980s (and presumably into the 1990s) beginning with the publication of Cherríe Moraga and Gloria Anzaldúa's *This Bridge Called My Back*. Gubar also finds blame in queer theory's postmodernist dodging of material realities, a claim she articulates most readily in relation to the work of Judith Butler. Two issues later, Robyn Wiegman, quite rightly and quite generously, takes Gubar to task. While Wiegman (1999, 376) responds point by point to the challenges of field coherence and field project, she also pointedly identifies the ways in which emotion saturates Gubar's text and "crafts whiteness as an injured identity throughout." As Wiegman argues, "From this victimized position, all analytical moves made by feminists of color are assaults against feminism, not crucial contributions to its self-examination and articulation" (378). In Wiegman's response to Gubar, she finds the lesbian as the threat to feminism's coherence: "In this context (of the battle between two kinds of feminism), we might understand the inconsistent role given to the lesbian, whose wavering presence (now you see her, now you don't) threatens to undermine from within the Edenic state of originary unity and sameness" (363). Gubar and Wiegman's exchange, and the generational tensions it signifies, echoes Linda Garber's argument in *Identity Poetics*. Garber identifies the generational anxieties that animate tension between the feminist and the queer across the 1990s. She maps these in relation to lesbian texts and lesbian politics but notes that the generational tension is specifically white. In so diagnosing, Garber rejects the claim that the generational tension is one of chronological rejection. Garber argues instead that new generations of scholars take seriously the works of lesbians of color and working-class lesbians that emerged across the 1970s and 1980s. Most damningly, Garber (2001, 5) accuses the previous generation of producing the generational schism through the "marginalization of working-class/lesbians of color." These three examples helpfully disrupt the narrative that the lesbian was left behind by the queer's ascendence. To the contrary, Wiegman and Garber help to identity both the lesbian's mobility and the attachments to whiteness that inform these anxieties.

25. Traub is citing Wiegman 2011.

26. In 2016, Traub and Lanser reconvened the Radcliffe group under the banner "Lesbian Studies in Queer Times" at the University of Michigan. I was a participant in this workshop.

27. See, for example, Martin 1994. For a succinct summary of the status of the lesbian in queer theory, see Huffer 2013.

28. For a deeper analysis of the construction of Black female sexuality as silence and the resulting assumption that lesbian is always white lesbian, see Hammonds 1994.

29. For a clear analysis of how the neoliberal politics of the 1990s subsumed liberal gay subjects, see Duggan 2004.

2. MARKED FOR LIFE

1. For a brief history of lesbian health in the United States, see Terry 1999.

2. For example, the 2020 Census (at least prior to the Trump administration) was slated to include a question of sexual identity.

3. For a summary and analysis of the various origin stories of the term *biopolitics*, see Mills 2015.

4. For more on the lesbian as a "kind of person," see Boyd 2013.

5. These narratives are by no means totalizing. Rather, they are representative of a multitude of social, political, and activist movements that brought these two diseases together.

6. For more on the rise of a gay health movement and its seed in 1970s politics and activism, see Batza 2018.

7. The catchphrase "slash, poison, and burn" was coined as a mode of critique by prominent breast cancer surgeon and activist Susan Love (2010). The phrase is a reference to long-standing treatment regimens that were often unnecessarily harming and disfiguring.

8. For more on the histories of ACT UP, see Gould 2009; Schulman 2022.

9. Zaps are a form of direct action protest with roots in the Gay Activists Alliance of the mid-twentieth century. As the name *zap* implies, the demonstrations were meant to provide an urgent and stinging disruption to business as usual in order to call attention to specific issues. ACT UP zaps are especially known for their creativity, theatrics, and art.

10. For a good analysis of the kind of neoliberal philanthropy as activism promulgated by organizations like the Komen Foundation and their many state-based and corporate partners, see King 2008.

11. An ongoing concern within the field of breast cancer research and prevention are the disproportionate rates of morbidity and mortality experienced by women of color. For example, a *New York Times* article (Parker-Pope 2014) notes the surprising, or perhaps all too unsurprising, statistic that Black women are less likely than their white counterparts to experience a breast cancer diagnosis but are more likely than white counterparts to die from breast cancer.

12. The difference between correlation and causation is especially important to note here, particularly in the regime of risk. *Correlation* states that as one variable—in this case, certain behaviors—increases or decreases, a second variable—in this case, incidence of breast cancer—increases or decreases at a similar rate. While such a connection between variables may imply a direct relation, it cannot be demonstrated that one variable produces an effect—that is to say, causes—a second variable to change. In the case of the Haynes study, the narrative of correlation is actually displaced through the lesbian. In effect, the Haynes study argues: lesbians are more likely to engage in these behaviors; these behaviors are noted to increase risk of breast cancer; thus, lesbians have a higher risk of breast cancer.

13. Ryan White was a hemophiliac teenager from Indiana who contracted HIV from a blood transfusion at age thirteen and passed away in 1990, at eighteen years old. White and his family became widely known for their fight to allow White to remain in public school at a time of heightened panic around HIV transmission. The Ryan White CARE (Comprehensive AIDS Resources Emergencies) Act was first passed in 1990 and remains the largest source of federal funding to support and care for people living with HIV/AIDS to this day.

14. For more on women and the early days of the HIV epidemic, see Patton and O'Sullivan 1990; Patton 1994.

15. Of course, many of the health behaviors noted here may be connected with lesbian bar culture that itself has historically been the site of lesbian political contestations around class respectability and the heteronormative implications of butch/femme dyads. See Jagose 1997.

16. See Mbembé and Meintjes 2003; Dibble, Roberts, and Nussey 2004; Meads and Moore 2013; Boehmer and Elk 2015.

17. See Boehmer et al. 2010.

18. See Hicks 2014.

19. For a history of the development of risk as a central analytic in the twentieth century, see Hacking 1990.

20. See Happe 2006.

21. See Simoni et al. 2017.

22. I am thinking here of the work of Grace Kyungwon Hong (2015), Roderick A. Ferguson (2003), and Chandan Reddy (2011), among others. This work, of course, builds on Mbembé and Meintjes 2003.

3. MURDEROUS LESBIAN SEPARATISM

1. I use the term *radical feminist* in reference to Alice Echols's (1989) *Daring to Be Bad: Radical Feminism in America, 1967–1975*. Echols identifies radical feminism as a specific movement within feminism and as part of the larger movement of 1960s radicalism. Building on Echols, I define *radical feminism* as a movement built largely around an ideology of separatism, specifically lesbian separatism, rather than assimilation. In doing so, I also mean to separate these terms from current instantiations of radical feminism, particularly in their essentialist and trans-exclusionary practices.

2. The allegations of bra burning at the 1968 Miss America protest remain an apocryphal event in the history of women's liberation. For more on the debates surrounding the veracity of the bra-burning claims, see Campbell 2010.

3. See Penner 2011; Winkiel 2013.

4. Solanas herself had a vexed relationship to being considered such a foundational figure for radical feminism, which included her own dismissal of the C.L.I.T. papers. See Fahs 2014.

5. See Winkiel 2013; Fahs 2014.

6. Though published anonymously, it is well known that the authors of the C.L.I.T. papers are Susan Cavin, Maricla Moyano, and Marcia Segerberg. See Jones 1998.

7. See Echols's biography of the Furies in Echols 1989.

8. These practices, at least as they are taken up in queer theory, are tacitly understood as related to gay male sex practices. And, I would argue, the implication is more readily connected to "risky" sex practices, such as barebacking, anonymous sex, and fisting, than to anal sex.

9. I am tempted here to call these figures "assholes"—and, indeed, they are—particularly following on the anality that is so prolific in the so-called antisocial strand

of queer theory. We might also call these figures "dicks," and, in doing so, perhaps shift their role in the sinthomosexual logic considered through radical feminism.

10. For more on the histories of trans women in radical feminist politics and spaces, see Enke 2018.

11. This is not to say that spaces and places are not central to finding lesbian feminism and lesbian politics. For more, see Enke 2007.

4. LESBIAN BED DEATH

1. See, especially, McGleughlin's (2021) reflection on this time. Here McGleughlin notes: "Conversations that once took place in consciousness-raising groups about sexual practice and desire were relegated again to private discussions to be had by an individual woman, or couple, with her/their therapist" (217). Later she notes, especially in relationship to engagement with butch–femme dynamics of the pre-Stonewall era, "that a discussion of private, intimate sexual life could not be separated from a discussion of public life, social life, and community" (218).

2. See, for example, Iasenza 2000; Mundy 2013; Bergner 2013; Rothblum and Hill 2014.

3. Although Blumstein is listed as the first author on the book, the phrase *lesbian bed death* is most frequently associated with Pepper Schwartz. Thus, I list Schwartz first when naming the authors.

4. See, for example, Cancian 1984; Goodman 1985; D'Emilio and Freedman 2012.

5. *New man* and *new woman* are terms that came about to describe the shift in gender roles and expectations as a result of the women's liberation movement and the shifting social landscape of post–World War II America. For a detailed account of the relationship between the United States' shifting social landscape, the rise of feminism, and the development of the "new man," see Ehrenreich 1983.

6. What is often left out of the conversation is Schwartz and Blumstein's further finding that lesbians experience more relationship turnover than the other three couples. So, even if one is to take the findings at face value, it does not measure a drop-off in lifetime sexual encounters. To the contrary, such findings may point to lesbians having a greater overall sexual frequency if they are consistently in new relationships.

7. The ways in which the women's movement has affected lesbian relationships is the focus of the case study of Natalie and Jill, two lesbians who met while living in a feminist, separatist collective. Within their case study, Schwartz and Blumstein highlight perceived and negotiated power differentials along the lines of both gendered expectations and class socialization (481–93).

8. See especially Frye 1990.

9. For a comprehensive summary of the literature on lesbian fusion, see Blyth and Straker 1996; Greene, Causby, and Miller 1999; Gold 2003; Frost and Eliason 2014.

10. The late 1980s and early 1990s saw a marked increase in sexological studies regarding lesbian sexual desire. For a representative sample, see Smalley 1987; Kurdek 1988; McKenzie 1992; Schreurs 1993; Bryant 1994; Hawton, Gath, and Day 1994; Downey and Friedman 1995; Blyth and Straker 1996; Greene, Causby, and Miller 1999.

11. Bowers v. Hardwick, 478 U.S. 186 (1986). This Supreme Court case upheld Georgia's sodomy laws, effectively criminalizing homosexual sex.

12. For more recent empirical studies of lesbian bed death, see van Rosmalen-Nooijens, Vergeer, and Lagro-Janssen 2008; Bridges and Horne 2007.

13. In feminist lore, many credit MacKinnon and Dworkin with the phrase "All sex is rape." The phrase, which does not appear in any of their writings, often stands in for their theoretical moves at the time. However, there is no clear citation to attribute the phrase to either thinker. Dworkin addresses this claim in the preface to the tenth anniversary edition of *Intercourse*. In her preface, Dworkin (2006, xxxii) addresses the misattribution with the following rhetorical question: "If one has eroticized a differential in power that allows for force as a natural and inevitable part of intercourse, how could one understand that this book does not say that all men are rapists or that all intercourse is rape?"

14. Lorna N. Bracewell's (2021) *Why We Lost the Sex Wars: Sexual Freedom in the #MeToo Era* troubles the distinction I make here. Bracewell demonstrates that antipornography feminist work in the 1970s was avowedly radical and highly skeptical of appeals to the state. Bracewell traces the shift to more liberal frameworks for both antipornography and sex-radical feminists through the influence of both classical liberalism and civil libertarianism.

15. Here, of course, is the animating tension of the sex wars—that between pleasure and danger. For more on how the tension of pleasure and danger marks this time in feminist memory, as well as the continued influence of this coupling today, see Walters 2016 and the *Signs* special issue "Pleasure and Danger: Sexual Freedom and Feminism in the Twenty-First Century" (42, no. 1 [Autumn 2016]).

16. Admittedly, I am sidestepping the importance of psychoanalysis for Bersani's argument. I am less concerned here with felicity to Bersani's argument than I am with connecting the pleasure that Halley finds in Bersani to the pleasures we might find in Dworkin.

17. Dworkin's identification as a lesbian leaves open the question of whether she agreed that an alternative mode of relationality, something akin to or modeled on a lesbian ideal, might offer an alternative.

18. S/M theorizing, particularly that which addresses why rape survivors might be interested in such play, does a particularly good job of parsing these distinctions. See Hammers 2014. However, the seemingly common praise of S/M's ability to let us have our danger and eat it too does little to address the persistence of such saturation in the lives of women and those perceived to be already ascribed to the subordinate position. For a sex-positive critique of S/M's transgressive promise, see Weiss 2011.

19. This is not to say that penetration is not a part of lesbian sexuality. Indeed, penetration was central to many of the debates and anxieties that informed the feminist sex wars. See, for example, Findlay 1992.

20. There has been a notable return to Dworkin recently. Specifically, a number of prominent third wave feminists have begun to ask about the effects of this disavowal. See especially Fateman 2014; Levy 2006. See also Dworkin 2019; Duberman 2020.

21. Growing out of her work on "governance feminism" in *Split Decisions,* Halley's (2016) work on consent is immensely informative for the very logic of sexual violence I engage here.

22. I must note here that Dworkin focuses instead—and, I would argue, dangerously—on obscenity laws that would result in censorship. Thus, I am not arguing that Dworkin thought there was no legislative mode to counter sexual violence. For more, see Sullivan, forthcoming.

23. By *carceral* I mean a logic that understands sexual violence as an abberant act commited by abberant individuals rather than an attention to the symbolic or structuring logics of heterosexuality that Dworkin draws out. Moreover, here I mean to point to impulses within feminist work, especially within the last forty years, that seek redress through the state, often to violent ends. See especially Bernstein 2007, 2010; Richie 2012; Whalley and Hackett 2017; Kim 2018.

24. For more on lesbian refusals to understand sex and sexuality through these logics, see Hollibaugh and Moraga 2000.

25. Here I echo Cvetkovich, who notes that Bersani's description of humiliation is a uniquely masculine experience of shame. Moreover, Cvetkovich argues, Bersani's argument relies on the "assumption that a coherent self is necessary and desirable, and dependent on avoiding the violation of penetration" (301n29).

26. For more on reading lesbian and queer women's identities as a rejection of heterosexuality, see Ward 2020.

5. KILLER LESBIANS

1. For a reading of the racialized meanings of the use of Grier's image, see Cvetkovich 2001.

2. By many accounts, lesbians of color did not find an easy home in the long-term projects of the Avengers. See Cogswell 2014.

3. The group has been variously called the New Jersey 7 or the Newark 7. On the night of the confrontation, seven women were arrested. However, because three pleaded guilty and spent less time incarcerated, the group was ultimately dubbed the New Jersey 4 in order to draw attention to the four women who went to trial and then spent years in prison. My analysis herein is drawn from the attention given to the New Jersey 4 in both local and national media and a subsequent documentary about their plight (Doroshwalther 2014).

4. Brief for Respondent at 26, People v. Dandridge, A.D.3d 779, 2006 N.Y. Slip Op. 791, 809 N.Y.S.2d 353 (N.Y. App. Div. 2006) at 18.

5. In 1989, five Black and Latino boys, ranging in age from fourteen to sixteen, were falsely accused and subsequently charged with and convicted of assaulting a twenty-eight-year-old white woman jogger in New York's Central Park. It took almost fifteen years for the boys to be exonerated and their convictions vacated. Media coverage of the boys' arrest and subsequent trial used similar language of "wilding" and "wolf pack." For more on the racialization of this language and its role in the public support for the boys' arrest and conviction, see Mexal 2013.

6. For more on same-race street harassment and the discursive forgetting of Black lesbians, see Fogg-Davis 2006.

7. In pairing aggression with lesbian identity in media responses to the case of the New Jersey 4, I am sidestepping an analysis of how some might claim "aggressive" as an identity or community marker. I am thinking here of "aggressive" as a Black, queer, masculine identity, especially as depicted in the 2005 documentary *The Aggressives* (Peddle 2012). See especially Keeling 2019. Here, I am focusing more on how media and even jurist perceptions of lesbians are racialized in ways that mark aggression as both obvious and willfully violent.

8. This is not to say that trans women are not vital parts of lesbian communities.

9. Importantly, as I demonstrate in chapter 1, the Lesbian Avengers have been central to rejecting antitrans policies and ideologies at Michfest and elsewhere. Indeed, Dyke Marches, an ongoing contribution of Lesbian Avengers' organizing, remain some of the sites where an avowedly trans-centering lesbian politics can happen.

CONCLUSION

1. This shirt, of course, reeks of feminist essentialism. Of note, Alix Dobkin famously signed on to a letter asking Olivia Records to fire Sandy Stone. Though Olivia refused to fire Stone, Stone ultimately left the collective. This event remains one of the touchstones for arguments about trans exclusion and lesbian feminism of this time. See especially Enke 2018.

2. Dictionary.com, s.v. "womxn," accessed April 8, 2022, https://www.dictionary.com/browse/womxn.

Bibliography

Aanerud, Rebecca. 2002. "Thinking Again: This Bridge Called My Back and the Challenge to Whiteness." In *This Bridge We Call Home: Radical Visions for Transformation*, edited by Gloria Anzaldúa and AnaLouise Keating, 69–77. New York: Routledge.

"A Collective Editorial." 2016. *TSQ: Transgender Studies Quarterly* 3 (1–2): 276–77. https://doi.org/10.1215/23289252-3334523.

Ahmed, Sara. 2010. *The Promise of Happiness*. Durham, N.C.: Duke University Press.

Ahmed, Sara. 2016. "An Affinity of Hammers." *TSQ: Transgender Studies Quarterly* 3 (1–2): 22–34. https://doi.org/10.1215/23289252-3334151.

Ahmed, Sara. 2017. *Living a Feminist Life*. Durham, N.C.: Duke University Press.

Allen, Leah Claire. 2016. "The Pleasures of Dangerous Criticism: Interpreting Andrea Dworkin as a Literary Critic." *Signs: Journal of Women in Culture and Society* 42 (1): 49–70. https://doi.org/10.1086/686977.

Allison, Dorothy. 1983. "Blumstein & Schwartz: A Massive Study of American Couples." *Advocate*, December 8, 1983.

Amin, Kadji. 2019. "Haunted by the 1990s: Queer Theory's Affective Histories." In *Imagining Queer Methods*, edited by Amin Ghaziani and Matt Brim, 277–93. New York: NYU Press.

Anderson, Aimee. 2015. "The Death of the Lesbian." *Huffington Post* (blog). July 1, 2015. https://www.huffingtonpost.com/aimee-anderson/the-death-of-the-lesbian_b_7699284.html.

Anzaldúa, Gloria. 1983. "La Prieta." In *This Bridge Called My Back: Writings by Radical Women of Color*, edited by Cherríe Moraga and Gloria Anzaldúa, 198–209. New York: Kitchen Table/Women of Color Press.

Associated Press. 1993a. "Study: AIDS Won't Shake Society." *Register-Guard*, February 5, 1993.

Associated Press. 1993b. "Study Suggests High Cancer Risk for Lesbians." *Great Falls Tribune*, February 5, 1993.

Batt, Sharon. 1994. *Patient No More: The Politics of Breast Cancer*. London: Scarlet Press.

Batza, Katie. 2018. *Before AIDS: Gay Health Politics in the 1970s.* Philadelphia: University of Pennsylvania Press.

Baus, Janet, and Su Friedrich, dir. 1993. *The Lesbian Avengers Eat Fire Too.* West Hollywood, Calif.: Stag Films, 2013.

Bazell, Robert. 1998. *Her-2: The Making of Herceptin, a Revolutionary Treatment for Breast Cancer.* New York: Random House.

Belenkaya, Veronica, Peter Kadushin, Austin Fenner, and Carrie Melago. 2006. "Girls Gone Wilding: Lesbians Locked Up in West Village Beating." *New York Daily News,* August 19, 2006.

Bennetts, Leslie. 1993. "k.d. Lang Cuts It Close." *Vanity Fair,* August 1993. https://www.vanityfair.com/style/1993/08/kd-lang-cover-story.

Bergner, Daniel. 2013. "Unexcited? There May Be a Pill for That." *New York Times,* May 22, 2013. http://www.nytimes.com/2013/05/26/magazine/unexcited-there-may-be-a-pill-for-that.html.

Bernstein, Elizabeth. 2007. "'The Sexual Politics of the 'New Abolitionism.'" *Differences* 18 (3): 128–51. https://doi.org/10.1215/10407391-2007-013.

Bernstein, Elizabeth. 2010. "Militarized Humanitarianism Meets Carceral Feminism: The Politics of Sex, Rights, and Freedom in Contemporary Antitrafficking Campaigns." *Signs: Journal of Women in Culture and Society* 36 (1): 45–71. https://doi.org/10.1086/652918.

Bersani, Leo. 2009. *Is the Rectum a Grave? And Other Essays.* Chicago: University of Chicago Press.

Bettcher, Talia Mae. 2007. "Evil Deceivers and Make-Believers: On Transphobic Violence and the Politics of Illusion." *Hypatia* 22 (3): 43–65. https://doi.org/10.1111/j.1527-2001.2007.tb01090.x.

Blumstein, Philip, and Pepper Schwartz. 1983. *American Couples: Money, Work, Sex.* New York: Pocket Books.

Blyth, Sue, and Gillian Straker. 1996. "Intimacy, Fusion, and Frequency of Sexual Contact in Lesbian Couples." *South African Journal of Psychology* 26 (4): 253–56. https://doi.org/10.1177/008124639602600409.

Boehmer, Ulrike, Melissa Clark, Mark Glickman, Alison Timm, Mairead Sullivan, Judy Bradford, and Deborah J. Bowen. 2010. "Using Cancer Registry Data for Recruitment of Sexual Minority Women: Successes and Limitations." *Journal of Women's Health* 19 (7): 1,289–97. https://doi.org/10.1089/jwh.2009.1744.

Boehmer, Ulrike, and Ronit Elk. 2015. *Cancer and the LGBT Community: Unique Perspectives from Risk to Survivorship.* Cham, Switzerland: Springer.

Boyd, Nan Alamilla. 2013. "The History of the Idea of the Lesbian as a Kind of Person." *Feminist Studies* 39 (2): 362–65.

Bracewell, Lorna N. 2021. *Why We Lost the Sex Wars: Sexual Freedom in the #MeToo Era.* Minneapolis: University of Minnesota Press.

Bradford, Judith B., and Caitlin C. Ryan. 2006. National Lesbian Health Care Survey, 1984–1985, Version 1. Inter-university Consortium for Political and Social Research, January 18, 2006. https://doi.org/10.3886/ICPSR08991.V1.

Bridges, Sara K., and Sharon G. Horne. 2007. "Sexual Satisfaction and Desire Discrepancy in Same Sex Women's Relationships." *Journal of Sex & Marital Therapy* 33 (1): 41–53. https://doi.org/10.1080/00926230600998466.

Brier, Jennifer. 2007. "Locating Lesbian and Feminist Responses to AIDS, 1982–1984." *Women's Studies Quarterly* 35 (1/2): 234–48.

Bronstein, Carolyn. 2011. *Battling Pornography: The American Feminist Anti-pornography Movement, 1976–1986*. Cambridge: Cambridge University Press.

Brown, Wendy. 1995. *States of Injury*. Princeton, N.J.: Princeton University Press.

Brown, Wendy. 1999. "Resisting Left Melancholy." *Boundary 2* 26 (3): 19–27.

Brown-Saracino, Japonica. 2017. *How Places Make Us: Novel LBQ Identities in Four Small Cities*. Chicago: University of Chicago Press.

Bryant, A. Steven. 1994. "Relationship Characteristics of American Gay and Lesbian Couples." *Journal of Gay & Lesbian Social Services* 1 (2): 101–17. https://doi.org/10.1300/J041v01n02_06.

Buckley, Cara, and Kate Hammer. 2006. "Man Is Stabbed in Attack After Admiring a Stranger." *New York Times*, August 19, 2006. http://www.nytimes.com/2006/08/19/nyregion/19stab.html.

Bunch, Charlotte. 1972. "Lesbians in Revolt." *The Furies: Lesbian Feminist Monthly* 1 (January): 8–9.

Burkholder, Nancy Jean. 1993. "A Kinder, Gentler Festival?" *TransSisters: The Journal of Transsexual Feminism* 2 (December): 4–5.

Cacho, Lisa Marie. 2012. *Social Death: Racialized Rightlessness and the Criminalization of the Unprotected*. New York: NYU Press.

Campbell, W. Joseph. 2010. *Getting It Wrong: Ten of the Greatest Misreported Stories in American Journalism*. Berkeley: University of California Press.

"Camp Trans Welcomes You." 1995. *TransSisters: The Journal of Transsexual Feminism*, no. 7 (Winter): 36–39.

Cancian, Francesca M. 1984. Review of *American Couples: Money, Work, Sex*, by Philip Blumstein and Pepper Schwartz. *American Journal of Sociology* 90 (3): 669–71.

Carney, Christina. 2012. "The Politics of Representation for Black Women and the Impossibility of Queering the New Jersey 4/7." In *Wish to Live: The Hip-Hop Feminism Pedagogy Reader*, edited by Ruth Nicole Brown and Chamara Jewel Kwakye, 71–79. New York: Peter Lang.

Cauterucci, Christina. 2016. "Lesbian No Longer Works for Many Young Queer Women. But Can a Community Exist without a Name?" *Slate*, December 20, 2016. https://slate.com/human-interest/2016/12/young-queer-women-dont-like-lesbian-as-a-name-heres-why.html.

Chow, Rey. 2002. *The Protestant Ethnic and the Spirit of Capitalism*. New York: Columbia University Press.

Ciasullo, Ann M. 2001. "Making Her (In)Visible: Cultural Representations of Lesbianism and the Lesbian Body in the 1990s." *Feminist Studies* 27 (3): 577–608. https://doi.org/10.2307/3178806.

Clarke, Cheryl. 1983. "Lesbianism: An Act of Resistance." In *This Bridge Called My Back: Writings by Radical Women of Color*, edited by Cherríe Moraga and Gloria Anzaldúa, 128–37. New York: Kitchen Table/Women of Color Press.

Clinton, Kate. 2016. "Commentary: What Caused Lesbian Extinction?" *Washington Blade*, April 28, 2016. https://www.washingtonblade.com/2016/04/28/what-caused-lesbian-extinction/.

C.L.I.T. 1974a. "C.L.I.T. Statement #1." *Off Our Backs* 4 (May): 16.

C.L.I.T. 1974b. "C.L.I.T. Statement #2." *Off Our Backs* 4 (July): 12–14.

C.L.I.T. 1976. "C.L.I.T. Collection No. 2." *DYKE, A Quarterly* 2:41–85.

Coffman, Chris. 2012. "The Sinthomosexual's Failed Challenge to (Hetero)Sexual Difference." *Culture, Theory and Critique* 54 (1): 56–73. https://doi.org/10.1080/14735781 4.2012.729704.

Cogswell, Kelly J. 2014. *Eating Fire: My Life as a Lesbian Avenger*. Minneapolis: University of Minnesota Press.

Cohen, Cathy J., and Sarah J. Jackson. 2015. "Ask a Feminist: A Conversation with Cathy Cohen on Black Lives Matter, Feminism, and Contemporary Activism." *Signs: Ask A Feminist* (blog). 2015. http://signsjournal.org/ask-a-feminist-cohen-jackson/.

Combahee River Collective. 1983. "A Black Feminist Statement." In *This Bridge Called My Back: Writings by Radical Women of Color*, edited by Cherríe Moraga and Gloria Anzaldúa, 210–18. New York: Kitchen Table: Women of Color Press.

Cooper, Julia. 2018. "50 Largest Bay Area LGBTQ-Owned Businesses." *San Francisco Business Times*, June 15, 2018. https://www.bizjournals.com/sanfrancisco/subscriber -only/2018/06/15/50-largest-bay-area-lgbtq-owned.html.

Corbman, Rachel. 2015. "The Scholars and the Feminists: The Barnard Sex Conference and the History of the Institutionalization of Feminism." *Feminist Formations* 27 (3): 49–80. https://doi.org/10.1353/ff.2016.0010.

Córdova, Jeanne. 2011. *When We Were Outlaws*. Midway, Fla.: Spinsters Ink.

Cossman, Brenda. 2021. *The New Sex Wars: Sexual Harm in the #MeToo Era*. New York: NYU Press.

Currans, Elizabeth. 2012. "Claiming Deviance and Honoring Community: Creating Resistant Spaces in U.S. Dyke Marches." *Feminist Formations* 24 (1): 73–101. https://doi.org/10.1353/ff.2012.0009.

Cvetkovich, Ann. 2001. "Fierce Pussies and Lesbian Avengers: Dyke Activism Meets Celebrity Culture." In *Feminist Consequences*, edited by Elisabeth Bronfen and Misha Kavka, 283–318. New York: Columbia University Press. https://doi.org/10.7312/bron11704.14.

Cvetkovich, Ann. 2003. *An Archive of Feelings: Trauma, Sexuality, and Lesbian Public Cultures*. Durham, N.C.: Duke University Press.

Day, Susie. 2007. "Killer Lesbians Mauled by Killer Court, Media Wolfpack." *Gay City News*, June 28, 2007. https://web.archive.org/web/20070713031412/http://www.gay citynews.com/site/news.cfm?newsid=18531149&BRD=2729&PAG=461&dept_id =585504&rfi=6.

D'Emilio, John. 2014. *In a New Century: Essays on Queer History, Politics, and Community Life*. Madison: University of Wisconsin Press.

D'Emilio, John, and Estelle B. Freedman. 2012. *Intimate Matters: A History of Sexuality in America*. Chicago: University of Chicago Press.

Dibble, Suzanne L., Stephanie A. Roberts, and Brenda Nussey. 2004. "Comparing Breast Cancer Risk between Lesbians and Their Heterosexual Sisters." *Women's Health Issues: Official Publication of the Jacobs Institute of Women's Health* 14 (2): 60–68. https://doi.org/10.1016/j.whi.2004.03.004.

Doroshwalther, Blair, dir. 2014. *Out in the Night*. New York: New Day Films. https://www.kanopy.com/en/product/241271.

Downey, Jennifer I., and Richard C. Friedman. 1995. "Internalized Homophobia in Lesbian Relationships." *Journal of the American Academy of Psychoanalysis* 23 (3): 435–47.

Doyle, Jennifer. 2009. "Blind Spots and Failed Performance: Abortion, Feminism, and Queer Theory." *Qui Parle: Critical Humanities and Social Sciences* 18 (1): 25–52. https://doi.org/10.1353/qui.0.0007.

Doyle, John. 2006. "Girl Gang Stabs Would-Be Romeo." *New York Post*, August 19, 2006.

Duberman, Martin. 2020. *Andrea Dworkin: The Feminist as Revolutionary*. New York: New Press.

Duggan, Lisa. 1998. "The Theory Wars, or Who's Afraid of Judith Butler?" *Journal of Women's History* 10 (1): 9–19. https://doi.org/10.1353/jowh.2010.0547.

Duggan, Lisa. 2001. *Sapphic Slashers: Sex, Violence, and American Modernity*. Durham, N.C.: Duke University Press.

Duggan, Lisa. 2004. *The Twilight of Equality? Neoliberalism, Cultural Politics, and the Attack on Democracy*. Boston: Beacon Press.

Duggan, Lisa, and Nan D. Hunter. 2006. *Sex Wars*. New York: Routledge.

Dworkin, Andrea. 2006. *Intercourse*. New York: Basic Books.

Dworkin, Andrea. 2019. *Last Days at Hot Slit: The Radical Feminism of Andrea Dworkin*. Edited by Johanna Fateman and Amy Scholder. South Pasadena, Calif.: Semiotext(e).

Echols, Alice. 1989. *Daring to Be Bad: Radical Feminism in America, 1967–1975*. Minneapolis: University of Minnesota Press.

Edelman, Lee. 2004. *No Future: Queer Theory and the Death Drive*. Durham, N.C.: Duke University Press.

Ehrenreich, Barbara. 1983. *The Hearts of Men: American Dreams and the Flight from Commitment*. Garden City, N.Y.: Anchor.

Eichhorn, Kate. 2015. "Feminism's There: On Post-ness and Nostalgia." *Feminist Theory* 16 (3): 251–64. https://doi.org/10.1177/1464700115604127.

Eloit, Ilana, and Clare Hemmings. 2019. "Lesbian Ghosts Feminism: An Introduction." *Feminist Theory* 20 (4): 351–60. https://doi.org/10.1177/1464700119871219.

El Rio. n.d. Accessed March 14, 2019. https://www.elriosf.com/.

Eng, David L., Jack Halberstam, and José Esteban Muñoz. 2005. "Introduction: What's Queer about Queer Studies Now." *Social Text* 23 (3–4 (84–85)): 1–17. https://doi.org/10.1215/01642472-23-3-4_84-85-1.

Enke, Finn. 2007. *Finding the Movement: Sexuality, Contested Space, and Feminist Activism*. Durham, N.C.: Duke University Press.

Enke, Finn. 2018. "Collective Memory and the Transfeminist 1970s: Toward a Less Plausible History." *TSQ: Transgender Studies Quarterly* 5 (1): 9–29. https://doi.org/10.1215/23289252-4291502.

Enszer, Julie R. 2016. "'How to Stop Choking to Death': Rethinking Lesbian Separatism as a Vibrant Political Theory and Feminist Practice." *Journal of Lesbian Studies* 20 (2): 180–96. https://doi.org/10.1080/10894160.2015.1083815.

Epstein, Steven. 2003. "Sexualizing Governance and Medicalizing Identities: The Emergence of 'State-Centered' LGBT Health Politics in the United States." *Sexualities* 6 (2): 131–71. https://doi.org/10.1177/1363460703006002001.

Epstein, Steven. 2009. *Inclusion: The Politics of Difference in Medical Research.* Chicago: University of Chicago Press.

Escoffir, Jeffrey. 1990. "Inside the Ivory Closet." *Out/Look: National Gay and Lesbian Quarterly* 10 (Fall): 40–48.

Fahs, Breanne. 2008. "The Radical Possibilities of Valerie Solanas." *Feminist Studies* 34 (3): 591–617.

Fahs, Breanne. 2014. *Valerie Solanas: The Defiant Life of the Woman Who Wrote SCUM.* New York: Feminist Press at CUNY.

Fateman, Johanna. 2014. "Johanna Fateman on Andrea Dworkin." In *Icon,* edited by Amy Scholder, 33–65. New York: Feminist Press at CUNY.

Ferguson, Roderick A. 2003. *Aberrations in Black: Toward a Queer of Color Critique.* Minneapolis: University of Minnesota Press.

Findlay, Heather. 1992. "Freud's 'Fetishism' and the Lesbian Dildo Debates." *Feminist Studies* 18 (3): 563–79. https://doi.org/10.2307/3178083.

Fogg-Davis, Hawley G. 2006. "Theorizing Black Lesbians within Black Feminism: A Critique of Same-Race Street Harassment." *Politics & Gender* 2 (1): 57–76. https://doi.org/10.1017/S1743923X06060028.

Fontenot, Andrea. 2006. Review of *No Future: Queer Theory and the Death Drive,* by Lee Edelman. *MFS Modern Fiction Studies* 52 (1): 252–56. https://doi.org/10.1353/mfs.2006.0024.

Foucault, Michel. 1978. *The History of Sexuality.* Vol. 1, *An Introduction.* New York: Vintage.

Franks, Mary Anne. 2007. "What's Left of Pleasure? A Book Review of Janet Halley's *Split Decisions: How and Why to Take a Break from Feminism.*" *Harvard Journal of Law and Gender* 30 (1): 257–67.

Fredrickson, Rica. 1993a. "MWMF Anti-TS Awareness: 1992 Gender Survey Results (130 Lines)." April 28, 1993. Email message. Available at https://groups.google.com/g/soc.motss/c/lfAgstey_SY/m/7rlqMQ-8FAEJ?pli=1.

Fredrickson, Rica. 1993b. "MWMF Anti-TS Awareness: Background Information," April 28, 1993. Email message. Available at https://groups.google.com/g/soc.motss/c/zw6Loc5VDWI/m/hx7WRadabEoJ?pli=1.

Freedman, Estelle B. 2006. *Feminism, Sexuality, and Politics: Essays by Estelle B. Freedman.* Chapel Hill: University of North Carolina Press.

Freeman, Elizabeth. 2010. *Time Binds: Queer Temporalities, Queer Histories.* Durham, N.C.: Duke University Press.

Frost, David M., and Michele J. Eliason. 2014. "Challenging the Assumption of Fusion in Female Same-Sex Relationships." *Psychology of Women Quarterly* 38 (1): 65–74. https://doi.org/10.1177/0361684313475877.

Frye, Marilyn. 1990. "Lesbian 'Sex.'" In *Lesbian Philosophies and Cultures: Issues in Philosophical Historiography,* edited by Jennifer Allen, 305–15. New York: SUNY Press.

"The Furies." 1972. *The Furies: Lesbian Feminist Monthly* 1 (January): 1.

Gabbatiss, Josh. 2018. "Anti-trans Activists Tried to Stop London's Pride Parade by Laying Down in the Street." *Independent,* July 8, 2018. https://www.independent.co.uk/news/uk/home-news/anti-trans-protest-london-pride-parade-lgbt-gay-2018-march-lesbian-gay-rights-a8436506.html.

Gallop, Jane. 1988. *Thinking through the Body.* New York: Columbia University Press.

Garber, Linda. 2001. *Identity Poetics: Race, Class, and the Lesbian-Feminist Roots of Queer Theory.* New York: Columbia University Press.

Get the L Out. 2019. "Lesbian Visibility, Lesbian Not Queer." *Get the L Out UK* (blog). June 25, 2019. https://www.gettheloutuk.com/blog/category/lesbian-visibility.html.

Gieseking, Jen Jack. 2020. *A Queer New York.* New York: NYU Press.

Giffney, Noreen, and Katherine O'Donnell. 2007. "Introduction." *Journal of Lesbian Studies* 11 (1–2): 1–18. https://doi.org/10.1300/J155v11n01_01.

Gold, Laura. 2003. "A Critical Analysis of Fusion in Lesbian Relationships." *Canadian Social Work Review/Revue Canadienne de Service Social* 20 (2): 259–71.

Goldberg, Michelle. 2014. "What Is a Woman?" *New Yorker,* August 4, 2014. https://www.newyorker.com/magazine/2014/08/04/woman-2.

Goodman, Norman. 1985. Review of *American Couples: Money, Work, Sex,* by Philip Blumstein and Pepper Schwartz. *Social Forces* 63 (3): 873–75. https://doi.org/10.2307/2578507.

Gould, Deborah B. 2009. *Moving Politics: Emotion and ACT UP's Fight against AIDS.* Chicago: University of Chicago Press.

Greene, Kathryn, Vickie Causby, and Diane Helene Miller. 1999. "The Nature and Function of Fusion in the Dynamics of Lesbian Relationships." *Affilia* 14 (1): 78–97.

Gubar, Susan. 1998. "What Ails Feminist Criticism?" *Critical Inquiry* 24 (4): 878–902.

Hacking, Ian. 1990. *The Taming of Chance.* Cambridge: Cambridge University Press.

Hagai, Ella Ben, and Nicole Seymour. 2022. "Is Lesbian Identity Obsolete?" *Journal of Lesbian Studies* 26 (1): 1–11. https://doi.org/10.1080/10894160.2021.2005231.

Halberstam, Jack. 1993. "Imagined Violence/Queer Violence: Representation, Rage, and Resistance." *Social Text* 37:187–201. https://doi.org/10.2307/466268.

Halberstam, Jack. 1998. *Female Masculinity.* Durham, N.C.: Duke University Press.

Halberstam, Jack. 2005. "Shame and White Gay Masculinity." *Social Text* 23 (3–4 (84–85)): 219–33. https://doi.org/10.1215/01642472-23-3-4_84-85-219.

Halberstam, Jack. 2008. "The Anti-social Turn in Queer Studies." *Graduate Journal of Social Science* 5 (2): 140–56.

Halberstam, Jack. 2011. *The Queer Art of Failure.* Durham, N.C.: Duke University Press.

Halley, Janet. 2006. *Split Decisions: How and Why to Take a Break from Feminism.* Princeton, N.J.: Princeton University Press.

Halley, Janet. 2016. "The Move to Affirmative Consent." *Signs: Journal of Women in Culture and Society* 42 (1): 257–79. https://doi.org/10.1086/686904.

Hammers, Corie. 2014. "Corporeality, Sadomasochism, and Sexual Trauma." *Body & Society* 20 (2): 68–90. https://doi.org/10.1177/1357034X13477159.

Hammonds, Evelynn. 1994. "Black (W)Holes and the Geometry of Black Female Sexuality." *Differences: A Journal of Feminist Cultural Studies* 6 (2–3): 126–46.

Hanhardt, Christina B. 2013. *Safe Space: Gay Neighborhood History and the Politics of Violence.* Durham, N.C.: Duke University Press.

Happe, Kelly E. 2006. "The Rhetoric of Race in Breast Cancer Research." *Patterns of Prejudice* 40 (4–5): 461–80. https://doi.org/10.1080/00313220601020171.

Harker, Jaime. 2018. *The Lesbian South: Southern Feminists, the Women in Print Movement, and the Queer Literary Canon.* Chapel Hill: University of North Carolina Press.

Hart, Lynda. 1994. *Fatal Women: Lesbian Sexuality and the Mark of Aggression.* Princeton, N.J.: Princeton University Press.

Hartocollis, Anemona. 2007. "Four Women Are Sentenced in Attack on Man in Village." *New York Times,* June 15, 2007. https://www.nytimes.com/2007/06/15/nyregion/15attack.html.

Hawton, Keith, Dennis Gath, and Ann Day. 1994. "Sexual Function in a Community Sample of Middle-Aged Women with Partners: Effects of Age, Marital, Socioeconomic, Psychiatric, Gynecological, and Menopausal Factors." *Archives of Sexual Behavior* 23 (4): 375–95. https://doi.org/10.1007/BF01541404.

Hayes, Eileen M. 2010. *Songs in Black and Lavender: Race, Sexual Politics, and Women's Music.* Urbana: University of Illinois Press.

Haynes, Suzanne. 1992. "Are Lesbians at a High Risk of Cancer?" Presentation given at 14th National Gay and Lesbian Health Foundation Conference, Los Angeles.

Heaney, Emma. 2016. "Women-Identified Women: Trans Women in 1970s Lesbian Feminist Organizing." *TSQ: Transgender Studies Quarterly* 3 (1–2): 137–45. https://doi.org/10.1215/23289252-3334295.

Hemmings, Clare. 2011. *Why Stories Matter: The Political Grammar of Feminist Theory.* Durham, N.C.: Duke University Press.

Henderson, Kevin. 2017. "Becoming Lesbian: Monique Wittig's Queer-Trans-Feminism." *Journal of Lesbian Studies* 22 (2): 185–203.

Hennessy, Rosemary. 2018. *Profit and Pleasure: Sexual Identities in Late Capitalism.* New York: Routledge.

Henry, Imani. 2007. "Lesbians Sentenced for Self-Defense: All-White Jury Convicts Black Women." *Workers World,* June 21, 2007. https://www.workers.org/2007/us/nj4-0628/.

Herring, Scott. 2010. *Another Country: Queer Anti-Urbanism.* New York: NYU Press.

Hesford, Victoria. 2013. *Feeling Women's Liberation.* Durham, N.C.: Duke University Press.

Heywood, Leslie, and Jennifer Drake. 1997. *Third Wave Agenda: Being Feminist, Doing Feminism.* Minneapolis: University of Minnesota Press.

Hicks, Josh. 2014. "Why the Federal Government Spent $3 Million to Study Lesbian Obesity." *Washington Post,* September 2, 2014. https://www.washingtonpost.com/news/federal-eye/wp/2014/09/02/why-the-federal-government-spent-3-million-to-study-lesbian-obesity/.

Hogan, Kristen. 2016. *The Feminist Bookstore Movement: Lesbian Antiracism and Feminist Accountability.* Durham, N.C.: Duke University Press.

Holden, Dominic. 2015. "Michigan Music Festival That Excluded Transgender People to Shut Down." *BuzzFeed News,* April 22, 2015. https://www.buzzfeednews.com/article/dominicholden/michigan-music-festival-that-excluded-transgender-peo ple-to.

Hollibaugh, Amber L., and Cherríe Moraga. 2000. "What We're Rollin Around in Bed With: Sexual Silences in Feminism—A Conversation toward Ending Them." In *My Dangerous Desires: A Queer Girl Dreaming Her Way Home,* by Amber L. Hollibaugh, 62–84. Durham, N.C.: Duke University Press.

Hong, Grace Kyungwon. 2015. *Death beyond Disavowal: The Impossible Politics of Difference.* Minneapolis: University of Minnesota Press.

HRC Foundation. 2021. "Violence Against the Transgender and Gender Nonconforming Community in 2020." https://www.hrc.org/resources/violence-against -the-trans-and-gender-non-conforming-community-in-2020.

Huffer, Lynne. 2013. *Are the Lips a Grave? A Queer Feminist on the Ethics of Sex.* New York: Columbia University Press.

Hull, Tupper. 1991. "Rally for Cancer Research Funding: Supporters Demand More Money to Study Breast Cancer." *San Francisco Examiner,* May 13, 1991.

Iasenza, Suzanne. 2000. "Lesbian Sexuality Post-Stonewall to Post-modernism: Putting the 'Lesbian Bed Death' Concept to Bed." *Journal of Sex Education and Therapy* 25 (1): 59–69. https://doi.org/10.1080/01614576.2000.11074330.

Iasenza, Suzanne. 2002. "Beyond 'Lesbian Bed Death.'" *Journal of Lesbian Studies* 6 (1): 111–20. https://doi.org/10.1300/J155v06n01_10.

Italiano, Laura. 2007. "Attack of the Killer Lesbians: Man Felt Like I Was Going to Die." *New York Post,* April 12, 2007. https://web.archive.org/web/20080218024758/http://www.nypost.com:80/seven/04122007/news/regionalnews/attack_of_ the_killer_lesbians_regionalnews_laura_italiano.htm.

Ivy, Veronica [Rachel McKinnon]. 2018. "The Epistemology of Propaganda." *Philosophy and Phenomenological Research* 96 (2): 483–89. https://doi.org/10.1111/phpr.12429.

Jagose, Annamarie. 1997. *Queer Theory: An Introduction.* New York: NYU Press.

Jay, Karla. 2000. *Tales of the Lavender Menace: A Memoir of Liberation.* New York: Basic Books.

Jeffreys, Sheila. 2014. *Gender Hurts: A Feminist Analysis of the Politics of Transgenderism.* Abingdon, U.K.: Routledge.

Jones, Lovell A., and Janice A. Chilton. 2002. "Impact of Breast Cancer on African American Women: Priority Areas for Research in the Next Decade." *American Journal of Public Health* 92 (4): 539–42.

Jones, Sonya L. 1998. *Gay and Lesbian Literature Since World War II: History and Memory.* Binghamton, N.Y.: Haworth Press.

Keeling, Kara. 2019. *Queer Times, Black Futures*. New York: NYU Press.

Kendall, Laurie J. 2013. *The Michigan Womyn's Music Festival: An Amazon Matrix of Meaning*. Christchurch, N.Z.: Spiral Womyn's Press.

Kershaw, Sarah. 2009. "My Sister's Keeper." *New York Times*, February 1, 2009. http://www.nytimes.com/2009/02/01/fashion/01womyn.html.

Kessler, Sarah. 2021. "Are You Being Sirred? Work in Progress, Nanette, Douglas, and the New Butch Middlebrow." *Film Quarterly* 74 (3): 46–55. https://doi.org/10.1525/fq.2021.74.3.46.

Kim, Mimi E. 2018. "From Carceral Feminism to Transformative Justice: Women-of-Color Feminism and Alternatives to Incarceration." *Journal of Ethnic & Cultural Diversity in Social Work* 27 (3): 219–33. https://doi.org/10.1080/15313204.2018.1474827.

King, Samantha. 2008. *Pink Ribbons, Inc.: Breast Cancer and the Politics of Philanthropy*. Minneapolis: University of Minnesota Press.

Kinsey, Alfred C., Wardell P. Pomeroy, and Clyde E. Martin. 1948. *Sexual Behavior in the Human Male*. Philadelphia: W. B. Saunders.

Kinsman, Gary. 1987. "Learning to Desire Passionately." *Rites for Lesbian and Gay Liberation*, December 1987, 5.

Klawiter, Maren. 2008. *The Biopolitics of Breast Cancer: Changing Cultures of Disease and Activism*. Minneapolis: University of Minnesota Press.

Koedt, Anne. 1970. "The Myth of the Vaginal Orgasm." In *Notes from the Second Year: Women's Liberation—Major Writings of the Radical Feminists*, 37–41. New York: Radical Feminism.

Koedt, Anne. 1973. "Lesbianism and Feminism." In *Radical Feminism*, edited by Anne Koedt, Ellen Levine, and Anita Rapone, 246–58. New York: Quadrangle Books.

Koyama, Emi. n.d. "Documents on Michigan/Trans Controversy." Eminism.org. Accessed on April 1, 2022. http://eminism.org/michigan/documents.html.

Koyama, Emi. 2003. *A Handbook on Discussing the Michigan Womyn's Music Festival for Trans Activists and Allies*. Portland, Ore.: Confluere Publications.

Kubala, Julie. 2020. "Teaching 'Bad Feminism': Mary Daly and the Legacy of '70s Lesbian-Feminism." *Feminist Formations* 32 (1): 117–36. https://doi.org/10.1353/ff.2020.0010.

Kurdek, Lawrence A. Kurdek. 1988. "Relationship Quality of Gay and Lesbian Cohabiting Couples." *Journal of Homosexuality* 15 (3–4): 93–118. https://doi.org/10.1300/J082v15n03_05.

Lee, Ntanya, Don Murphy, and Lisa North. 1994. "Sexuality, Multicultural Education, and the New York City Public Schools." *Radical Teacher* 45: 12–16.

Levy, Ariel. 2006. Introduction to *Intercourse*, by Andrea Dworkin, xi–xxvii. New York: Basic Books.

Loulan, JoAnn. 1984. *Lesbian Sex*. San Francisco: Spinsters Ink.

Love, Heather. 2007. "Wedding Crashers." *GLQ: A Journal of Lesbian and Gay Studies* 13 (1): 125–39.

Love, Heather. 2009. *Feeling Backward: Loss and the Politics of Queer History*. Cambridge, Mass.: Harvard University Press.

Love, Heather. 2011. "Queers _____ This." In *After Sex? On Writing Since Queer Theory,* edited by Janet Halley and Andrew Parker, 180–91. Durham, N.C.: Duke University Press.

Love, Susan. 2010. *Dr. Susan Love's Breast Book.* Cambridge, Mass.: Da Capo Lifelong Books.

Luis, Keridwen N. 2018. *Herlands: Exploring the Women's Land Movement in the United States.* Minneapolis: University of Minnesota Press.

Luo, Tian, and Philip B. Stark. 2014. "Only the Bad Die Young: Restaurant Mortality in the Western US." ArXiv:1410.8603 [stat.AP]. October 31, 2014. http://arxiv.org/abs/1410.8603.

Manalansan, Martin F. 2005. "Race, Violence, and Neoliberal Spatial Politics in the Global City." *Social Text* 23 (3–4 (84–85)): 141–55. https://doi.org/10.1215/01642472-23-3-4_84-85-141.

Martin, Biddy. 1994. "Sexualities without Genders and Other Queer Utopias." *Diacritics* 24 (2/3): 104–21. https://doi.org/10.2307/465167.

Martinez, Jose. 2007. "Lesbian Wolf Pack Guilty: Jersey Girl Gang Gets Lockup in Beatdown." *NY Daily News,* April 19, 2007. https://web.archive.org/web/20071214195523/http://www.nydailynews.com/news/ny_crime/2007/04/19/2007-04-19_lesbian_wolf_pack_guilty.html.

Mason, Tim, dir. 2019. *Work in Progress.* Season 1, episode 2, "176, 172, 171." Aired December 15, 2019, on Showtime.

Mattson, Greggor. 2015. "Style and the Value of Gay Nightlife: Homonormative Placemaking in San Francisco." *Urban Studies* 52 (16): 3,144–59. https://doi.org/10.1177/0042098014555630.

Mattson, Greggor. 2019. "Are Gay Bars Closing? Trends in United States Gay Bar Listings, 1977–2017." SocArXiv, February 26, 2019. https://doi.org/10.31235/osf.io/ju786.

Mbembé, J.-A., and Libby Meintjes. 2003. "Necropolitics." *Public Culture* 15 (1): 11–40.

McGleughlin, Jade. 1987. "Proposal." Series I. Internal Files: Executive Directors: Urvashi Vaid: Subject Files: NGLTF History: Town Meetings on Sex and Politics. Archives of Sexuality and Gender, Cornell University Libraries.

McGleughlin, Jade. 2021. "Full Circle with Chodorow: Reflections on Women's Desire and Lesbian Sexuality." In *Nancy Chodorow and the Reproduction of Mothering: Forty Years On,* edited by Petra Bueskens, 205–36. Cham, Switzerland: Springer International Publishing. https://doi.org/10.1007/978-3-030-55590-0_11.

Mckenna, Susan E. 2002. "The Queer Insistence of Ally McBeal: Lesbian Chic, Postfeminism, and Lesbian Reception." *Communication Review* 5 (4): 285–314. https://doi.org/10.1080/10714420214691.

McKenzie, Susan. 1992. "Merger in Lesbian Relationships." *Women & Therapy* 12 (1–2): 151–60. https://doi.org/10.1300/J015V12N01_12.

McKinney, Cait. 2020. *Information Activism: A Queer History of Lesbian Media Technologies.* Durham, N.C.: Duke University Press.

McLean, Barbara. 1973. "Diary of a Mad Organizer." *Lesbian Tide,* June 30, 1973, 16–17, 28, 36–38.

Meads, Catherine, and David Moore. 2013. "Breast Cancer in Lesbians and Bisexual Women: Systematic Review of Incidence, Prevalence, and Risk Studies." *BMC Public Health* 13:1127. https://doi.org/10.1186/1471-2458-13-1127.

Mexal, Stephen J. 2013. "The Roots of 'Wilding': Black Literary Naturalism, the Language of Wilderness, and Hip Hop in the Central Park Jogger Rape." *African American Review* 46 (1): 101–15. https://doi.org/10.1353/afa.2013.0010.

Mills, Catherine. 2015. "Biopolitics and the Concept of Life." In *Biopower: Foucault and Beyond,* edited by Vernon W. Cisney and Nicolae Morar, 82–101. Chicago: University of Chicago Press.

Moraga, Cherríe. 1983. Preface to *This Bridge Called My Back: Writings by Radical Women of Color,* edited by Cherríe Moraga and Gloria Anzaldúa, xiii–xix. New York: Kitchen Table/Women of Color Press.

Moraga, Cherríe, and Gloria Anzaldúa, eds. 1983. *This Bridge Called My Back: Writings by Radical Women of Color.* New York: Kitchen Table/Women of Color Press.

Morris, Bonnie J. 1999. *Eden Built by Eves: The Culture of Women's Music Festivals.* Boston: Alyson Books.

Morris, Bonnie J. 2016. *The Disappearing L: Erasure of Lesbian Spaces and Culture.* Albany: SUNY Press.

Mundy, Liza. 2013. "The Gay Guide to Wedded Bliss." *Atlantic,* June 2013. http://www.theatlantic.com/magazine/archive/2013/06/the-gay-guide-to-wedded-bliss/309317/.

Muñoz, José Esteban. 1999. *Disidentifications: Queers of Color and the Performance of Politics.* Minneapolis: University of Minnesota Press.

Muñoz, José Esteban. 2006. "Thinking Beyond Anti-relationality and Antiutopianism in Queer Critique." *PMLA* 121 (3): 825–26.

Muñoz, José Esteban. 2009. *Cruising Utopia: The Then and There of Queer Futurity.* New York: NYU Press.

Munt, Sally R. 2007. "A Seat at the Table." *Journal of Lesbian Studies* 11 (1–2): 53–67. https://doi.org/10.1300/J155v11n01_04.

Musser, Amber Jamilla. 2015. "Lesbians, Tea, and the Vernacular of Fluids." *Women & Performance: A Journal of Feminist Theory* 25 (1): 23–40. https://doi.org/10.1080/0740770X.2014.994841.

Musser, Amber Jamilla. 2018. *Sensual Excess: Queer Femininity and Brown Jouissance.* New York: NYU Press.

Nash, Jennifer C. 2019. *Black Feminism Reimagined: After Intersectionality.* Durham, N.C.: Duke University Press.

Nash, Jennifer C., and Samantha Pinto. 2020. "Stories That Matter Now: Feminist Classics & Feminist Desire in the Contemporary Classroom." *Feminist Formations* 32 (1): ix–xiii. https://doi.org/10.1353/ff.2020.0000.

Nettick, Geri, and Beth Elliott. 2011. *Mirrors: Portrait of a Lesbian Transsexual.* CreateSpace Independent Publishing Platform.

NGLTF. 1987. "Project Description." The National Gay and Lesbian Taskforce Records, 1973–2000. Box 100, Folder 70. LGBTQ History and Culture since 1940, Part II. Cornell University Libraries.

Noss, Kaitlin. 2013. "Queering Utopia: Deep Lez and the Future of Hope." *WSQ: Women's Studies Quarterly* 40 (3): 126–45. https://doi.org/10.1353/wsq.2013.0029.

Olivia. n.d. "Our Vacations." Accessed March 14, 2019. https://www.olivia.com/our-vacations.

O'Mara, Michelle. 2012. "The Correlation of Sexual Frequency and Relationship Satisfaction among Lesbians." PhD diss., American Academy of Clinical Sexologists. https://micheleomara.com/wp-content/uploads/2019/04/0.0-lesbian-sexual-frequency-dissertation.pdf.

Parker, Pat. 1983. "Revolution: It's Not Neat or Pretty or Quick." In *This Bridge Called My Back: Writings by Radical Women of Color,* edited by Cherríe Moraga and Gloria Anzaldúa, 238–42. New York: Kitchen Table/Women of Color Press.

Parker-Pope, Tara. 2014. "The Breast Cancer Racial Gap." *Well* (blog). March 3, 2014. http://well.blogs.nytimes.com/2014/03/03/the-breast-cancer-racial-gap/.

Patton, Cindy. 1994. *Last Served? Gendering the HIV Pandemic.* London: Taylor & Francis.

Patton, Cindy, and Sue O'Sullivan. 1990. "Mapping: Lesbians, AIDS, and Sexuality." *Feminist Review* 34 (1): 120–33. https://doi.org/10.1057/fr.1990.16.

Pearce, Ruth, Sonja Erikainen, and Ben Vincent. 2020. "TERF Wars: An Introduction." *Sociological Review* 68 (4): 677–98. https://doi.org/10.1177/0038026120934713.

Peddle, Daniel, dir. 2012. *The Aggressives.* San Francisco: Breaking Glass Pictures. https://www.kanopy.com/en/product/121515.

Penner, James. 2011. *Pinks, Pansies, and Punks: The Rhetoric of Masculinity in American Literary Culture.* Bloomington: Indiana University Press.

Placzek, Jessica. 2015. "Goodbye Lexington: Owner to Shut Doors to Beloved Lesbian Bar." *KQED,* April 25, 2015, https://www.kqed.org/news/10501545/goodbye-lexington-owner-to-shut-doors-to-beloved-lesbian-bar.

Podmore, Julie A. 2006. "Gone 'Underground'? Lesbian Visibility and the Consolidation of Queer Space in Montréal." *Social & Cultural Geography* 7 (4): 595–625. https://doi.org/10.1080/14649360600825737.

Post, Laura. 1990. "The First Olivia Cruise Maiden Voyage." *Hot Wire: The Journal of Women's Music and Culture* (September).

Przybylo, Ela. 2019. *Asexual Erotics: Intimate Readings of Compulsory Sexuality.* Columbus: Ohio State University Press.

Puar, Jasbir. 2007. *Terrorist Assemblages: Homonationalism in Queer Times.* Durham, N.C.: Duke University Press.

Radicalesbians. 2018. "The Woman-Identified Woman." In *Feminist Manifestos: A Global Documentary Reader,* edited by Penny A. Weiss, 221–26. New York: NYU Press.

Ramirez, Roque. 2003. "'That's My Place!': Negotiating Racial, Sexual, and Gender Politics in San Francisco's Gay Latino Alliance, 1975–1983." *Journal of the History of Sexuality* 12 (2): 224–58. https://doi.org/10.1353/sex.2003.0078.

Rand, Erin J. 2013. "An Appetite for Activism: The Lesbian Avengers and the Queer Politics of Visibility." *Women's Studies in Communication* 36 (2): 121–41. https://doi.org/10.1080/07491409.2013.794754.

Raymond, Janice G. 1994. *The Transsexual Empire: The Making of the She-Male.* New York: Teachers College Press.

Reddy, Chandan. 2011. *Freedom with Violence: Race, Sexuality, and the US State.* Durham, N.C.: Duke University Press.

Retter, Yolanda, Anne-Marie Bouthillette, and Gordon Brent Ingram, eds. 1997. *Queers in Space: Communities, Public Places, Sites of Resistance.* Seattle, Wash.: Bay Press.

Rich, Adrienne. 1995. *Of Woman Born: Motherhood as Experience and Institution.* New York: W. W. Norton.

Richie, Beth E. 2012. *Arrested Justice: Black Women, Violence, and America's Prison Nation.* New York: NYU Press.

Rodríguez, Juana María. 2014. *Sexual Futures, Queer Gestures, and Other Latina Longings.* New York: NYU Press.

Ronell, Avital. 2004. "The Deviant Payback: The Aims of Valerie Solanas." Introduction to *SCUM Manifesto.* New York: Verso.

Rose, Nikolas. 2006. *The Politics of Life Itself: Biomedicine, Power, and Subjectivity in the Twenty-First Century.* Princeton, N.J.: Princeton University Press.

Ross, Barbara, and Tracy Connor. 2007. "The Case of the Lesbian Beatdown." *New York Daily News,* April 12, 2007. https://web.archive.org/web/20090515025124/http://www.nydailynews.com/news/ny_crime/2007/04/12/2007-04-12_the_case_of_the_lesbian_beatdown-2.html.

Rothblum, Esther D., and Marcia Hill. 2014. *Couples Therapy: Feminist Perspectives.* New York: Routledge.

Rubin, Gayle S. 2011. "Thinking Sex." In *Deviations: A Gayle Rubin Reader.* Durham, N.C.: Duke University Press.

Rudy, Kathy. 2001. "Radical Feminism, Lesbian Separatism, and Queer Theory." *Feminist Studies* 27 (1): 191–222. https://doi.org/10.2307/3178457.

Rupp, Leila J. 2013. "Thinking About 'Lesbian History.'" *Feminist Studies* 39 (2): 357–61.

Ryan, Caitlin, and Judith Bradford. 1999. "Conducting the National Lesbian Health Care Survey: First of Its Kind." *Journal of the Gay and Lesbian Medical Association* 3 (3): 91–97. https://doi.org/10.1023/A:1022240011658.

Salholz, Eloise, and Daniel Glick. 1993. "The Power and the Pride." *Newsweek,* June 20, 1993.

Samek, Alyssa A. 2016. "Violence and Identity Politics: 1970s Lesbian-Feminist Discourse and Robin Morgan's 1973 West Coast Lesbian Conference Keynote Address." *Communication and Critical/Cultural Studies* 13 (3): 232–49. https://doi.org/10.1080/14791420.2015.1127400.

Samer, Rox. 2022. *Lesbian Potentiality and Feminist Media in the 1970s.* Durham, N.C.: Duke University Press.

Schreurs, Karlein M. G. 1993. "Sexuality in Lesbian Couples: The Importance of Gender." *Annual Review of Sex Research* 4 (1): 49–66. https://doi.org/10.1080/10532528.1993.10559884.

Schulman, Sarah. 1994. *My American History: Lesbian and Gay Life during the Reagan/Bush Years.* New York: Routledge.

Schulman, Sarah. 2004. "What Became of 'Freedom Summer'?" *Gay & Lesbian Review Worldwide* 11 (1): 20–21.

Schulman, Sarah. 2022. *Let the Record Show: A Political History of ACT UP New York, 1987–1993.* London: Picador.

Serano, Julia. 2016. *Whipping Girl: A Transsexual Woman on Sexism and the Scapegoating of Femininity.* Emeryville, Calif.: Seal Press.

Shrier, Abigail. 2020. *Irreversible Damage: The Transgender Craze Seducing Our Daughters.* New York: Simon and Schuster.

Simoni, Jane M., Laramie Smith, Kathryn M. Oost, Keren Lehavot, and Karen Fredriksen-Goldsen. 2017. "Disparities in Physical Health Conditions among Lesbian and Bisexual Women: A Systematic Review of Population-Based Studies." *Journal of Homosexuality* 64 (1): 32–44. https://doi.org/10.1080/00918369.2016.1174021.

Smalley, Sondra. 1987. "Dependency Issues in Lesbian Relationships." *Journal of Homosexuality* 14 (1–2): 125–35. https://doi.org/10.1300/J082v14n01_10.

Smith, Barbara. 1978. "Toward a Black Feminist Criticism." *Radical Teacher* 7:20–27.

Smith, Barbara. 1999. "Blacks and Gays: Healing the Great Divide." In *Dangerous Liaisons: Blacks, Gays, and the Struggle for Equality,* edited by Eric Brandt, 15–24. New York: New Press.

Smith, Barbara, and Beverly Smith. 1983. "Across the Kitchen Table: A Sister-to-Sister Dialogue." In *This Bridge Called My Back: Writings by Radical Women of Color,* edited by Cherríe Moraga and Gloria Anzaldúa, 113–27. New York: Kitchen Table/Women of Color Press.

Smythe, Viv. 2008. "An Apology and a Promise." *Finally, Feminism 101* (blog). August 19, 2008. https://finallyfeminism101.wordpress.com/2008/08/19/an-apology-and-a-promise/.

Solanas, Valerie. 2004. *SCUM Manifesto.* New York: Verso.

Solarz, Andrea L. 1999. *Lesbian Health: Current Assessment and Directions for the Future.* The National Academies Collection: Reports Funded by National Institutes of Health. Washington, D.C.: National Academies Press. http://www.ncbi.nlm.nih.gov/books/NBK45100/.

Stein, Arlene, ed. 1993. *Sisters, Sexperts, Queers: Beyond the Lesbian Nation.* New York: Plume.

Stein, Arlene. 1997. *Sex and Sensibility: Stories of a Lesbian Generation.* Berkeley: University of California Press.

Stein, Arlene. 2010. "The Incredible Shrinking Lesbian World and Other Queer Conundra." *Sexualities* 13 (1): 21–32. https://doi.org/10.1177/1363460709352724.

Steinmetz, Katy. 2014. "The Transgender Tipping Point." *Time,* June 9, 2014. https://time.com/135480/transgender-tipping-point/.

Stoller, Nancy E. 1997. *Lessons from the Damned: Queers, Whores, and Junkies Respond to AIDS.* London: Routledge.

Strongman, SaraEllen. 2018. "'Creating Justice between Us': Audre Lorde's Theory of the Erotic as Coalitional Politics in the Women's Movement." *Feminist Theory* 19 (1): 41–59. https://doi.org/10.1177/1464700117742870.

Sullivan, Mairead. Forthcoming. "Grossed Out: The Carceral Logics of Disgust and the Demands of #MeToo." *Signs: Journal of Women in Culture and Society.*

Swisher, Kara. 1993. "We Love Lesbians! Or Do We? 'Hot' Subculture—Or Just New Hurtful Stereotypes?" *Washington Post*, July 18, 1993. https://www.washington post.com/archive/opinions/1993/07/18/we-love-lesbians-or-do-we-hot-subcul ture-or-just-new-hurtful-stereotypes/c04ac909-7af7-4fe6-965f-546c72f768dd/.

Sycamore, Mattilda Bernstein. 2013. *The End of San Francisco*. San Francisco: City Lights Publishers.

Terry, Jennifer. 1999. "Agendas for Lesbian Health: Countering the Ills of Homopho- bia." In *Revisioning Women, Health, and Healing: Feminist, Cultural, and Technoscience Perspectives*, edited by Adele E. Clarke and Virginia Olesen, 324–42. New York: Routledge.

Tompkins, Kyla Wazana. 2015. "Intersections of Race, Gender, and Sexuality." In *The Cambridge Companion to American Gay and Lesbian Literature*, edited by Scott Her- ring, 173–89. Cambridge: Cambridge University Press.

Tongson, Karen. 2011. *Relocations: Queer Suburban Imaginaries*. New York: NYU Press.

Traub, Valerie. 2016. *Thinking Sex with the Early Moderns*. Philadelphia: University of Pennsylvania Press.

Trigilio, Jo. 2016. "Complicated and Messy Politics of Inclusion: Michfest and the Boston Dyke March." *Journal of Lesbian Studies* 20 (2): 234–50. https://doi.org/10.1 080/10894160.2016.1083835.

Trump, Donald. 2016. "Transcript: Donald Trump's Taped Comments About Women." Transcript. *New York Times*, October 8, 2016. https://www.nytimes.com/2016/10/ 08/us/donald-trump-tape-transcript.html.

Vance, Carole S., ed. 1984. *Pleasure and Danger: Exploring Female Sexuality*. Boston: Routledge and Kegan Paul.

van Rosmalen-Nooijens, Karin, Marianne Vergeer, and Antoinette L. M. Lagro-Janssen. 2008. "Bed Death and Other Lesbian Sexual Problems Unraveled: A Qualitative Study of the Sexual Health of Lesbian Women Involved in a Relationship." *Women & Health* 48 (3): 339–62. https://doi.org/10.1080/03630240802463343.

Villarejo, Amy. 2003. *Lesbian Rule: Cultural Criticism and the Value of Desire*. Durham, N.C.: Duke University Press.

Vogel, Lisa. 2014. "Michfest Responds: We Have a Few Demands of Our Own." *Pride Source* (blog). August 18, 2014. https://pridesource.com/article/67561-2/.

Walker, Rebecca, ed. 1995. *To Be Real: Telling the Truth and Changing the Face of Femi- nism*. New York: Anchor.

Walters, Suzanna Danuta. 1996. "From Here to Queer: Radical Feminism, Postmod- ernism, and the Lesbian Menace (Or, Why Can't a Woman Be More like a Fag?)." *Signs* 21 (4): 830–69.

Walters, Suzanna Danuta. 2003. *All the Rage: The Story of Gay Visibility in America*. Chicago: University of Chicago Press.

Walters, Suzanna Danuta. 2016. "Introduction: The Dangers of a Metaphor—Beyond the Battlefield in the Sex Wars." *Signs: Journal of Women in Culture and Society* 42 (1): 1–9. https://doi.org/10.1086/686750.

Ward, Jane. 2020. *The Tragedy of Heterosexuality*. New York: NYU Press.

Warner, Sara. 2013. *Acts of Gaiety: LGBT Performance and the Politics of Pleasure.* Ann Arbor: University of Michigan Press.

Weiss, Margot. 2011. *Techniques of Pleasure: BDSM and the Circuits of Sexuality.* Durham, N.C.: Duke University Press.

Whalley, Elizabeth, and Colleen Hackett. 2017. "Carceral Feminisms: The Abolitionist Project and Undoing Dominant Feminisms." *Contemporary Justice Review* 20 (4): 456–73. https://doi.org/10.1080/10282580.2017.1383762.

Wheeler, Rod. 2007. "Violent Lesbian Gangs a Growing Problem." Interview by Bill O'Reilly. *The O'Reilly Factor.* Fox News Media Transcript. https://web.archive .org/web/20090328125726/http://www6.lexisnexis.com/publisher/EndUser?Act ion=UserDisplayFullDocument&orgId=574&topicId=100007214&docId=l:630549 858&start=2.

Wiegman, Robyn. 1999. "What Ails Feminist Criticism? A Second Opinion." *Critical Inquiry* 25 (2): 362–79.

Wiegman, Robyn. 2000. "Feminism's Apocalyptic Futures." *New Literary History* 31 (4): 805–25. https://doi.org/10.1353/nlh.2000.0053.

Wiegman, Robyn. 2011. "Afterword: The Lesbian Premodern Meets the Lesbian Postmodern." In *The Lesbian Premodern,* edited by N. Giffney, M. Sauer, and P. D. Watt, 203–12. New York: Palgrave Macmillan.

Wiegman, Robyn. 2012. *Object Lessons.* Durham, N.C.: Duke University Press.

Wildhawk. n.d. "The Story." Accessed April 1, 2022. https://www.wildhawksf.com/ about.

Willey, Angela. 2016. *Undoing Monogamy: The Politics of Science and the Possibilities of Biology.* Durham, N.C.: Duke University Press.

Willey, Angela. 2017. "Lesbians, Life, and Antiracist Ethics." *Feminist Formations* 29 (3): 150–55. https://doi.org/10.1353/ff.2017.0035.

Wilson, Elizabeth A. 2015. *Gut Feminism.* Durham, N.C.: Duke University Press.

Wilson, Lena. 2018. "Do I Have to Give Up Lesbian History to Participate in Queer Culture?" *Slate,* August 16, 2018. https://slate.com/human-interest/2018/08/les bian-history-terfs-and-queer-culture-do-queer-women-have-to-reject-all-second -wave-feminism-to-be-inclusive.html.

Winkiel, Laura. 2013. "The 'Sweet Assassin' and the Performative Politics of SCUM Manifesto." In *The Queer Sixties,* edited by Patricia Juliana Smith, 62–86. New York: Routledge.

Winnow, Jackie. 1992. "Lesbians Evolving Health Care: Cancer and AIDS." *Feminist Review* 41: 68–76. https://doi.org/10.2307/1395233.

Index

MAIREAD SULLIVAN is associate professor of women's and gender studies at Loyola Marymount University.

Printed and bound by CPI Group (UK) Ltd, Croydon, CR0 4YY

13/04/2025

14656503-0002